1,251 INCREDIBLE & FUN HOCKEY FACTS

TYLER THOMPSON

© Copyright 2022 – Tyler Thompson

www.tylerthompson.online
tthompson@tylerthompson.online

It is not legal to reproduce, duplicate, or transmit any part of this document in either electronic means or in printed format. Recording of this publication is strictly prohibited and any storage of this document is not al owed unless with written permission from the publisher except for the use of brief quotations in a book review.

This book is a work of fiction. Any resemblance to persons, living or dead, or places, events or locations is purely coincidental.

CONTENT

INTRODUCTION	**5**
HISTORY OF hockey	**7**
HISTORY OF HOCKEY	*8*
Early Competitions	*22*
Expansion and Popularity	*31*
LEGENDARY PLAYERS	**40**
Sidney Crosby	*40*
Bobby Hull	*42*
Guy Lafleur	*43*
Mark Messier	*45*
Jean Beliveau	*47*
Maurice Richard	*49*
Mario Lemieux	*50*
Bobby Orr	*51*
Wayne Gretzky	*53*
Gordie Howe	*54*
AMAZING RECORDS	**56**
Scoring Records	*56*
Goalie Records	*64*
Playoff Records	*72*
GREATEST HOCKEY TEAMS OF ALL TIME	**89**
Montreal Canadiens	*89*
Detroit Red Wings	*94*
Toronto Maple Leafs	*98*
ICONIC ARENAS	**104**
Madison Square Garden	*104*
Maple Leaf Gardens	*110*
Bell Centre	*119*
UNFORGETTABLE EVENTS	**128**
Stanley Cup Upsets	*128*
Olympic Hockey Showdowns	*135*
Miraculous On-Ice Comebacks	*141*

CULTURE AND TRADITIONS — **146**
- *Hockey Slang and Expressions* — *146*
- *Classic Hockey Foods* — *149*
- *Fan Chants and Rituals* — *153*

GREAT NHL MOMENTS — **158**
- *Incredible Goalie Saves* — *158*
- *Dramatic Overtime Goals* — *165*
- *Fierce Rivalries* — *171*

INTRODUCTION

Step up to the plate, young baseball fanatics, because have we got a treat for you! If you can't get enough of the diamond, the dugouts, and the dramatic home runs, then you've just hit a grand slam by picking up this book! Welcome to "Super Interesting Baseball Facts for Kids: 2150 Mind-Blowing Secrets from the Diamond - Exploring Legends, Iconic Plays, Epic Moments, Legendary Fields, and the Science Behind Majestic Home Runs!"

This isn't just another baseball book; this is your VIP ticket to the heart and soul of the game. Get ready to dive head-first into the most epic, jaw-dropping, and yeah, even mind-blowing baseball facts you've ever encountered. Ever wonder how Babe Ruth became the Sultan of Swat? Or how Jackie Robinson smashed racial barriers as easily as he smashed baseballs? All your burning questions are answered right

But hang on, this ride doesn't stop at the Hall of Fame. Nope! We're taking you behind the scenes, into the locker rooms, and even into the brains of baseball players to reveal what makes them tick—and swing, and hit, and run! Have you ever asked yourself how a curveball curves, or why a fast pitch is so fast? You're about to find out, and trust us, you'll be so amazed that you might even forget to eat your Cracker Jacks!

This book is jam-packed with chapters that are as irresistible as a perfect pitch. From the legendary players who changed the game forever to the unforgettable events that made baseball history, we've got it all. Learn about the iconic stadiums that have hosted the heroes of the game, discover the traditions that make baseball more than just a sport, and relive some of the MLB's greatest moments!

Sure, you might know the basic rules: three strikes and you're out, nine innings in a game, and never, ever forget to touch base. But do you know about the superstitions that players swear by or the quirky traditions that make the game a cultural treasure? Get ready to find out!

So, batter up, future baseball legends! It's time to chew your gum, adjust your cap, and dig your cleats into the dirt. With this book in your hands, you're not just a fan—you're part of the game.

Let's play ball!.

HISTORY OF HOCKEY

HISTORY OF HOCKEY

Origins of Hockey
1: The Ice Age of Hockey
Long before smartphones and video games, back in the 1800s, kids in Canada didn't just build snowmen – they were busy inventing hockey! Imagine playing on a frozen pond, using frozen cow dung as pucks. Yes, you read that right! Before the shiny black pucks we know today, early hockey players had to make do with what they had, and sometimes, that meant using cow dung. Just think, the next time you're watching a hockey game, how far the puck has come!

2: Hockey's Multicultural Hat Trick

Hockey is like the cool kid at the sports party that everyone wants to hang out with, but did you know it has roots in several cultures? It's like a sports stew, with ingredients from Irish hurling, English field hockey, and Native American lacrosse. Back in the 18th century, these games blended in Canada to create what we now know as hockey. So, when you cheer for your favorite team, remember you're celebrating a global mashup!

3: The First Indoor Hockey Game
On March 3, 1875, Montreal witnessed a game-changing event – the first-ever indoor hockey game! Played at the Victoria Skating Rink, this game had it all: two teams of nine players, a wooden puck, and a crowd that had no idea they were witnessing history. Just imagine skating around in woolen sweaters and without helmets, trying not to slip on the ice. Talk about a throwback Thursday!

4: Stanley Cup's Humble Beginnings
The Stanley Cup, now a towering trophy that every NHL player dreams of hoisting, started as a small salad bowl. Lord Stanley of Preston, the Governor General of Canada in 1892, bought it for 10 guineas (about $50 today). He probably never imagined it would grow into the iconic symbol of hockey excellence it is today. So next time you're eating salad, just think, you could be holding the next big sports trophy!

5: The Zamboni's Grand Entrance
In 1949, the world of hockey got a shiny new toy: the Zamboni. Before this ice-resurfacing machine made its debut, smoothing out the ice was a tedious job that took several workers and hours to complete. The first Zamboni, affectionately known as the Model A, turned what used to be a chore into a spectacle, with fans cheering as it cleaned the ice. Now, it's not just about the game; it's about waiting for the Zamboni to make its grand entrance!

6: The Masked Revolution
Picture this: it's 1959, and you're a hockey goalie with nothing but a leather cap for protection. Sounds scary, right? That all changed when Jacques Plante, a goalie for the Montreal Canadiens, decided enough was enough after a puck hit his face. He stepped onto the ice wearing a face mask, and although people thought it looked odd, it revolutionized goalie gear. Now, goalies look like they're ready for battle, and it's all thanks to Plante's bold move.

7: The Miracle on Ice
In 1980, at the Winter Olympics in Lake Placid, New York, the U.S. hockey team, made up of college students and amateurs, did the unthinkable – they beat the Soviet Union, a team that had won nearly every world championship and Olympic tournament since 1954. This victory was so surprising it was dubbed the "Miracle on Ice." Imagine being one of those students, going from college

exams to defeating a world superpower on ice!

8: The Longest Game Ever Played
Hockey games usually last about 60 minutes, but on March 24, 1936, the Detroit Red Wings and the Montreal Maroons decided they just couldn't get enough hockey. Their playoff game went into six overtime periods, lasting a total of 176 minutes and 30 seconds of game time. That's nearly three regular games back-to-back! Players were so exhausted that they probably slept in their skates after the game.

9: The Birth of the NHL
In 1917, five teams decided to form a league, and thus, the NHL was born. But it wasn't all smooth sailing; the league faced many challenges, including teams folding and the 1919 Spanish Flu epidemic, which canceled the Stanley Cup finals. It's like the NHL was the little league that could, overcoming obstacles to become the major international sports league we know today.

10: Hockey's Hall of Fame
The Hockey Hall of Fame, located in Toronto, Canada, is like the treasure chest of hockey. Established in 1943, it's home to the most significant collection of hockey memorabilia and the stories of the legends who have shaped the game. Walking through the Hall of Fame is like scrolling through the greatest moments in hockey history, except you can't swipe left!

11: Women's Hockey Scores
Women's hockey has been skating its way into history for over a century, with the first recorded game in 1892 in Ottawa. But it wasn't until 1998 that women's hockey made its Olympic debut in Nagano, Japan, proving that these athletes could shoot and score with the best of them. So, next time you're watching a women's hockey game, remember you're witnessing pioneers on ice!

12: The First Professional Hockey Players
In 1904, the Portage Lakes Hockey Club in Michigan decided to do something radical – pay their players. This move not only changed the game for those players but also marked the birth of professional hockey. Imagine going from playing for fun to getting paid to skate and score. It was a game-changer, literally!

13: The Origin of the Word "Hockey"
The word "hockey" has a mysterious origin, with several theories floating around. One popular story suggests it comes from the French word "hoquet," meaning shepherd's stick. So next time you pick up a hockey stick, think of it as your shepherd's staff, guiding your team to victory!

14: The Lightning Fast Shot
Did you know the fastest hockey shot ever recorded was a blistering 110.3 mph by Zdeno Chara in 2012? That's faster than a speeding car on the highway! Imagine trying to catch that with just a glove. Goalies, you have our respect.

15: The Golden Goal
In the 2010 Winter Olympics, Sidney Crosby scored the "golden goal" against the USA, winning the gold medal for Canada in overtime. This moment was so epic, Canadians everywhere remember exactly where they were when it happened. It's like the hockey version of landing on the moon!

16: The Night of the Flying Octopus
In 1952, Detroit Red Wings fans started a quirky tradition that continues to this day: throwing an octopus onto the ice during playoff games. The eight legs of the octopus symbolized the eight wins needed to secure the Stanley Cup at the time. Imagine being at a game and suddenly seeing an octopus flying over your head!

17: The Invisible Puck Problem
Ever watch a hockey game and lose track of the puck? You're not alone. In the late 1990s, Fox Sports introduced the "glow puck" with a comet-like tail on TV broadcasts to make it easier to follow. While it looked like something out of a video game, traditionalists weren't fans, and the idea was shelved. It's like trying to put ketchup on a hot dog in Chicago!

18: The Goalie Who Scored
Goalies are known for stopping goals, not scoring them. But in 1979, Billy Smith of the New York Islanders became the first NHL goalie to be credited with a goal. It was actually an own goal by the opposing team, but since Smith was the last Islander to touch the puck, he got the credit. Talk about being in the right place at the right time!

19: The Hockey Stick Curve Craze
In the 1960s, NHL player Stan Mikita accidentally broke the blade of his hockey stick during practice. When he noticed the curve helped control the puck better, it sparked a trend. Soon, players were curving their sticks like bananas, leading the NHL to implement rules on just how curvy those sticks could be. It's like discovering a cheat code in real life!

20: The NHL's Expansion South
In 1993, the NHL made a bold move by expanding into Florida with the Tampa Bay Lightning. Critics doubted hockey could thrive in the sunshine state, but the team proved them wrong by winning the Stanley Cup in 2004 and 2020. It's like finding out penguins can live in the desert!

21: The Birth of the Air Hockey Table
In 1969, a group of Brunswick Billiards employees invented air hockey as a way to create a game that wasn't affected by friction. Little did they know, they were creating a future arcade staple. Imagine playing hockey with a puck that floats on air – it's like magic!

22: The Great One's Unbreakable Record
Wayne Gretzky, known as "The Great One," holds a record that seems almost impossible to break: 2,857 career points. To put that in perspective, a player would need to average about 100 points a season for 29 seasons to match it. It's like being so good at video games that no one else can even get on the scoreboard.

23: The Penalty Box's Nickname
The penalty box in hockey is affectionately known as the "sin bin." It's where players go to think about what they've done after breaking the rules. Imagine a timeout corner, but with millions of people watching. It's the ultimate "think about your actions" spot!

24: The First Woman in the NHL
In 1992, Manon Rhéaume broke barriers by becoming the first woman to play in an NHL preseason game as a goaltender for the Tampa Bay Lightning. While she didn't make the regular-season roster, she paved the way for future generations of female athletes. It's like stepping onto the moon for women's sports!

25: The Oldest Professional Hockey Player
Gordie Howe, affectionately known as "Mr. Hockey," played his final NHL game in 1980 at the age of 52. He's a legend on the ice, proving that age is just a number when it comes to the game you love. Imagine playing in the big leagues when most people are thinking about retirement!

26: Hockey Under the Midnight Sun

In the far north of Canada, there's a place where the sun barely sets in summer. Here, kids play an annual hockey game that starts late at night and ends in the early hours of the morning, all under natural light! It's like having a sleepover with your friends, but instead of watching movies, you're playing the coolest game on ice.

27: The Hockey Jersey Swap
Did you know that after a hard-fought international hockey tournament, players often swap jerseys with their opponents? It's a sign of respect and friendship, showing that even though they battle on the ice, they're all part of the big hockey family. Next time you trade cards or video games with your friend, think of it as your own jersey swap.

28: The Goal That Broke the Glass
Hockey pucks can fly at incredible speeds, but in 2011, a slapshot was so powerful it shattered the glass behind the goal. Fans were showered in glass shards, but don't worry, everyone was okay, and it became a legendary moment in hockey history. It's like hitting a home run, but instead of the ball going over the fence, it breaks it!

29: The Referee's Special Skate Blades
Referees in hockey have a tough job keeping up with the play, so they wear specially designed skate blades that are slightly longer and have less of a curve. This helps them glide smoothly over the ice and keep up with the action without getting in the way. Imagine having super shoes that make you run faster and jump higher during a game of tag!

30: The Mascot Hall of Fame
Yes, there's a Hall of Fame for mascots, and several hockey mascots have been inducted. These furry and feathery friends do more than just entertain the crowd; they embody the spirit of their teams and bring smiles to fans of all ages. It's like being the class clown, but instead of detention, you get a trophy!

31: The First Outdoor NHL Game
In 2003, the NHL took the game back to its roots by hosting the Heritage Classic, an outdoor game in Edmonton, Canada. It was a throwback to pond hockey, played in freezing temperatures in front of thousands of bundled-up fans. It's like having a snowball fight with your friends, but on a much, much bigger scale.

32: The Stanley Cup's Lost Names
The Stanley Cup has been around for over a century, and every year, the winning team's players have their names engraved on it. But, due to spelling errors and name corrections, some players have their names on the Cup more than once! It's like getting a gold star from your teacher, but she spells your name wrong – twice.

33: The Lucky Loonie
During the 2002 Winter Olympics in Salt Lake City, a Canadian ice maker secretly placed a loonie (Canadian $1 coin) at center ice. Both the men's and women's Canadian hockey teams won gold medals, and the loonie was credited with bringing them luck. It's like finding a four-leaf clover before a big test and acing it!

34: The Ice Hockey World Championships' Surprise Winner
In 1936, Great Britain won the Ice Hockey World Championships, surprising everyone since Britain isn't known for its ice hockey prowess. It was like the underdog team in a movie pulling off a miracle win – the kind that makes you stand up and cheer!

35: The Player Who Played for Both Teams in One Game
In the early days of the NHL, teams sometimes didn't have backup goalies. So, if a goalie was injured, they would borrow one from the opposing team. This led to the odd situation where a player could play for both teams in the same game. It's like playing a video game with

your friend and then suddenly switching controllers in the middle of the game.

36: The Sudden Death Overtime Origin
The term "sudden death" to describe overtime in hockey was first used in the 1930s. It sounds pretty dramatic, but it just means the first team to score wins the game immediately. It's like playing a game of tag where the next person you tag becomes "it" for the next round, no questions asked.

37: The NHL's Forgotten Team
The Montreal Maroons were an NHL team from 1924 to 1938, winning the Stanley Cup twice. However, as the Great Depression took its toll, the team folded and is now a forgotten chapter in hockey history. It's like discovering a secret level in your favorite game that no one else knows about.

38: The Most Penalties in One Game
In a 1981 game between the Boston Bruins and the Minnesota North Stars, the teams combined for a record 406 penalty minutes, including 12 fights. It was more like a brawl than a hockey game, with players spending more time in the "sin bin" than on the ice. It's like playing a game of dodgeball where everyone forgets about the ball and just starts arguing.

39: The Longest Name on the Stanley Cup
With a name that stretches 24 letters long, Wally Van Allan has the longest name ever engraved on the Stanley Cup. It's so long, you'd need to take a breath halfway through saying it. Imagine if every time you scored a goal, the announcer had to pause for a breath before finishing your name!

40: The Hockey Night Tradition
"Hockey Night in Canada" has been a Saturday night tradition since 1952, bringing games to Canadians coast to coast. It's like the weekly movie night, but instead of picking a film, everyone knows it's going to be hockey, every Saturday, without fail.

41: The Youngest NHL Player
At just 15 years old, Armand "Bep" Guidolin became the youngest player to ever play in the NHL, making his debut in 1942. It's like being promoted to the big leagues of school recess when you're still in kindergarten!

42: The First Black NHL Player
In 1958, Willie O'Ree broke the color barrier in the NHL, playing for the Boston Bruins. He faced many challenges but paved the way for future generations of players from diverse backgrounds. It's like being the first kid to climb the highest tree in the park, showing everyone it can be done.

43: The Hockey Game That Never Ended
Well, not exactly, but in 1932, a game between the Detroit Red Wings and the Montreal Canadiens was called off after three overtime periods due to a curfew, with no winner declared. It's like playing a game of hide and seek that goes on so long, everyone just decides to go home for dinner.

44: The Oldest NHL Rookie
At 38 years old, Connie Madigan became the oldest rookie to ever play in the NHL, making his debut in 1973. It shows you're never too old to chase your dreams, even if it means lacing up skates and hitting the ice with players half your age.

45: The Hockey Hall of Fame's First Female Inductee
In 2010, Cammi Granato and Angela James became the first women inducted into the Hockey Hall of Fame, breaking the ice ceiling for female players

everywhere. It's like being chosen first for the team, not just among the girls, but among everyone.

46: The Stanley Cup's Misspelled Names
Despite the honor of having one's name engraved on the Stanley Cup, there have been over a dozen spelling errors over the years, including legendary names like Jacques Plante and the Boston Bruins. It's like getting a trophy with your name on it, but they call you "Bob" instead of "Rob."

47: The Goalie Who Scored in His Own Net
In an attempt to clear the puck, goalie Ron Hextall accidentally scored in his own net during a 1987 game. It's a reminder that even pros can have an "oops" moment, just like accidentally scoring an own goal in a soccer game with friends.

48: The NHL's First European Captain to Win the Stanley Cup
In 2008, Nicklas Lidstrom of the Detroit Red Wings became the first European captain to lift the Stanley Cup, showing that leadership and skill know no borders. It's like being the captain of your school project team and leading them to an A+.

49: The Player Who Won the Most Stanley Cups
Henri Richard of the Montreal Canadiens holds the record for the most Stanley Cup wins by a player, with 11 championships. It's like winning the school spelling bee 11 times in a row – a streak that's hard to beat!

50: The Annual Teddy Bear Toss
In a heartwarming tradition, fans throw teddy bears onto the ice after the home team scores its first goal. The bears are then collected and donated to children's hospitals. It's a beautiful way to spread joy and love, showing that hockey is more than just a game.

51: The Record for Most Teams Played For
Mike Sillinger holds the NHL record for playing on the most teams throughout his career. From 1990 to 2009, he laced up skates for 12 different teams! It's like going to a new school every year and having to make new friends each time.

52: The First NHL Game Broadcast on TV
The first NHL game ever broadcast on television was in 1952, between the Montreal Canadiens and the Detroit Red Wings. Viewers watched the game on small, grainy screens, a far cry from today's high-definition broadcasts. It's like going from playing video games on your phone to a giant arcade screen.

53: The Birth of the Playoff Beard Tradition
The tradition of growing a "playoff beard" began in the 1980s with the New York Islanders. Players wouldn't shave until their team was either eliminated or won the Stanley Cup. It's like having a lucky charm, but instead of carrying it in your pocket, you grow it on your face!

54: The Fastest Goal in NHL History
The fastest goal in NHL history was scored just 2 seconds into a game. This record is held by Doug Smail of the Winnipeg Jets and Bryan Trottier of the New York Islanders. It's like scoring a point in a game before your opponent even knows the game has started.

55: The Invention of the Hockey Helmet
While helmets were not mandatory in the early days of hockey, the first player to regularly wear one was George Owen in the 1928-1929 NHL season. It took until 1979 for the NHL to require all new players to wear helmets, showing how attitudes towards safety evolve. It's like being the only kid wearing knee pads and elbow guards at the skate park,

but soon everyone realizes it's a good idea.

56: The Youngest Team Captain to Win a Stanley Cup 🏆👶
Sidney Crosby became the youngest team captain in NHL history to win the Stanley Cup in 2009 with the Pittsburgh Penguins at the age of 21. It's like being voted class president in elementary school and then actually getting to run the school for a day.

57: The Origin of the Term "Hat Trick" 🎩
The term "hat trick" is used when a player scores three goals in a game. It originated from cricket in England but became popular in hockey when fans would throw hats onto the ice to celebrate the achievement. It's like getting a high-five, but with hats, and a lot more of them.

58: The First Indoor Ice Rink 🏠
The first indoor ice rink opened in London in 1876, paving the way for hockey to be played year-round, regardless of the weather outside. It's like discovering you can have ice cream any time, not just in summer.

59: The Longest NHL Career ⏳
Gordie Howe holds the record for the longest NHL career, playing 26 seasons from 1946 to 1980. He's a true example of longevity and passion for the game, like your favorite toy from childhood that you still enjoy as a teenager.

60: The NHL's First Broadcast in Color 📺
The first NHL game broadcast in color was on November 25, 1966, allowing fans to see their teams' colors on TV for the first time. It's like watching your favorite black and white cartoon and suddenly seeing it in full color.

61: The First Player to Score 50 Goals in a Season 🏒
Maurice "Rocket" Richard was the first NHL player to score 50 goals in a single season (1944-45). Achieving this milestone set a new standard for scoring excellence in the league. It's like being the first kid in class to finish a book reading challenge.

62: The Creation of the Goalie Mask 🥅
Jacques Plante was the first NHL goaltender to wear a protective mask in a regular-season game on November 1, 1959. This innovation forever changed the position, making it safer for goalies. It's like being the first person to bring an umbrella to school on a rainy day, showing everyone how useful it can be.

63: The Origin of the NHL 🏒
The National Hockey League (NHL) was founded on November 26, 1917, in Montreal, Quebec, Canada, with four original teams. It's like starting a club with your friends that grows into the most popular club at school.

64: The First Female NHL Coach 👩🏒
In 1992, Manon Rhéaume became not only the first woman to play in an NHL preseason game but also later went on to coach in a professional men's hockey league, breaking yet another gender barrier in the sport. It's like the girl who not only joins the boys' soccer team but also becomes the team captain.

65: The Most Consecutive Stanley Cup Wins 🏆
The Montreal Canadiens hold the record for the most consecutive Stanley Cup wins, with five championships from 1956 to 1960. It's like winning the school talent show every year from kindergarten to fourth grade.

66: The First NHL Player of Asian Descent 🏒

Larry Kwong was the first NHL player of Asian descent, breaking the ice for the league's diversity when he played for the New York Rangers in 1948. It's like being the first person from your neighborhood to be featured on a popular TV show.

67: The NHL's Expansion Beyond Six Teams

In 1967, the NHL expanded beyond the "Original Six" by adding six more teams, doubling the league's size and beginning its transformation into the diverse and widespread league it is today. It's like your small club at school suddenly welcoming a bunch of new members and becoming one of the biggest clubs around.

68: The First Outdoor NHL Game in the Modern Era

The 2003 Heritage Classic in Edmonton was the first regular-season outdoor NHL game in the modern era, reviving the tradition of playing hockey in its original, outdoor setting. It's like taking your video game console outside to play in the backyard for the first time.

69: The Goalie Without a Mask

Andy Brown was the last NHL goalie to play without a mask, doing so until retiring in 1974. Playing one of the most dangerous positions without today's standard protective gear is like riding a bike downhill with no helmet!

70: The First African-American NHL Player

Willie O'Ree, who broke the NHL's color barrier in 1958, is often referred to as the "Jackie Robinson of ice hockey." His pioneering role opened the door for players of all races and backgrounds to compete at the highest levels of the sport. It's like being the first kid from your town to compete in a national competition, setting the stage for others to follow.

71: The Highest-Scoring Game

The highest-scoring NHL game ever took place on January 10, 1920, between the Montreal Canadiens and the Toronto St. Pats, with a final score of 14-7. It was like a video game match where defense was an afterthought, and every shot turned into a goal!

72: The Origin of the Penalty Shot

The penalty shot was introduced to the NHL in the 1934-35 season as a way to penalize a team for committing a foul that prevented a clear scoring opportunity. It's like getting a free throw in basketball because someone stopped you from making a sure basket.

73: The First NHL Player to Reach 1,000 Points

Gordie Howe was the first player in NHL history to reach 1,000 career points, achieving this milestone on November 27, 1960. It's like being the first person to reach the top level in a video game that everyone in your school is trying to beat.

74: The Evolution of the Hockey Puck

Early hockey pucks were made from wood and even frozen cow dung before settling on the vulcanized rubber we use today. This evolution was crucial for the game's development, much like how upgrading your gear in a game helps you achieve better results.

75: The Introduction of the Forward Pass

The forward pass was not always allowed in hockey. It was introduced to the NHL in the 1929-30 season, radically changing the strategy and speed of the game. It's like introducing a new rule in tag that allows you to teleport, completely changing how the game is played.

76: The Longest Unbeaten Streak

The 1979-80 Philadelphia Flyers hold the record for the longest unbeaten streak in NHL history, going 35 games without a loss. It's like playing a game on the hardest difficulty and not losing a single life for weeks.

77: The First NHL Game Played in Europe
The NHL's first regular-season games in Europe were played in 2007, when the Los Angeles Kings and the Anaheim Ducks faced off in London, England. It marked the beginning of the league's efforts to grow the game internationally, similar to going on an epic quest that takes you to new, unexplored lands.

78: The Oldest Rookie to Score a Goal
Gordie Howe, at 52 years and 11 days old, is the oldest player to score a goal in the NHL, proving that age is just a number when it comes to talent and passion. It's like your grandparent beating you at your favorite video game and showing you they've still got it.

79: The First Winter Classic
The first NHL Winter Classic, an outdoor game played on New Year's Day, took place in 2008 between the Buffalo Sabres and the Pittsburgh Penguins. This event has since become a beloved annual tradition, akin to waking up on your birthday knowing something special is going to happen.

80: The Stanley Cup's Travel Adventures
The Stanley Cup has traveled the world, including visits to the Arctic Circle, the White House, and even a live combat zone in Afghanistan. It's the most well-traveled trophy in sports, much like that one friend who always seems to be visiting someplace new.

81: The First All-Star Game
The NHL's first All-Star Game was held in 1947 as a benefit for the players' pension fund. It featured the previous season's Stanley Cup champions against a selection of players from the other teams, similar to assembling a dream team in your favorite sports video game.

82: The NHL's Integration of Advanced Stats
In recent years, the NHL has embraced advanced statistics ("analytics") to evaluate players and strategies more effectively, akin to using a high-tech gadget to find hidden treasures in a game.

83: The Record for Most Saves in a Playoff Game
Goalie Kelly Hrudey made 73 saves for the New York Islanders in a 1987 playoff game against the Washington Capitals, the most in an NHL playoff game. It was like a marathon where every step was a potential stumble, but he never fell.

84: The First Helmeted NHL Team
The Boston Bruins became the first NHL team to have all its players wearing helmets during a game in 1979, leading the way in player safety. It's like being the first in your neighborhood to wear the coolest new fashion trend, and then everyone else starts wearing it too.

85: The First Broadcasted NHL Game in HD
The NHL entered the high-definition era in 2003, with the first game broadcasted in HD, offering fans a clearer and more immersive viewing experience, much like switching from a standard TV to a cinema screen.

86: The Creation of the Presidents' Trophy
Introduced in the 1985-86 season, the Presidents' Trophy is awarded to the NHL team that finishes the regular season with the most points. It's like getting a bonus prize for being the best player throughout the game, not just at the end.

87: The First NHL Video Game
The first officially licensed NHL video game was "NHL Hockey" by EA Sports, released in 1991. It marked the beginning of a beloved series that has introduced countless fans to the sport, akin to how a gateway hobby can lead to a lifelong passion.

88: The Most Goals by a Defenseman in One Season
Paul Coffey set the record for most goals by a defenseman in a single season with 48 goals in 1985-86. It's like breaking the high score in a game where no one thought it was possible to get that many points.

89: The NHL's First Female Full-Time Coach
In 2016, Dawn Braid became the first female full-time coach in the NHL when she was hired as a skating coach by the Arizona Coyotes, breaking new ground for women in the sport. It's like unlocking a character in a game that no one knew existed.

90: The Fastest Skate in NHL History
Connor McDavid set a new NHL record during the 2019 Skills Competition, skating a lap in just 13.378 seconds. It's like using a speed boost in a racing game that propels you far ahead of the competition.

91: The First Brother Duo in the Hall of Fame
Maurice "Rocket" Richard and Henri Richard were the first siblings to be inducted into the Hockey Hall of Fame. Their incredible careers with the Montreal Canadiens left a lasting legacy, much like being the first two kids from the same family to win the school's annual talent show.

92: The Shortest Player to Play in the NHL
Roy Worters, standing at 5 feet 3 inches, was the shortest player ever to play in the NHL. Despite his stature, he had a remarkable career as a goaltender, proving that in hockey, skill and determination outweigh size, akin to the smallest player on the playground being the fastest or most agile.

93: The NHL's First Outdoor Game at a Military Service Academy
The 2018 NHL Stadium Series featured the first outdoor game held at a U.S. military service academy, between the Washington Capitals and the Toronto Maple Leafs at the Naval Academy in Annapolis, Maryland. It was a unique blend of sports and service, like when your school sports day is held at a local army base.

94: The First NHL Player to Defect from the Soviet Union
In 1989, Alexander Mogilny became the first player to defect from the Soviet Union to play in the NHL, joining the Buffalo Sabres. His brave move opened the door for other Eastern European players, akin to being the first person to explore uncharted territory in a video game.

95: The Creation of the NHL Players' Association
The NHL Players' Association (NHLPA) was founded in 1967 to advocate for players' rights and improve their working conditions, much like forming a guild in a multiplayer game to ensure fair treatment for all members.

96: The First Use of Instant Replay in the NHL
In 1991, the NHL introduced instant replay to help referees make the right call on contentious goals. It was a game-changer, ensuring fairness and accuracy, similar to using a replay feature in video games to perfect your strategy.

97: The NHL's First Outdoor Game in a Prison Yard

In a unique twist, the 2012 "Big House" Winter Classic was held at Michigan Stadium, affectionately known as the "Big House." Though not an actual prison, the nickname adds a quirky element, like playing a sports game in the most unexpected of settings in a video game world.

98: The First Helmeted Goalie
Jacques Plante was not only pioneering in wearing a face mask but also was among the first goalies to regularly wear a helmet beneath his mask, enhancing safety in a role where bravery meets skill, akin to equipping your character with the best armor in a role-playing game.

99: The NHL's First Expansion Team to Win the Stanley Cup
The Philadelphia Flyers, one of the six teams added during the 1967 NHL expansion, were the first expansion team to win the Stanley Cup in 1974, showing that new teams could compete at the highest level, much like a rookie player winning a tournament against seasoned veterans.

100: The Introduction of the Coach's Challenge
Introduced in the 2015-2016 season, the coach's challenge allows teams to request a review of certain officiating decisions, bringing strategy and a new layer of fairness to the game, similar to having a second chance to complete a mission in a game after initially failing.

101: The NHL's First Game Broadcast in 3D
In 2010, the NHL entered the 3D broadcasting era, offering fans a new, immersive way to watch hockey, enhancing the viewing experience much like the jump from 2D to 3D gaming revolutionized video games.

102: The Longest Serving NHL Captain
Steve Yzerman served as the captain of the Detroit Red Wings for 19 seasons (1986-2006), making him the longest-serving captain of any team in NHL history, a testament to leadership and loyalty, akin to a player sticking with their team through every level of a challenging game.

103: The Most Penalties in a Single NHL Season
During the 1974-1975 season, the Philadelphia Flyers, known as the "Broad Street Bullies," accumulated the most penalties in a single NHL season, showcasing their aggressive style of play, like choosing the most belligerent character in a fighting game.

104: The NHL's First Triple Overtime Stanley Cup Final Game
The first triple overtime game in Stanley Cup Final history took place in 1931 between the Chicago Blackhawks and the Montreal Canadiens, showcasing the endurance and determination of the players, akin to a marathon gaming session that stretches into the wee hours.

105: The First NHL Mascot
In 1976, the Philadelphia Flyers introduced the NHL's first mascot, "Slapshot," paving the way for the league's teams to adopt their own unique mascots, adding fun and entertainment to the game experience, much like unlockable characters add to a video game's replay value.

106: The First NHL Game Broadcast Coast-to-Coast
The first NHL game to be broadcast coast-to-coast in the United States took place on January 18, 1953. This monumental broadcast between the Boston Bruins and the Montreal Canadiens allowed fans across the nation

to partake in the excitement of hockey, much like a viral live stream that captivates audiences everywhere.

107: The Highest Altitude NHL Game
The 2020 NHL Stadium Series game at the Air Force Academy's Falcon Stadium was one of the highest-altitude games ever played, at over 6,600 feet above sea level. The unique setting tested the players' endurance and showcased the sport's adaptability, similar to playing a game level designed with extreme environmental challenges.

108: The First NHL Player to Kneel During the National Anthem
In 2020, Matt Dumba became the first NHL player to take a knee during the national anthem, highlighting the sport's growing awareness and involvement in social justice movements, much like a pivotal moment in a narrative-driven game that challenges players' perspectives.

109: The NHL's First Foray into Virtual Reality
The NHL has experimented with virtual reality (VR) to bring fans closer to the action, offering VR experiences that allow users to feel as though they're on the ice with the players, similar to immersive VR gaming that transports players to new worlds.

110: The Oldest NHL Team Never to Win the Stanley Cup
The Vancouver Canucks, established in 1970, are among the oldest teams in the NHL never to have won the Stanley Cup, exemplifying the perseverance and loyal fanbase akin to players who stick with a challenging game, determined to see it through to the end.

111: The First NHL Player Born in the Bahamas
Andre Deveaux, born in the Bahamas, became the first NHL player from the tropical archipelago when he debuted in the 2008-2009 season, showcasing hockey's global appeal, similar to a globally popular game that attracts players from every corner of the world.

112: The NHL's Greenest Arena
The Seattle Kraken's Climate Pledge Arena is considered the greenest arena in the NHL, emphasizing sustainability and environmental consciousness, much like eco-friendly gaming consoles and peripherals aim to reduce the environmental impact of gaming.

113: The First NHL Outdoor Game in Canada
The 2003 Heritage Classic in Edmonton was the first official outdoor NHL game in Canada, pitting the Oilers against the Montreal Canadiens in frigid temperatures, reminiscent of playing a game mode that tests survival skills in extreme conditions.

114: The Most Goals Scored by a Team in a Single Game
The Montreal Canadiens set the record for the most goals scored by a team in a single NHL game with 16 goals against the Quebec Bulldogs on March 3, 1920, showcasing an offensive powerhouse similar to achieving a high score in an arcade game that seems unbeatable.

115: The NHL's Contribution to War Effort
During World War II, numerous NHL players paused their hockey careers to serve in the military, demonstrating the league's commitment to broader societal responsibilities, akin to games that include themes of sacrifice and heroism.

116: The First Helmeted Player in the NHL
In the 1940s, Boston Bruins' forward George Owen became one of the first players to regularly wear a helmet during NHL games, paving the way for player safety innovations, similar to the introduction of new safety features in game controllers to prevent injuries.

117: The NHL's Introduction of the Shootout
The shootout was introduced in the 2005-2006 season to resolve ties in regular-season games, adding a dramatic conclusion to matches akin to a sudden-death round in a competitive game.

118: The First NHL Team to Fly to a Game
The Detroit Red Wings became the first NHL team to fly to an away game when they chartered a flight in 1950, marking a new era in sports travel that mirrored the expansive reach of gaming through online multiplayer experiences.

119: The First Indigenous NHL Player
Fred Sasakamoose became one of the first Indigenous players in the NHL when he debuted with the Chicago Blackhawks in 1953, breaking barriers and inspiring future generations, much like groundbreaking characters and stories in video games that celebrate diversity

120: The Invention of the Curved Hockey Stick Blade
In the 1960s, Stan Mikita and Bobby Hull are credited with popularizing the curved blade, revolutionizing how players shoot and handle the puck. This innovation allowed for more unpredictable and powerful shots, akin to discovering a game-changing strategy in a competitive video game that shifts the balance of play.

121: The NHL's Integration of Women into Broadcasting
In 1978, Robin Herman and Marcel St. Cyr became the first female reporters to enter an NHL locker room, breaking gender barriers in sports journalism. Their pioneering efforts paved the way for future generations, similar to the inclusion of female protagonists in video games, offering more diversity and representation.

122: The Creation of the NHL Draft Lottery
Introduced in 1995, the NHL Draft Lottery was designed to discourage teams from losing on purpose to secure the first overall draft pick. This system ensures a fair and exciting process for teams to acquire top talent, much like randomized loot systems in games that keep every player's experience unique and engaging.

123: The Fastest Three Goals by a Single Player
Bill Mosienko holds the record for the fastest three goals by a single player, scoring them in just 21 seconds during a game in 1952. This feat is akin to achieving a rare and difficult achievement in a game that few players can claim.

124: The Introduction of Glow Pucks
In an attempt to make hockey more viewer-friendly on television, Fox Sports introduced the "glow puck" in the 1990s. This innovation, which highlighted the puck's location with a glowing halo, was like adding a visual aid in a video game to enhance player experience, though it received mixed reviews from fans.

125: The First NHL Outdoor Game Broadcast in 4K
The NHL entered the ultra-high-definition era with the broadcast of the 2016 Winter Classic in 4K resolution, offering fans an unprecedented level of detail and immersion, similar to the leap in graphics fidelity seen with the latest generation of gaming consoles.

126: The Most Career NHL Games Played
Gordie Howe holds the record for the most NHL games played in a career, with

1,767 regular-season games. This longevity is akin to a gamer who has logged thousands of hours in a single game, mastering its every aspect.

127: The NHL's First-Ever Tie Game

The first recorded tie in NHL history occurred on December 8, 1917, between the Montreal Wanderers and the Toronto Arenas, ending in a 10-10 deadlock. This was before the era of overtime and shootouts, much like early video games that would end in a draw if neither player could secure a win within the time limit.

128: The Development of Synthetic Ice Surfaces

Advancements in technology have led to the creation of high-quality synthetic ice surfaces, allowing for hockey training and play in climates and locations where natural ice is not feasible, akin to how advancements in VR technology have expanded the accessibility and types of gaming experiences available.

129: The Youngest Captain to Lift the Stanley Cup

Sidney Crosby became the youngest captain in NHL history to win the Stanley Cup at the age of 21 years and 10 months in 2009. This achievement is like a young esports player leading their team to victory in a major tournament, showcasing talent and leadership beyond their years.

130: The Use of RFID Technology in Pucks and Players' Jerseys

The NHL has experimented with Radio Frequency Identification (RFID) technology to track player movements and puck location in real time, providing a wealth of data for analytics. This innovation is akin to real-time strategy elements in video games that allow players to analyze and adjust their tactics on the fly.

131: First NHL Player to Score on His Own Net During a Power Play

Steve Smith infamously scored on his own net during Game 7 of the 1986 Smythe Division Finals on his 23rd birthday, inadvertently helping the Calgary Flames eliminate his team, the Edmonton Oilers. This event is reminiscent of a critical error in a video game that leads to an unexpected defeat, showcasing the unpredictability of sports and games alike.

132: The Most Consecutive Wins by a Goalie

Between February 9 and March 6, 2016, Braden Holtby of the Washington Capitals tied the NHL record for the most consecutive wins by a goaltender, with 11 straight victories. This streak mirrors a player on a winning spree in competitive gaming, where momentum seems unstoppable.

133: The Inaugural Outdoor NHL Game Played in a Prison Yard

A lesser-known piece of hockey lore is the outdoor game played in 1954 at the Marquette Branch Prison in Michigan. This unique setting for an exhibition match between the Detroit Red Wings and prison inmates is akin to a hidden level or easter egg in a video game, offering a unique experience outside the main storyline.

134: The First NHL Player to Reach 2,000 Penalty Minutes

Tiger Williams is renowned for his toughness, becoming the first NHL player to accumulate over 2,000 penalty minutes in his career. This record is a testament to his role as an enforcer on the ice, similar to a character in a video game known for their high-risk, high-reward playstyle.

135: The Introduction of the Two-Line Pass Rule

The NHL eliminated the two-line offside pass rule before the 2005-2006 season, leading to a faster, more open game. This change is akin to a game update that tweaks the mechanics for a more fluid and dynamic player experience.

136: Oldest Player to Win a Stanley Cup
Chris Chelios was 46 years old when he won his last Stanley Cup with the Detroit Red Wings in 2008, showcasing that age is but a number in the pursuit of excellence, much like veteran gamers who remain competitive in the esports scene.

137: First NHL Game Played in Europe
The NHL's first regular-season games played in Europe occurred in October 2007, with the Anaheim Ducks and the Los Angeles Kings facing off in London, England. This expansion is similar to global online multiplayer games that unite players from various continents in a shared gaming experience.

138: The First Use of a Siren to Signal the End of a Period
Originally, the end of a period in an NHL game was signaled by a bell or a whistle. The transition to using a loud siren is a notable evolution in the game's presentation, enhancing the spectator experience in a manner akin to the development of immersive sound effects in video gaming.

139: The First NHL Player of South Asian Descent
Robin Bawa made history as the first player of South Asian descent to play in the NHL, debuting in 1989. His groundbreaking presence in the league paved the way for greater diversity in hockey, reflecting the growing inclusivity found in the global gaming community.

140: The Longest Gap Between Stanley Cup Championships
The New York Rangers ended a 54-year championship drought by winning the Stanley Cup in 1994, a narrative of perseverance and eventual triumph akin to completing a notoriously difficult game or level after numerous attempts.

141: The First NHL Player to Win Consecutive MVP Awards with Different Teams
Dominik Hasek won the Hart Trophy as the league's MVP in consecutive seasons (1997 and 1998) while playing for two different teams, showcasing a level of individual excellence and adaptability that mirrors a top player dominating in different gaming genres or titles.

142: The Invention of the Goal Judge's Light
The goal judge's light, used to signal when a goal has been scored, was introduced to enhance the accuracy of scoring calls, much like feedback systems in video games that confirm achievements or successes to players.

EARLY COMPETITIONS

1: The Stanley Cup's Mysterious Beginnings
Did you know the Stanley Cup was originally just a bowl? Yep, in 1892, Lord Stanley of Preston decided hockey players needed a trophy and bought a silver bowl for about $50. Imagine winning the biggest hockey tournament and being handed a salad bowl!

2: The First Winner's Surprise
The Montreal Amateur Athletic Association (MAAA) was the first team to win the Stanley Cup in 1893. But here's the kicker: there was no championship game! They were just declared the best team. It's like winning a video game tournament because you have the coolest username.

3: The Cup Gets Lost!
In 1905, the Ottawa Silver Seven were so excited about winning the Stanley

Cup, they decided to kick it across the Rideau Canal. The next day, they realized it was missing but luckily found it in a snowbank. Talk about a cold victory!

4: The Stanley Cup Goes to War
During World War I, the 1919 Stanley Cup Finals were cancelled because of the Spanish Flu epidemic. It's like trying to play hockey in a swimming pool, not very effective and definitely not recommended.

5: The Cup's Traveling Tales
The Stanley Cup has seen more of the world than most people, including a dip in Mario Lemieux's swimming pool and a visit to a strip club. It's the most adventurous trophy ever, probably with more stories than a globe-trotting grandparent!

6: The First Women's Name on the Cup
In 1992, the Cup broke tradition! Marguerite Norris, the first female NHL executive as president of the Detroit Red Wings, got her name engraved on the Stanley Cup. It's like discovering a secret level in a game that was supposed to be boys-only.

7: The Cup Survives a Fire!
In 1962, the Montreal Canadiens' home arena caught fire, but the Stanley Cup was saved from the flames. It's like that one toy that survives every cleanup, no matter how much chaos ensues.

8: The World Championships' Humble Beginnings
The first Ice Hockey World Championships were held in 1920 during the Summer Olympics. That's right, hockey in summer! It's like playing beach volleyball in a snowstorm.

9: No Ice, No Problem!
In 1912, at the first European Ice Hockey Championship, they had to play the final game on a frozen lake because there was no indoor ice rink available. Talk about a home-ice advantage!

10: A Trophy Full of Names
The Stanley Cup has so many names engraved on it that it now stands at nearly three feet tall. If trophies were like trees, the Stanley Cup would be the tallest in the forest, with each name a leaf on its branches.

11: The Challenge Cup Era
Before the NHL took control, the Stanley Cup was a challenge cup, meaning any team could challenge the current holder for a shot at glory. It's like being the king of the hill in your backyard, where anyone can try to dethrone you.

12: The One-Time Wonders
The Victoria Cougars are the last non-NHL team to win the Stanley Cup, back in 1925. Imagine being the ultimate underdogs and taking home the biggest prize in hockey. It's like winning a race on a tricycle against fancy sports cars.

13: A Cup for a Dentist?
In the early days, the Stanley Cup was so obscure that it was once left in a photographer's studio, which later became a dentist's office. So for a while, the most coveted trophy in hockey might have watched over some tooth extractions!

14: The Amateur Era Champions
Before the NHL monopolized the Stanley Cup, it was amateur teams who battled for the title. It's like your school's dodgeball tournament suddenly becoming a national competition.

15: The First International Face-Off
The 1920 Olympics featured the first international hockey competition, making it a true battle of the nations on ice. It's like inviting your online gaming friends from around the world for a local tournament.

16: The Cup's Forgotten Champions
Several teams that won the Stanley Cup in the early days are no longer active, like the Kenora Thistles. It's like being the champion of a game that's no longer popular, but the glory still feels good.

17: The Stanley Cup's Edible Replica
A chocolate company once made a life-size Stanley Cup replica. That's right, a trophy you can eat! It's every kid's dream: winning a championship and then eating the prize.

18: The Non-Stop Party Cup
The Stanley Cup has been to more parties than any other trophy, often filled with all kinds of beverages. It's like the popular kid at school who's invited to every birthday bash.

19: The Handoff Tradition
The tradition of players handing the Stanley Cup directly to each other started with the New York Islanders in the 1980s. It's like passing down a legendary sword in a video game from one hero to another.

20: The Cup's Summer Vacation
Every winning player gets a day with the Stanley Cup, taking it on adventures from fishing trips to mountaintop. It's like the most interesting pet that everyone gets to babysit for a day.

21: A Trophy That Grows
Unlike most trophies, the Stanley Cup gets taller as more rings are added to the bottom. It's like a plant that grows with each victory, except you can't water this one.

22: The Accidental Swim
The Stanley Cup has accidentally fallen into swimming pools more than once during celebrations. It's like that friend who always ends up in the pool with their clothes on at parties.

23: The DIY Repairs
The Cup has been dented and damaged so many times that it's undergone numerous repairs. It's like that one toy you keep fixing because you can't bear to part with it.

24: The Stolen Cup Caper
In 1970, the Stanley Cup was stolen from the Hockey Hall of Fame, only to be mysteriously returned. It's like the plot of a detective movie, but with a happy ending.

25: The First Stanley Cup Parade
The tradition of parading the Stanley Cup through the winning city started with the Montreal Canadiens. It's like taking your trophy on a victory lap around the neighborhood, showing off to all your friends.

26: The Cup's Day Off
Believe it or not, the Stanley Cup once got forgotten by the side of the road! The 1905 Ottawa Silver Seven, perhaps too jubilant from their win, left it behind. It's like leaving your lunchbox at the park, but way, way more valuable.

27: The Mini Stanley Cup
Did you know there's a mini version of the Stanley Cup? In 1997, the Detroit Red Wings made a pint-sized replica for the team mascot. It's like having a mini-me that's cool enough to have its own mini-adventures!

28: The Animal Encounter
The Stanley Cup has met more animals than a zookeeper! It's been nibbled by horses, cuddled by dogs, and even encountered a penguin. Imagine telling a penguin, "No sliding with the Cup!"

29: The Invisible Stanley Cup

In 1907, the Montreal Wanderers' rink burned down, and the Cup was thought to be lost in the fire. Turns out, it was safe all along in a bank vault. It's like finding your "lost" video game under the couch.

30: The Top-Secret Formula
The exact metal blend used to make the Stanley Cup is a closely guarded secret. It's like the recipe for your grandma's famous cookies – everyone loves it, but only she knows how to make it just right.

31: The Cup's Name Corrections
Mistakes happen, and the Stanley Cup has a few misspelled names engraved on it. When they're noticed, sometimes they get corrected, sometimes not. It's like autocorrect gone wrong but in metal.

32: The Unofficial Swim Team
The Stanley Cup has taken more swims than a fish, often ending up in players' pools. It's like that one friend who always ends up pushing everyone into the pool at parties.

33: The Kidnapped Cup
In 1962, the Cup was "kidnapped" by Toronto Maple Leafs fans demanding a better team. The ransom? A winning squad. It's like holding your video game hostage until it agrees to give you unlimited lives.

34: The Double Duty Cup
Not just for hoisting, the Stanley Cup has been used to baptize babies and even as a giant cereal bowl. Imagine eating your morning Cheerios out of a trophy!

35: The Most Traveled Trophy
With all its adventures, the Stanley Cup is likely the most traveled sports trophy in the world, visiting over 25 countries. It's like that one classmate who's been everywhere and has the coolest stories.

36: The Oldest Professional Athlete Trophy
The Stanley Cup is the oldest professional sports trophy in North America, making it the great-grandparent of championship awards. It's seen more games than any living fan!

37: The Cup's Bodyguard
Yes, the Stanley Cup has its own bodyguard! Wherever it goes, there's someone making sure it doesn't end up on another unexpected adventure. It's like having a personal chaperone for the most popular kid in school.

38: The "Stolen" Cup
In 1907, the Kenora Thistles briefly "stole" the Cup to engrave their names on it because they weren't added fast enough. It's like sneaking your name onto the top scorer list when no one's looking.

39: The Mystery of the Missing Ring
The original bowl of the Stanley Cup has had several bands added to fit more names. But as space runs out, older bands are removed, making it a trophy with a changing history. It's like editing your character's backstory in a role-playing game.

40: The First Women Champions
The first women to officially get their names on the Cup were the Edmonton Grads, a women's basketball team honored in 1924 for their international achievements, showing the Cup's love for all athletes.

41: The Stanley Cup Goes to the Movies
The Cup has had cameo appearances in movies and TV shows, making it more famous than some actors. It's like when your favorite video game character shows up in another game.

42: The Cup's Day in Court

The Stanley Cup has been the subject of legal battles, including who owns it and who can compete for it. It's like arguing over who gets to be player one in a video game. 🎮👤⚖️

43: The Cup's Clone 🏆👽
There's an exact replica of the Stanley Cup kept at the Hockey Hall of Fame for display when the original is traveling. It's like having a stunt double in a dangerous movie scene. 🎬🏆

44: The Signature Inside the Cup ✒️🏆
Players sometimes sneak their signatures inside the Cup's bowl or bands. It's like leaving a secret message in a hidden spot, hoping someone someday will find it. 🔑🔍

45: The Stanley Cup's Secret Keeper 👁️🏆
The names of all the winners are engraved on the bands, but only a select few know the stories behind each engraving. It's like being part of an exclusive club where every member has an epic tale. 📚🎟️

46: The Cup's Accidental Trip to Russia 🇷🇺🏆
In 1997, the Cup accidentally ended up on a flight to Russia when a player took the wrong plane. It's like your luggage going on a vacation without you. 🧳✈️

47: The Stanley Cup's Diet 🏆🍇
From popcorn to poutine, the Cup has held a smorgasbord of snacks and dishes during celebrations. It's like the ultimate party guest who brings the dish everyone wants to try. 🍿🍴

48: The Cup's Visit to the Top of the World 🏔️🏆
The Stanley Cup has been to the Arctic Circle, proving it's not just cool—it's Arctic cool. It's like unlocking the final, secret level in a game and finding out it's cooler than you imagined. ❄️🎮

49: The Cup's Close Call with Disaster 💥🏆
Despite its travels and adventures, the Stanley Cup has never been seriously damaged or lost. It's like the character in a game who has an invincibility cheat code. 🛡️🎮

50: The Ultimate Hockey Honor 🏒🏆
Winning the Stanley Cup is considered the ultimate honor in hockey, a dream that every player chases from the moment they lace up their first pair of skates. It's like reaching the final level in a game and realizing the journey was the best part. 🎮🖤

51: The Cup's Underwater Adventure 🏆🐠
The Stanley Cup has been on more than one underwater escapade, including being taken scuba diving. It's as if it has a secret life as a mermaid, exploring coral reefs and making friends with fish. 🐟🐙

52: The Midnight Sun Game ☀️🏒
In Dawson City, Yukon, a game of hockey under the midnight sun is a tradition, where players can experience the game in daylight at midnight. It's like playing your favorite video game with a never-ending power supply, where night never falls. 🌙🎮

53: The Smallest Town for a Big Win 🏆🏘️
In 1907, the Kenora Thistles from Kenora, Ontario (population of just a few thousand), won the Stanley Cup. It's like the smallest school at the spelling bee taking home the grand prize. 🐝🏆

54: The Goalie Who Scored a Goal 🥅🏒
Goalies hardly ever score, but Ron Hextall of the Philadelphia Flyers did just that in 1987, firing the puck into an empty net. It's like the quiet kid in class answering the toughest question

correctly, to everyone's amazement.

55: The First Broadcasted Ice Hockey Game
In 1923, a Canadian radio station broadcasted an ice hockey game for the first time. It was like streaming before the internet, where listeners had to imagine the icy action in their living rooms.

56: The Cup as a Cereal Bowl
Yes, players have eaten breakfast out of the Stanley Cup! It's like your bowl at home suddenly becoming the coolest dish ever, making even oatmeal taste like victory.

57: The Zamboni's Debut
The first Zamboni machine hit the ice in 1949, forever changing how ice rinks were resurfaced. It's like when video games introduced the reset button, making everything smooth and playable again.

58: The Stanley Cup's Day at the Derby
The Cup has also attended the Kentucky Derby, proving it's not just a fan of ice but also enjoys a day out at the races. It's like taking your skateboard to a bike race and still having a blast.

59: A Presidential Encounter
The Stanley Cup has visited the White House multiple times, meeting various U.S. Presidents. It's like being the most popular kid in school, where even the principal wants to shake your hand.

60: The Cup's Missing Day
There was a day when the Stanley Cup was lost in a nightclub, only to be found the next day under a table. It's like when you misplace your favorite game cartridge but find it just in time for the weekend.

61: The First Women to Play in the World Championships
Women's ice hockey debuted at the World Championships in 1990, marking a significant moment in the sport's history. It's like unlocking a new level in a game where the action gets even more exciting.

62: The Oldest Ice Hockey Rink
The oldest indoor ice hockey rink still in use today is Matthews Arena in Boston, opened in 1910. It's like playing in a historic castle, where every game feels like a knightly tournament.

63: The Longest Game Ever Played
In 1936, the Detroit Red Wings and the Montreal Maroons played the longest NHL game, lasting over 116 minutes of overtime. It's like a marathon gaming session that goes on all night, where no one wants to hit the pause button.

64: The Cup in Combat Zones
The Stanley Cup has visited troops in combat zones, bringing a piece of home to those serving far away. It's like sending your favorite game character on a mission to boost everyone's spirits.

65: The Trophy That Wasn't Just for Hockey
Initially, the Stanley Cup wasn't exclusive to hockey; it was meant for Canada's top-ranking amateur ice hockey club, which could include curling or other sports teams challenging for it. It's like a multi-game arcade cabinet that offers more than just one type of game.

66: The First Official Indoor Hockey Game
The first recorded indoor ice hockey game took place on March 3, 1875, in Montreal, paving the way for the sport's future. Imagine transitioning from playing in the cold to being indoors, like when gaming moved from arcades to living rooms.

67: The Stanley Cup's Logbook
Every adventure of the Stanley Cup is carefully logged by its handlers, creating

a diary filled with tales of joy, celebration, and sometimes, misadventure. It's like having a save file that records every step of your epic journey in a game.

68: The Cup as a Bonding Tool
Winning teams often bring the Stanley Cup to their hometowns, sharing their victory with family, friends, and fans. It's like sharing your highest game score with your friends, uniting everyone in a moment of pride.

69: The Youngest and Oldest Winners
The Stanley Cup has been hoisted by some of the youngest and oldest players in NHL history, showing that when it comes to hockey, age is just a number. It's like in video games, where both kids and adults can achieve greatness.

70: The Cup's Symbol of Resilience
Through pandemics, wars, and natural disasters, the Stanley Cup has endured, symbolizing the resilience and passion of the hockey community. It's like the save button that ensures no matter what happens, the game goes on.

71: The Cup's Accidental Tourist Trap
Believe it or not, the Stanley Cup once made an unexpected stop at a local bowling alley. Left behind by celebrating players, it became the star attraction among bowlers. Imagine rolling a strike and then getting to hoist the Cup as your prize.

72: The Ice Hockey World Championships' Unlikely Hero
In 1938, the British ice hockey team, composed largely of Canadian players living in the UK, won the World Championships. It's like your favorite video game character winning a battle in another game's universe.

73: The First Professional Ice Hockey Game
The first game considered to be professional ice hockey was played in 1904 in Houghton, Michigan. Players were actually paid, making it a pivotal moment in hockey history. It's like when gamers first realized they could make a career out of esports.

74: The Goal That Wasn't
During the 1999 Stanley Cup Finals, a controversial goal by Brett Hull of the Dallas Stars ended the series, despite debates over its legality according to the rules at the time. It's akin to winning a game on a technicality, sparking debates in every gaming forum online.

75: The Stanley Cup's Namesake's Never-Won Irony
Lord Stanley of Preston, the Governor General of Canada who donated the Stanley Cup, never actually saw a championship game or even knew the overwhelming success the trophy would achieve. It's like creating a viral video game but never playing it yourself.

76: The National Women's Hockey Team's Dominance
The Canadian women's national ice hockey team has an impressive track record at the World Championships, showcasing the growth and dominance of women in the sport. It's like a player who consistently tops the leaderboards, becoming a legend in their own right.

77: The Tradition of Playoff Beards
The tradition where players refrain from shaving during the playoffs has become a superstitious practice in hockey, symbolizing unity and focus. It's like equipping a lucky charm in a game for an extra boost.

78: The Oldest Stanley Cup Winner

Chris Chelios was 46 years old when he won his last Cup, making him one of the oldest players to ever win. It's like playing a marathon gaming session well into the night and coming out victorious as the sun rises.

79: The Instant Replay Revolution
The NHL was among the first major sports leagues to adopt instant replay technology in 1991, changing how games were officiated. It's akin to a game update that fixes all the previous bugs, making everything fairer for players.

80: The Youngest League MVP
Sidney Crosby won the Hart Trophy as the NHL MVP at the age of 19, showcasing the incredible talent and potential of young players. It's like unlocking the most challenging achievement in a game while still learning the controls.

81: The Multi-Sport Athletes
Some early hockey players were multi-sport athletes, competing in both ice hockey and other sports such as lacrosse or football. It's like mastering several genres of video games, from RPGs to FPS, and being awesome at all of them.

82: The Stanley Cup's Botanical Adventure
The Cup has been used as a flower pot more than once during its travels. Imagine the most prestigious trophy in hockey doubling as decor in someone's living room.

83: The Spontaneous Street Hockey Game
There's a tradition among some winning teams to play a spontaneous game of street hockey with the Cup present, bringing the sport back to its grassroots. It's like when gamers organize impromptu LAN parties to celebrate a big win.

84: The Mystery of the 1940 Engraving
Legend has it that a mischievous engraving related to a curse was hidden on the Cup by a disgruntled engraver in 1940. It's the kind of Easter egg that gamers might spend hours trying to find in their favorite game.

85: The Cup's International Diplomacy
The Stanley Cup has played a role in international diplomacy, being displayed in countries around the world as a symbol of peace and friendship through sports. It's like when gaming communities come together for charity streams, uniting for a common cause.

86: The Emergency Goalie Rule
In hockey, there's a rule that allows an emergency goalie (often a staff member or fan) to suit up and play if both team goalies are injured. It's like being called up from the audience to play on stage at a gaming convention.

87: The Unbreakable Records
Some early hockey records are considered unbreakable due to changes in the sport's dynamics and rules. It's like having a high score in a classic arcade game that stands the test of time.

88: The Fan Who Named the Ducks
The Anaheim Ducks were named after a fan contest following their depiction in the popular "Mighty Ducks" movies, showing the influence of pop culture on the sport. It's akin to video game fans voting on the name of a new character or game title.

89: The Referee's Unique Signal Language
Hockey referees use a unique set of hand signals to indicate penalties, resembling a silent language all their own. It's like learning cheat codes for a video game, where each combination has a specific outcome.

90: The Goal That Changed the Rules
After a controversial goal was allowed in the 1999 Stanley Cup Finals, the NHL reviewed and changed its rules regarding goal crease violations. It's like a game patch that fixes a glitch everyone's been complaining about.

91: The Multi-Talented Stanley Cup
The Stanley Cup isn't just a sports trophy; it's a movie star! It has appeared in several films and TV shows, sometimes playing itself, other times just casually hanging out in the background. It's like that versatile actor who's equally good in dramas and comedies, except shinier and more beloved by hockey fans.

92: The Reluctant Champions
In the early days of the Stanley Cup, winning teams weren't always eager to claim their prize. One year, the Cup was left at the home of a team's trustee because the winning team simply forgot to take it with them. It's like finishing first in a marathon and leaving without your medal because you were too tired to remember it.

93: The Cup's Secret Keeper
There's one man whose job is to keep the Stanley Cup safe and sound, traveling with it everywhere it goes. He's like a modern-day knight, except his armor is a suit, and his sword is a polishing cloth. Imagine having "Protector of the Cup" on your business cards!

94: The Stanley Cup's Day at School
Winners of the Stanley Cup have taken it to schools, sharing their victory with excited students. It turns a regular school day into an unforgettable experience, kind of like when the principal cancels classes for a surprise assembly, but infinitely cooler.

95: The Longest Overtime in Playoff History
The record for the longest overtime in NHL playoff history goes to a game between the Detroit Red Wings and the Montreal Maroons in 1936, lasting a whopping six overtime periods. It's like playing the final level of a video game, and it just keeps going and going, testing the limits of your endurance and snack supplies.

96: The Most Goals by One Team in a Stanley Cup Final Game
The most goals scored by a single team in a Stanley Cup Final game is 13, achieved by the Edmonton Oilers in 1985. Scoring 13 goals in a single game is like achieving a high score so high that even the game can't believe it.

97: The Stanley Cup's Visit to the Arctic Circle
Yes, the Cup has traveled to the Arctic Circle, proving its appeal is truly universal. It's met with fans in some of the coldest, most remote communities on earth, where ice hockey is a way of life. It's like your favorite game character showing up in real life for an epic adventure in your hometown.

98: The Cup's Custom Travel Case
The Stanley Cup has its own custom travel case, designed to keep it safe and secure no matter where in the world it goes. It's the VIP of luggage, with more stamps in its passport than most people dream of. It's like that special protective case you have for your most prized gaming console, but for the most famous trophy in sports.

99: The First Woman to Have Her Name Engraved on the Cup
In 1992, Marguerite Norris became the first woman to have her name engraved

on the Stanley Cup as president of the Detroit Red Wings. It was a groundbreaking moment, showing that the ice ceiling could be broken. It's like unlocking a previously unachievable achievement in a game, changing the rules for everyone who plays after you. 🎮

100: The Cup's Close Call with Fire ⚔️🏆
The Stanley Cup has survived many adventures, including being in a building when a fire broke out. Thankfully, it was rescued unscathed, proving its resilience. It's like that one character in every adventure movie who manages to escape every tricky situation without a scratch. 🎬🔥

EXPANSION AND POPULARITY

1: The Original Ice Breakers 🏒
Did you know the NHL started with only four teams, not six, in 1917? That's right! The Montreal Canadiens, Montreal Wanderers, Ottawa Senators, and Toronto Arenas were the cool kids on the block. Imagine playing against the same three teams all season. Talk about a small playground!

2: The Great Expansion 🌐
Fast forward to 1967, and the NHL decided it was time to invite more friends to the party. Doubling in size, it welcomed six new teams: Los Angeles Kings, California Seals, Philadelphia Flyers, Pittsburgh Penguins, St. Louis Blues, and Minnesota North Stars. Suddenly, the NHL's playground got a lot bigger!

3: From Sea to Shining Sea 🇺🇸🇨🇦
Hockey wasn't just a Canadian pastime. By 1924, the Boston Bruins became the first American team to join the NHL, making the league an international affair. Imagine crossing the border to play hockey and calling it a "work trip."

4: The Missing Teams Mystery 🕵️‍♂️
Ever heard of the Montreal Maroons or the New York Americans? They were part of the NHL's "Original Eleven" before the league settled on the "Original Six." These teams vanished like a puck in a snowstorm, leaving behind tales of hockey heroics and mystery.

5: The Stanley Cup's Wild Ride 🏆
The Stanley Cup has been around even longer than the NHL, first awarded in 1893. It's been lost, found, left by the roadside, and even used as a flower pot! Talk about a trophy with a story to tell.

6: The Flying Puck 🚀
The fastest slapshot ever recorded zipped at an eye-watering 108.8 mph by Zdeno Chara in 2012. That's faster than a speeding car on the highway—without a traffic ticket!

7: The Longest Game 🕰️
In 1936, the Detroit Red Wings and the Montreal Maroons played the longest game in NHL history, lasting over 176 minutes! That's like watching "The Lion King" nearly four times back-to-back. Hope they packed snacks!

8: The Goalie Mask Revolution 😷
Jacques Plante changed the game forever in 1959 by being the first goalie to wear a mask regularly. Before that, goalies faced flying pucks with nothing but hope and courage. Talk about a face-saving move!

9: The Birth of the Zamboni 🚜
In 1949, Frank Zamboni invented the first ice resurfacing machine, making choppy ice smooth again. Before that, smoothing the ice was a job that took a team of people with towels and squeegees. Thanks, Frank, for saving our arms and our ice!

10: Miracle on Ice 🇺🇸

In 1980, the U.S. Olympic hockey team, made of amateurs and college players, defeated the Soviet Union's professional team in what's known as the "Miracle on Ice." It was like David vs. Goliath, but with hockey sticks and a lot of ice.

11: Hockey Goes Global
The NHL truly went global when it started drafting players from all over the world. In 1973, Borje Salming from Sweden and Inge Hammarstrom from Sweden joined the Toronto Maple Leafs, opening the door for international players to shine on the ice in the NHL.

12: The Hockey Hall of Fame
Located in Toronto, Canada, the Hockey Hall of Fame was established in 1943 to honor the best of the best in hockey. Imagine a museum where instead of quiet whispers, you hear the sounds of cheers and slapshots!

13: The Women's Hockey Boom
Women's hockey has seen a massive surge in popularity, with the first Women's World Championship held in 1990. Since then, the sport has grown exponentially, proving that hockey isn't just a boys' club.

14: The Outdoor Game Returns
In 2003, the NHL hosted its first modern outdoor game, the Heritage Classic, in Edmonton, Alberta. It was like taking hockey back to its roots, playing on a frozen pond, but with thousands of fans watching!

15: The Mascot Madness
Every NHL team has a mascot, from a 7-foot-tall orange fuzzy creature named Gritty for the Philadelphia Flyers to a saber-toothed tiger named Sabretooth for the Buffalo Sabres. These characters add fun and excitement for fans, especially the younger ones, making every game an adventure.

16: The Record for Most Teams
The NHL has grown from its original four teams to 32 teams as of 2021, with the Seattle Kraken joining the league. The NHL's expansion shows how the love for hockey has spread like wildfire across North America.

17: The Youngest NHL Player
Sidney Crosby was only 18 years old when he joined the NHL in 2005, quickly becoming one of the league's brightest stars. Imagine being in high school and also a professional hockey player!

18: The Sudden Death Overtime
Introduced in the 1983-84 season, sudden death overtime added extra excitement to NHL games. Now, if a game is tied at the end of regulation, the next goal wins, making every shot thrilling!

19: The Penalty Box Tradition
Hockey is the only major sport with a "penalty box," where players take a time-out for breaking the rules. It's like being sent to the corner to think about what you've done, but with millions of people watching.

20: The Original Six Era
The "Original Six" era from 1942 to 1967 saw the Montreal Canadiens, Toronto Maple Leafs, Boston Bruins, Chicago Blackhawks, Detroit Red Wings, and New York Rangers dominate the league. This period is considered the golden age of hockey, with fierce rivalries and legendary players shaping the game's history.

21: The First NHL Game Broadcast
The first NHL game broadcast on television took place in 1952. Now, imagine trying to follow a tiny black-and-white puck on a small TV screen. Talk about a challenge!

22: The Helmet Revolution
It wasn't until 1979 that the NHL made wearing helmets mandatory for all new players. Before that, players relied on their hairdos for protection. Safety first, fashion second!

23: The Four-Goal "Hat Trick"
While a "hat trick" usually means scoring three goals in a game, Joe Malone holds the record for scoring seven goals in a single game in 1920. That's a hat trick plus a little extra for good measure!

24: The First African-American NHL Player
In 1958, Willie O'Ree broke the color barrier in the NHL, playing for the Boston Bruins. He paved the way for future generations, proving that talent knows no color.

25: The Longest Stanley Cup Drought
The Toronto Maple Leafs haven't won the Stanley Cup since 1967, holding the longest drought in NHL history. Leafs fans are still waiting for the spring to come after a very long winter.

26: The Unbreakable Record
Glenn Hall, a legendary goalie, played 502 consecutive complete games from 1955 to 1962. That's like showing up to every single day of school for almost 3 years straight—without ever calling in sick!

27: The First Broadcast in Color
Hockey fans saw the game in a whole new light when the first NHL game was broadcast in color in 1966. It was like going from watching a game in a snowstorm to suddenly seeing the ice and jerseys in vivid detail.

28: The Mascot Who Came from Comics
You've heard of superheroes in comics, but did you know the Philadelphia Flyers' mascot, Gritty, has his own comic book? It's the ultimate crossover—where sports meet superhero sagas!

29: The NHL's Leap Across the Pond
In 2007, the NHL played its first regular-season games in Europe, with the Los Angeles Kings and the Anaheim Ducks facing off in London. It was like a "British invasion," but with hockey sticks and pucks instead of guitars.

30: The Goalie Who Scored
Goalies are known for stopping goals, but in 1979, Billy Smith of the New York Islanders became the first NHL goalie to be credited with scoring a goal. Talk about a role reversal!

31: The Stanley Cup's Pool Party
The Stanley Cup has seen its fair share of adventures, including being thrown into Mario Lemieux's swimming pool. It's probably the only trophy with a built-in swim routine.

32: The Zeroes on the Board
The Montreal Canadiens and the Toronto Maple Leafs hold the record for the longest game without a goal, playing over 176 minutes in 1936 before a goal was finally scored. It was a true test of patience for both players and fans!

33: The Draft Pick from a Fictional Place

In 1974, the Buffalo Sabres drafted Taro Tsujimoto from the Tokyo Katanas as a joke, fooling the NHL and fans. Taro became the most famous player never to play in the league, from a team that never existed.

34: The Most Decorated Team
The Montreal Canadiens hold the record for the most Stanley Cup victories, with 24 wins. It's like having a trophy room the size of a hockey rink!

35: The Referee's Signature Stripes
Referees didn't always wear stripes. The black-and-white striped uniform was introduced in 1956 to distinguish them from the players. Before that, it was anyone's guess who was in charge of the game.

36: The Fan Who Changed the Game
In 1959, a fan struck by a puck led to the installation of protective netting around the rink areas. It was a literal "heads-up" that improved safety for everyone.

37: The Oldest Rookie
At the age of 27, Sergei Makarov was named the NHL's Rookie of the Year in 1990, proving that it's never too late to start your NHL journey. Age is just a number, especially on the ice!

38: The Shortest Game on Record
Due to a curfew in 1939, a game between the Boston Bruins and the Montreal Canadiens was called off after just one period. It was the NHL's version of a "bedtime" for hockey.

39: The Player with a Day Job
In the early days of the NHL, players often had day jobs in the offseason. Imagine winning the Stanley Cup and then clocking in at the factory the next day!

40: The Team That Never Was
The San Francisco Seals were supposed to join the NHL in 1967, but financial issues kept them out. It's like being invited to the biggest party of the year and then missing your flight.

41: The Goalie Without a Mask
Andy Brown was the last NHL goalie to play without a mask in 1974. It's like riding a bike downhill with no brakes—thrilling but definitely not recommended.

42: The Penalty Shot Origin
Penalty shots were introduced in 1934 as a way to punish teams for fouling a player on a clear scoring opportunity. It's the ultimate showdown—just the player, the goalie, and the puck.

43: The Night of the Fans
In 1928, the New York Rangers won the Stanley Cup with a roster filled with injuries, even using their coach as a player. It was like calling someone from the stands to suit up and play!

44: The Fastest Three Goals
Bill Mosienko holds the record for the fastest three goals, scoring them in just 21 seconds in 1952. It was quicker than making a sandwich!

45: The Puck's Evolution
Originally, hockey was played with a ball. The puck was introduced to prevent the ball from bouncing out of the outdoor rinks. It's like deciding to roll instead of bounce through life.

46: The Team That Folded During the Finals
The Montreal Maroons made it to the Stanley Cup Finals in 1938 but folded before the next season started. It's like making it to the last level of a video game and then the power goes out.

47: The Player Turned Spy
During World War II, goaltender Walter "Turk" Broda doubled as a spy for the Canadian government. Hockey skills by day, espionage by night!

48: The Birth of the "Hockey Night in Canada"
"Hockey Night in Canada" first aired on the radio in 1931, becoming one of the longest-running sports broadcasts in history. It's like the grandfather of all sports shows.

49: The First Female to Play in the NHL
Manon Rheaume broke the gender barrier in 1992, playing as a goalie in an NHL preseason game for the Tampa Bay Lightning. It was a slapshot for equality!

50: The Accidental Trophy

The Stanley Cup was originally bought as a decorative bowl before becoming the most coveted trophy in hockey. It's like buying a vase and ending up with the most famous sports trophy in the world.

And there you have it—50 unique and entertaining hockey facts to delight and inform. Let me know if there's anything else you'd like to explore!

51: The Indoor Snowfall
In 1996, the Florida Panthers celebrated goals with a unique tradition: fans throwing plastic rats onto the ice, a nod to player Scott Mellanby's rat-slaying shot in the locker room. It was like a Florida snowstorm, but with rats instead of snowflakes!

52: The Longest Name on the Cup
With 24 letters, the longest name ever engraved on the Stanley Cup belongs to Jean-Sébastien Giguère. Imagine trying to fit that on a jersey!

53: The Team That Came Back from the Dead
The Ottawa Senators of today are not the original team. The first Senators, founded in 1883, won 11 Stanley Cups before dissolving in 1934. The current team was resurrected in 1992, proving you can't keep a good team down.

54: The First Outdoor NHL Game on Record
The first officially recorded outdoor NHL game took place not in the 21st century, but in 1954, when the Detroit Red Wings faced off against inmates at the Marquette Branch Prison. It was quite literally a game behind bars!

55: The Stanley Cup's Misadventures
The Stanley Cup has been through a lot, including being left on the side of the road, getting lost on a flight, and even being found at the bottom of Mario Lemieux's pool. This trophy might have more adventures than Indiana Jones!

56: The NHL's First European Player
Swede Ulf Sterner made history in 1965 as the first European-trained player to hit the ice in an NHL game, paving the way for a flood of international talent to enter the league in the following decades.

57: The Highest Scoring Game
The highest scoring NHL game ever recorded was between the Edmonton Oilers and the Chicago Blackhawks in 1985, with a total of 21 goals scored. The final score was 12-9, making it seem more like a baseball score than a hockey game!

58: The Goalie Who Scored in His Own Net
In an attempt to clear the puck, Billy Smith of the New York Islanders inadvertently scored on his own net in 1977, becoming the first NHL goalie to score an own goal. Talk about an oops moment!

59: The First Helmeted Player
George Owen of the Boston Bruins became the first NHL player to regularly wear a helmet in 1928, way ahead of his time considering helmets didn't become mandatory until 1979. Safety first!

60: The Most Penalties in a Single Game
The Philadelphia Flyers and the Ottawa Senators set the record for the most penalty minutes in a single game with 419 minutes in 2004. It was less of a hockey game and more of a penalty parade!

61: The Player Who Won the Most Stanley Cups
Henri Richard, the "Pocket Rocket," won the Stanley Cup 11 times with the Montreal Canadiens, the most by any player in NHL history. That's enough rings to deck out both hands and still have one left over!

62: The Team That Changed Names Overnight 🔄
The Mighty Ducks of Anaheim rebranded to the Anaheim Ducks in 2006, shedding their Disney-inspired name and logo for a more streamlined look. It was like waking up and deciding to change your name from Mickey to Mike!

63: The NHL's First Black Captain 🎖
In 2003, Jarome Iginla became the first black captain in NHL history, leading the Calgary Flames. Breaking barriers on the ice, Iginla showed leadership knows no color.

64: The Team That Traveled the Farthest for a Game ✈
In 2010, the NHL played its farthest game from North America in Helsinki, Finland, between the Carolina Hurricanes and the Minnesota Wild. It was a home game for Finnish players but a field trip for everyone else.

65: The Coldest NHL Game ❄
The 2014 Winter Classic between the Toronto Maple Leafs and the Detroit Red Wings was played in a chilling -10°C (14°F). Fans and players alike bundled up for what felt like a hockey game in a freezer!

66: The Most Consecutive Playoff Appearances 🏒
The Boston Bruins hold the record for the most consecutive playoff appearances, making the postseason 29 years in a row from 1968 to 1996. It's like getting an invite to every party for nearly three decades!

67: The First NHL Player to Defect 🛂
In 1980, Czechoslovakian star Peter Stastny defected to Canada to play for the Quebec Nordiques, becoming one of the first players from the Eastern Bloc to join the NHL during the Cold War.

68: The First Father-Son to Win the Stanley Cup 🏆👨‍👦
Bobby and Brett Hull became the first father-son duo to both win the Stanley Cup, sharing more than just genetics but also championship rings.

69: The Most Goals by a Goalie 🥅
Martin Brodeur holds the record for the most goals scored by a goalie, with three in the regular season and one in the playoffs. Who says goalies can't score?

70: The First Game Broadcast in VR 🕶
In 2016, the NHL entered the virtual reality era, broadcasting a game in VR for the first time, allowing fans to experience the action as if they were standing on the ice themselves.

71: The Player with the Longest Name 📛
With 14 letters, Jonathan Cheechoo holds the record for the longest last name of any player in NHL history. Imagine the announcer trying to fit that on a game-winning goal call!

72: The Team with No Home Wins 🏠🚫
The 1930-31 Philadelphia Quakers hold the dubious distinction of being the only NHL team to go an entire season without winning a single home game. Talk about tough love from the home crowd!

73: The NHL's First All-Star Game ⭐
The NHL's first All-Star Game was held in 1947, not for exhibition but to raise funds for the family of Ace Bailey, whose career ended early due to injury. It was a game played for a good cause, turning stars into heroes off the ice.

74: The Oldest Player to Win the Stanley Cup ⏰
Chris Chelios was 46 years old when he lifted the Stanley Cup with the Detroit Red Wings in 2008, proving that in hockey, age is but a number if you've got the heart (and the stamina) to keep skating.

75: The First NHL Team in the Sun Belt

The Los Angeles Kings were part of the NHL's first expansion into the Sun Belt in 1967, bringing ice hockey to the land of sun and surf and forever changing the landscape of the league.

76: The Shortest Player to Ever Play

Roy "Shrimp" Worters stood at just 5 feet 3 inches tall, making him the shortest player in NHL history. Despite his stature, Worters was a giant in goal, proving that heart and skill matter more than size on the ice.

77: The First NHL Game Not Played on Ice

In a bizarre twist of events, a preseason game in 1991 between the Los Angeles Kings and the New York Rangers was played in Las Vegas, outdoors, at Caesars Palace. It wasn't the ice melting in the desert heat that was odd, but the that it was the first NHL game played on artificial ice outdoors!

78: The Team That Became a Dynasty

The New York Islanders won four consecutive Stanley Cups from 1980 to 1983, becoming only the second team in NHL history to achieve such a feat. It was a reign of ice that solidified their place as one of the greatest dynasties in hockey.

79: The Player Who Became a Coach Mid-Season

In 1979, player-coach Al Arbour took off his skates and stepped behind the bench mid-season to lead the New York Islanders to their first of four consecutive Stanley Cups. It's like switching from playing a video game to controlling the whole tournament!

80: The Most Lopsided Trade in History

In what's considered one of the most lopsided trades in NHL history, the Quebec Nordiques traded Eric Lindros to the Philadelphia Flyers in 1992 for players, draft picks, and $15 million. This trade shaped the future of both franchises and is a tale of caution in the trading game.

81: The Team That Almost Wasn't

The Chicago Blackhawks nearly folded during the Great Depression but were saved by a last-minute infusion of cash from the Norris family. It's like hitting the jackpot just when you think you're out of coins.

82: The First Live Broadcast of an NHL Game

The first live broadcast of an NHL game was in 1952, between the Detroit Red Wings and the Montreal Canadiens. Fans for the first time could cheer from their living rooms, transforming how people experienced the game.

83: The Most Games Played Without Winning the Stanley Cup

Phil Housley holds the record for the most NHL games played without winning the Stanley Cup, with 1,495 games under his belt. It's a bittersweet record that highlights both endurance and the elusive nature of championship glory.

84: The First NHL Player to Kneel During the National Anthem

In 2020, Matt Dumba became the first NHL player to kneel during the national anthem, taking a stand for social justice and marking a moment of significant cultural impact within the sport.

85: The Team with a Curse

The Toronto Maple Leafs are said to be cursed by the "Curse of 1967," the last year they won the Stanley Cup. Superstitious fans blame various events for the team's lengthy championship drought, from trading away key players to moving from the Maple Leaf Gardens.

86: The Game That Ended in a Tie Due to Lights Out

A game between the Boston Bruins and the Montreal Canadiens in 1950 had to be called off and ended in a tie when a power outage at the Boston Garden left the rink in darkness. It was a night when the players literally couldn't find the back of the net.

87: The Oldest Player Ever to Play in the NHL
Gordie Howe is the oldest player ever to play in the NHL, retiring at the age of 52. His career spanned five decades, earning him the nickname "Mr. Hockey."

88: The First NHL Player to Reach 50 Goals in a Season
Maurice "Rocket" Richard was the first NHL player to score 50 goals in a single season, achieving this feat in 1945. His explosive scoring ability earned him his nickname and changed the game forever.

89: The Team That Played Without a Name
In 1925, the Pittsburgh Pirates joined the NHL but played their first season without an official team name. Fans and newspapers referred to them simply as "the Pittsburgh NHL team," a true no-name squad.

90: The Goalie Who Played with a Broken Neck
Playing one of the most demanding positions in sports, Boston Bruins' goalie Tuukka Rask once finished a game despite having a broken neck. It's a testament to the toughness required to guard the net in the NHL.

91: The Fastest Hat Trick by a Rookie
Auston Matthews set the record for the fastest hat trick by a rookie in his NHL debut in 2016, scoring four goals for the Toronto Maple Leafs. It was like showing up for your first day at work and completing a month's worth of assignments by lunchtime.

92: The Most Penalty Minutes by a Single Player in One Season
Dave "Tiger" Williams holds the record for the most penalty minutes in a single season, racking up 442 minutes in the penalty box in 1977-1978. It's a record that's as tough as nails, just like Tiger himself.

93: The Team That Won After Relocation
The Colorado Avalanche won the Stanley Cup in their first season after relocating from Quebec in 1995, proving that a change of scenery can indeed lead to success.

94: The Player with the Most Consecutive Games Scored In
Wayne Gretzky holds the record for the most consecutive games with at least one point, scoring in 51 straight games during the 1983-84 season. It's like hitting a home run every time you're at bat for half the season.

95: The Goal That Wasn't Seen
In 2004, during the Stanley Cup Finals, Calgary Flames' Martin Gelinas scored a goal that would have won the game, but it wasn't seen by the officials and wasn't counted. It remains one of the most controversial moments in NHL history.

96: The Player Who Played for the Most Teams
Mike Sillinger holds the record for playing on the most NHL teams, dressing for 12 different squads throughout his career. He's the epitome of "have skates, will travel."

97: The Most Overtime Goals in Playoff History
Joe Sakic holds the record for the most overtime goals in NHL playoff history, with 8 sudden-death winners. Clutch moments seemed to find Sakic just as much as he found the back of the net.

98: The First NHL Mascot

In 1976, the Philadelphia Flyers introduced the NHL to its first mascot, "Slapshot," a pioneering move that would lead to the league's wide array of beloved team mascots today.

99: The Player with the Most Stanley Cup Wins as a Captain 🏆
Jean Béliveau holds the record for the most Stanley Cup wins as a captain, leading the Montreal Canadiens to 5 championships. His leadership on and off the ice set a standard for what it means to wear the "C."

100: The NHL's First Triple Overtime Game in the Finals
The first triple overtime game in Stanley Cup Finals history happened in 1936 between the Detroit Red Wings and the Montreal Maroons. Mud Bruneteau of the Red Wings scored the game-winning goal, ending the marathon match and securing a place in hockey lore.

LEGENDARY PLAYERS

SIDNEY CROSBY

1: The Kid Who Became The Captain
Once upon a time, a young boy named Sidney Crosby dreamed of playing in the NHL. Not just playing, but shining bright! Fast forward to 2005, and this dream came true when the Pittsburgh Penguins said, "We choose you!" making him the first overall pick. By the age of 19, he wasn't just a player; he was the captain, the youngest in NHL history at the time. Imagine being in charge of a whole team of grown-ups before you're even old enough to rent a car!

2: The Golden Goal
In 2010, at the Winter Olympics in Vancouver, Sidney did something so cool it's frozen in time. He scored "The Golden Goal" against the USA, winning Canada the gold medal. It was like hitting the winning home run in the bottom of the ninth inning of the World Series, but with icier stakes!

3: Sid the Kid's Superstitions
Sidney might skate like a superhero, but he has his quirks too. Before every game, he eats the same meal: a peanut butter and jelly sandwich. And talk about a routine! He always ties his left skate before the right one. It's like having a lucky charm, but for your feet.

4: The Sid Work Ethic
This hockey legend is known for his incredible work ethic. He's the first one to hit the ice at practice and the last one to leave. It's like he's trying to make sure the ice doesn't get too lonely without him. His dedication is so intense, it makes normal hard work look like a vacation.

5: The Man Behind the Ice
Off the ice, Sidney's just as impressive. He's not just about slapshots and checking; he's got brains too. Did you know he scored 1200 out of 1600 on his SATs? That's like acing a test without even needing to study. Well, maybe he studied a little.

6: Crosby's Good Deeds
Sidney isn't just a hero on the ice; he's also one off it. His foundation, the Sidney Crosby Foundation, helps children all over the world. It's like he's passing the puck to kids everywhere, giving them a shot at a better life.

7: The Comeback Kid
In 2011, Crosby faced a huge challenge. He suffered from concussions that kept him off the ice for almost a year. But like a true hero in a sports movie, he made a comeback, proving that not even a bumpy ride can keep a good player down.

8: Sid's Secret Talent
When he's not scoring goals or winning trophies, Sidney has a secret talent: he's a pretty good singer! He once belted out "I Will Always Love You" by Whitney Houston in a karaoke challenge. Imagine the surprise of finding out that the guy scoring goals on the ice can also score big on the karaoke stage!

9: The Record Breaker
Throughout his career, Sidney has broken so many records, it's like he's got a personal vendetta against them. For instance, he's the youngest player to win the Art Ross Trophy as the NHL's leading scorer. It's like he's playing a video game on easy mode, but in real life.

10: Sid's Penguin Loyalty
Since being drafted in 2005, Sidney has never worn another NHL team's jersey. He's as loyal to the Pittsburgh Penguins as a dog is to its human. It's like he and the Penguins are in a "BFFs Forever" kind of relationship.

11: The Prankster
Off the ice, Sidney's known for his sense of humor, especially his love for pranks. He once filled a teammate's car with so many foam peanuts, it looked like a giant snow globe! It's all fun and games until you need to find your car keys.

12: The Milestone Man
Crosby hit the 1,000-point milestone in 2017, joining the ranks of hockey royalty faster than most. It's like he sprinted to the top of Mount Everest while everyone else was taking the scenic route.

13: Sid's Love for the Game
Even after achieving so much, Sidney's love for hockey remains as pure as when he first started. He once said if he wasn't playing in the NHL, he'd still be playing hockey somewhere, somehow. It's like the ice calls to him, and he just can't help but answer.

14: The Tim Hortons Connection
Sidney has a sweet spot for Tim Hortons, a famous Canadian coffee shop. He starred in a commercial for them, showing that his Canadian roots run deep. It's like being so Canadian, even your coffee preference is a national symbol.

15: The International Ice Ambassador
Crosby has represented Canada in international competitions, spreading his hockey magic across the world. It's like he's on a mission to show every corner of the globe how it's done, Canadian style.

16: The Young Achiever
Sidney was so good, so young, he was dubbed "The Next One," a nod to Wayne Gretzky's "The Great One." It's like being handed the torch while you're still roasting marshmallows over the campfire.

17: Sid's Sneaker Collection

Away from the rink, Sidney has a thing for sneakers. He's got a collection that would make any sneakerhead jealous. It's like every pair tells a story, from overtime wins to just chilling out.

18: The Captain's Cup 🏆🏒
Under Sidney's leadership, the Penguins have won the Stanley Cup three times. It's like he's not just part of the team; he's steering the ship through stormy seas to treasure island.

19: Crosby's Quiet Life 🏠📚
Despite his fame, Sidney prefers a quiet life. He enjoys reading and spending time at home. It's like he's a superhero who, after saving the world, just wants to curl up with a good book.

20: The Jersey Number Mystery 🔢🤔
Why does Sidney wear number 87? He was born on August 7, 1987 (8/7/87), and his jersey reflects that special date. It's like wearing your birthday on your back, but making it look cool.

21: Sid the Role Model 🌈👶
Crosby is a role model for kids everywhere, showing that with hard work and dedication, dreams can come true. It's like he's the captain not just of a team, but of a whole generation of future players.

22: The Overtime Oracle ⏱️🏒
Sidney has a knack for scoring in overtime, making him the guy you want on the ice when the game's on the line. It's like he has a crystal ball, and it always says, "Score the next goal."

23: Sid's Dry Sense of Humor 😄🌵
Despite his serious work ethic, Sidney has a dry sense of humor that keeps his teammates laughing. It's like he's as skilled with jokes as he is with a hockey stick.

24: The Philanthropic Heart 💚🌍

Beyond his foundation, Sidney's philanthropy extends to various causes, from supporting children's hospitals to disaster relief efforts. It's like his heart is as big as his trophy case.

25: The Living Legend 🐐
Sidney Crosby isn't just a player; he's a living legend, inspiring countless kids to lace up and hit the ice. It's like he's not just playing the game; he's changing it, one goal at a time.

BOBBY HULL

1: The Blonde Bomber 💣👱♂️
Bobby Hull, also known as "The Golden Jet" for his speedy skating and golden locks, had a shot so powerful it once broke through the netting of the goal. Imagine shooting a puck so hard, it decides to make its own exit! It's like his hockey stick was a magic wand, and the puck was under a speeding spell.

2: Record Smasher 🏒💥
In the 1965-66 season, Hull smashed records by scoring 54 goals, becoming the first NHL player to break the 50-goal mark in a single season. It was like he turned the hockey rink into a personal goal-scoring party, and the puck was always invited.

3: A Family Affair 🏒❤️
Hockey talent runs in the Hull family. Bobby's son, Brett Hull, also became an NHL legend, making them the first father-son duo to each score over 600 NHL goals. It's like scoring goals was their family business, and business was booming!

4: The Million Dollar Man 💰👤
Bobby Hull made headlines in 1972 when he signed a contract with the Winnipeg Jets of the World Hockey Association

(WHA) for a whopping $1.75 million, making him the highest-paid player at the time. It was like he hit the jackpot, but instead of a slot machine, he used a hockey stick.

5: Off-Ice Hero
Beyond the rink, Hull was known for his charitable work, especially for children with disabilities. His heart was as golden as his hair, showing that heroes come in all forms, not all wear capes, some wield hockey sticks.

6: The Inventor of the Curved Stick
Hull was one of the first players to experiment with a curved stick blade, revolutionizing the game. His slapshot with this curved stick was so fierce, goalies would quiver at the sight. It was like he had a secret weapon hidden under the ice.

7: A Stamp of Approval
Bobby Hull was so legendary that Canada issued a postage stamp in his honor in 2014. It's like he went from delivering goals on the ice to delivering letters in style.

8: The Ambassador of Hockey
After retiring, Hull became an ambassador for the sport, spreading his love for hockey around the world. It was like he switched from scoring goals to scoring hearts, making new fans wherever he went.

9: The Art of Skating
Hull's skating was so powerful and graceful, fans would come just to watch him glide across the ice. It was like he was part athlete, part ballet dancer, and the ice was his stage.

10: The Power of the Puck
Legend has it that Hull could shoot the puck at speeds over 118 miles per hour. That's so fast, if his puck were a car, it would get a speeding ticket on most highways!

11: The Hull Trophy Case
Over his career, Hull collected awards like they were going out of style: two Hart Trophies (MVP), three Art Ross Trophies (leading scorer), and a Lady Byng Trophy for gentlemanly conduct. His trophy case was so crowded, it's a wonder it didn't collapse!

12: Hull's Record-Breaking Deal
When Hull signed with the WHA, it wasn't just any contract; it was a record-breaker that sent shockwaves through professional sports. It was like he scored a goal so big, it landed in the bank!

13: The Hull Shot Heard Around the World
Hull's slapshot was so notorious, it inspired goalies to wear more protective gear. It was like every time he wound up for a shot, goalies wished they had an extra layer of armor.

14: The Unstoppable Force
On the ice, Hull was like a freight train: once he got going, there was no stopping him. Opponents knew that trying to halt his charge was like trying to stop a speeding train with a hockey stick.

15: The Leader of the Jets
As a leader on and off the ice, Hull captained the Winnipeg Jets to three Avco World Trophy championships in the WHA. It was like he was the pilot guiding his team to victory, no turbulence allowed.

GUY LAFLEUR

1: The Flower That Bloomed on Ice
Guy Lafleur, affectionately known as "The Flower," wasn't just any player; he was a hockey icon who blossomed with the Montreal Canadiens. Drafted first overall in 1971, Lafleur grew into an NHL

superstar, proving that flowers could indeed thrive in cold ice arenas.

2: A Trophy Garden 🏆🌷
Lafleur's career was like a well-tended garden, blooming with awards. He won the Hart Trophy (MVP) twice, the Art Ross Trophy (scoring leader) three times, and the Conn Smythe Trophy (playoff MVP) once. It's as if every season, he decided to add a new trophy to his collection, just for fun!

3: The Golden Mane 🦁💇‍♂️
Known for his flowing locks as much as his scoring touch, Lafleur's hair became almost as legendary as his hockey skills. When he sped down the ice, his golden mane flew behind him like a comet's tail, making fans wonder if he was part hockey player, part rock star.

4: The Comeback Kid 👶🏒
After retiring in 1984, Lafleur couldn't stay away from the ice. He made a stunning return to the NHL with the New York Rangers in 1988, and later with the Quebec Nordiques, proving that you can't keep a good Flower down. It was like he missed the cold so much, he just had to come back for more.

5: A Heart As Golden As His Hair ♡🏒
Off the ice, Lafleur's heart was as big as his trophy case. He dedicated much of his time to charity work, especially for children. It's like he decided if he could make goals happen on the ice, he could make dreams come true off it too.

6: The Speed Demon 🏎️💨
Lafleur was known for his incredible speed on the ice, earning him another nickname, "Le Démon Blond." He could zoom past defenders as if they were standing still, making it look like he had rockets instead of skates.

7: Record Breaker Extraordinaire 📚💔
Lafleur was the first player in the NHL to score 50 goals and 100 points in six consecutive seasons. It's like he treated the record book like his personal diary, filling it with his own incredible achievements.

8: The Airport Tribute ✈️
In 2017, to honor his contributions to hockey and society, Montreal renamed a portion of the Trans-Canada Highway and an airport terminal after Lafleur. Imagine being so beloved that even airplanes tip their wings to you as they fly by!

9: The Practical Joker 😂🎭
Lafleur had a notorious sense of humor, often pulling pranks on teammates. Whether it was hiding their equipment or surprising them with a bucket of ice water, Lafleur made sure laughter was always part of the game plan.

10: The Video Game Star 🎮
Lafleur was one of the first hockey players to be featured in a video game. In the 1980s, "Le Démon Blond" brought his on-ice magic to the digital world, allowing kids to control their idol with the push of a button. It was like bringing The Flower into your living room, minus the ice and cold.

11: The Wine Connoisseur 🍷🍇
In his life away from hockey, Lafleur developed a passion for wine, even releasing his own brand. It seems his taste for scoring goals translated into a taste for fine wines. It's like he decided if he could dazzle on the ice, why not dazzle in the vineyard too?

12: The Philanthropic Power Play 🌍💚
Through his Guy Lafleur Fund of Excellence, he supported students in health sciences, blending his love for hockey with a commitment to education and healthcare. It's as if he was scoring

goals for a better future, one scholarship at a time.

13: The Enduring Legacy
Lafleur's impact on hockey is immortalized in the Hockey Hall of Fame, ensuring that The Flower's legacy will continue to inspire future generations. It's like he planted seeds of inspiration that will grow in the hearts of young players everywhere.

14: The Beloved Broadcaster
After hanging up his skates, Lafleur didn't stray far from the ice, turning to broadcasting to share his insights on the game. It's like he switched from scoring goals to scoring points with viewers, proving his hockey IQ was as impressive as his playing skills.

MARK MESSIER

1: The Leader with Six Rings
Mark Messier, known as "The Moose" for his strength and power on the ice, is one of the few players to have his name engraved on the Stanley Cup six times! It's like he decided one ring wasn't enough for each finger on his hockey glove hand, so he went ahead and collected a half dozen.

2: The Guarantee That Became Legendary
During the 1994 Eastern Conference Finals, with the New York Rangers down in the series, Messier boldly guaranteed a Game 6 victory against the New Jersey Devils. Then, like a true hero in a sports movie, he delivered by scoring a hat trick to win the game. It was like saying, "I'll do my homework and then some," and ending up inventing a new math formula.

3: The Messier Leadership Award
Messier's leadership was so inspirational that the NHL created the Mark Messier Leadership Award in his honor, given to the player who exemplifies great leadership qualities to his team. It's like being so good at being the captain, they make a captaincy award just for you.

4: A Star Beyond the Ice
Off the ice, Messier is known for his philanthropic efforts, including working with the New York Police and Fire Widows' and Children's Benefit Fund. It's like he not only scored goals but also aimed to score big-hearted wins for those in need.

5: The Voice of Reason
Messier was so respected that when he spoke in the locker room, everyone listened. It was as if the coach called a timeout, but instead, it was Messier time—a moment when even the Zamboni driver would stop to listen.

6: The Edmonton Dynasty Builder
Messier was a key player in the Edmonton Oilers' dynasty in the 1980s, helping the team clinch five Stanley Cups. It's like he was building a castle, but instead of bricks, he used hockey pucks.

7: The Man of Many Teams
Over his illustrious career, Messier played for the Edmonton Oilers, New York Rangers, and Vancouver Canucks, leaving an indelible mark on each. It's like he went on a tour of Canada and New York, but instead of souvenirs, he collected fans' hearts.

8: The Second to Gretzky
Messier is second only to Wayne Gretzky in total NHL points scored, making him hockey royalty. It's like being the Robin to Batman, but for hockey, and with a lot more ice.

9: The First New York Rangers' Cup in 54 Years
In 1994, Messier led the New York Rangers to their first Stanley Cup in 54 years, ending one of the longest championship droughts in history. It was

as if he was a rain dancer for hockey, bringing the Cup showers to New York.

10: The Man Who Moved a Mountain 🏔️🚚
Messier's leadership was so effective, it was like he could move mountains with his motivation. If Mount Everest were a hockey team, Messier would have it winning the Stanley Cup in no time.

11: The Skater Who Could Fly Without Wings 🪶⛸️
Messier's skating speed was legendary, earning him the nickname "The Moose" not just for his strength, but for his surprising speed. It was as if he had invisible wings on his skates, zooming past defenders as if they were standing still.

12: A Face on the Mountain 🏔️🖼️
In 1997, a Canadian mountain was named after Messier, Mount Messier, in British Columbia. It's not every day you get a mountain named after you—usually, you're lucky if it's a small hill or a goldfish.

13: The Mentor to Many 🐣🏰
Messier was known for mentoring younger players, sharing wisdom gained from his years on the ice. It was like he ran a "How to Be Awesome at Hockey" class, and the lessons were always sold out.

14: The Man with a Plan 📋
Even in high-pressure situations, Messier was known for his strategic thinking, often seen advising coaches on game plans. It's like he had a crystal ball, predicting play outcomes before they happened.

15: The Never-Ending Career ⏳
Messier's NHL career spanned 25 seasons, making him one of the longest-serving players in league history. It's like he loved hockey so much, he refused to hang up his skates until they practically fell apart.

16: A Taste for Acting 🎭📺
Messier tried his hand at acting, appearing in commercials and TV shows. It's like he thought, "I've conquered hockey, now let's see about Hollywood."

17: The Captain of Captains 🚢
Messier served as captain for two different Stanley Cup-winning teams, a rare feat. It's like being voted "Most Likely to Succeed" in high school and then actually doing it twice.

18: The Oiler Forever 🖤🤍
Despite playing for multiple teams, Messier is often most fondly remembered as an Edmonton Oiler, where his NHL journey began. It's like having a first love in hockey, and no matter where you go, a piece of your heart remains with them.

19: A Heart as Big as His Career ♥️
Known for his generosity, Messier often visited children in hospitals, bringing smiles and lifting spirits. It's as if he scored goals on the ice and in the hearts of kids everywhere.

20: The Legendary Number 11 🏒
Messier's number 11 jersey was retired by both the New York Rangers and the Edmonton Oilers, a testament to his impact on both teams. It's like getting two standing ovations at the end of a performance because once wasn't enough.

21: The Fitness Fanatic 🏋️♂️🍎
Messier was known for his rigorous fitness regime, which contributed to his longevity in the sport. It's as if he treated his body like a high-performance sports car, always fine-tuning it for peak performance.

22: The Ice to Boardroom Transition
After retiring, Messier transitioned into business and leadership roles, applying his on-ice leadership to the boardroom. It's like he decided if he could lead a team to victory, why not a company?

23: The Inspiration to Many
Messier's career has inspired countless young hockey players to pursue their dreams, showing that hard work and determination pay off. It's like he lit a beacon for aspiring hockey stars, guiding them toward their goals.

24: The Hockey Hall of Famer
Messier was inducted into the Hockey Hall of Fame in 2007, cementing his legacy in the sport. It's like hockey itself gave him a high-five and said, "Welcome to immortality."

25: The Ultimate Team Player
Above all, Messier was the ultimate team player, known for elevating his teammates' play and fostering a winning culture. It's as if he knew the secret recipe for success and wasn't afraid to share it with the whole team.

JEAN BELIVEAU

1: The Gentleman of Hockey
Jean Beliveau, known as "Le Gros Bill," wasn't just a hockey player; he was the epitome of a gentleman on and off the ice. Imagine a player so respected that even the referees would think twice before calling a penalty on him. It was like he had a permanent "good guy" badge pinned to his jersey.

2: A Trophy Case Like No Other
Beliveau's trophy case was so stuffed, it could be its own museum. With 10 Stanley Cups as a player and 7 more as an executive with the Montreal Canadiens, it's like he had a season pass to the Stanley Cup Finals. Some people collect stamps; Beliveau collected Stanley Cups.

3: The Record Setter
Beliveau was the first player in the NHL to score 1,000 points, a milestone that made headlines. It's as if he climbed Mount Everest but decided to do it on skates, setting the bar high for those who followed.

4: Captain Fantastic
Beliveau served as the captain of the Montreal Canadiens for 10 seasons, the longest captaincy in team history at the time. Leading by example, he was more than just a player; he was like the wise sage of hockey, guiding his team through battles on the ice.

5: A Heart as Big as the Rink
Off the ice, Beliveau's heart matched his stature. He was known for his extensive charity work, particularly with children. It's as if he decided that since he was scoring goals for fun, he might as well score some good karma points too.

6: The Signature Move
Beliveau's signature on the ice wasn't just his autograph; it was his ability to score with grace and power. Watching him score was like watching a master painter, except his brush was a hockey stick, and the canvas was the opponent's net.

7: The NHL's Gentle Giant
Standing at 6 feet 3 inches tall, Beliveau was a towering presence on the ice. But despite his size, he was known for his gentle nature, proving that you don't have to be rough to be tough. It's like he was a friendly giant, except instead of a beanstalk, he climbed the boards of the rink.

8: A Pioneer for Players' Rights
Beliveau was instrumental in establishing the NHL Players' Association, advocating for players' rights and benefits. It was like he was not just playing for the team

on his jersey but for every player in the league.

9: The Man of Many Firsts
Jean Beliveau was the first player to win the Conn Smythe Trophy as the Most Valuable Player in the playoffs, setting yet another standard for excellence. It's as if every time the NHL invented a new award, they just assumed Beliveau would win it first.

10: Beliveau's Legacy Lives On
Even after his passing, Beliveau's legacy continues to impact the sport and the community, with the Jean Beliveau Foundation supporting various charitable causes. It's like he passed the puck of kindness forward, ensuring that his legacy would go beyond just goals and assists.

11: The Respect of a Nation
Such was Beliveau's impact that upon his passing, the Canadian government offered a state funeral, a rare honor for a sports figure. It's as if the entire country wanted to give him one last standing ovation.

12: The Idol of Idols
Beliveau was idolized not just by fans but also by other hockey players, including the great Wayne Gretzky. Gretzky admired Beliveau so much that meeting him was like meeting his own hero. It's like Superman getting an autograph from Hercules.

13: A True Leader in Every Sense
Beliveau's leadership was not just about wearing the "C" on his jersey; it was about setting a moral compass for the team. He led with integrity, making him the captain not just of a team but of the sport itself.

14: The Face of the Franchise
Beliveau's image was so synonymous with the Montreal Canadiens that for many, he was the face of the franchise. It's like he was the superhero mascot for the team, but instead of a cape, he wore skates.

15: The Quintessential Canadian
Jean Beliveau embodied the spirit of Canadian hockey: skilled, humble, and gracious. It's like he was the human form of Canada, if Canada could deke and score.

16: The Fan Favorite
Beliveau's popularity transcended rivalries, making him one of the few players beloved by fans across all teams. It was like he had a universal fan club, and everyone was invited to join.

17: Hockey's Ambassador
Beyond his on-ice achievements, Beliveau served as an ambassador for hockey, spreading his love for the game worldwide. It's as if he was on a mission to make sure everyone, everywhere, could experience the joy of hockey.

18: The Stamp of Greatness
Beliveau was honored with his own postage stamp in Canada, a nod to his status as a national icon. It's like he was so legendary, even the mail wanted his autograph.

19: A Model of Consistency
Throughout his career, Beliveau was a model of consistency, always performing at the highest level. It's like he decided early on that being amazing would be his normal.

20: The Ovation That Said It All
Upon his retirement, Beliveau received one of the longest standing ovations in sports history, lasting several minutes. It was like the applause had its own intermission.

21: The Power of Beliveau's Presence

Beliveau had a presence that could light up a room or an arena. When he entered, it was like someone turned on the high beams, illuminating everything and everyone around him.

22: A Talent Recognized Early
Beliveau's talent was recognized early in his life, dominating youth leagues to such an extent that he seemed destined for greatness. It's like he was born with a hockey stick in his hand, ready to take on the world.

23: The Voice of Reason and Compassion
Beliveau was known for his wisdom and compassion, often sought after by teammates and fans alike for advice. It was like he was the team's unofficial therapist, counselor, and life coach rolled into one.

24: The Ultimate Teammate and Opponent
Beliveau was respected by teammates and opponents alike for his sportsmanship and fair play. Playing against him was like going against a legend; you wanted to win but couldn't help but admire him.

25: The Endless Love Affair with Hockey
For Beliveau, hockey was more than a game; it was a lifelong love affair. Even after his playing days were over, his passion for the sport never waned. It's like he and hockey had taken a vow: till death do us part.

MAURICE RICHARD

1: The Rocket's Launch
Maurice Richard, known as "The Rocket" for his explosive speed, was the first NHL player to score 50 goals in a single season, and he did it in just 50 games during the 1944-45 season. It's like he was playing a video game on easy mode, but there were no video games back then, so he just dazzled fans in real life instead.

2: A Fiery Competitor
Richard's fiery temper was as famous as his scoring ability. One time, he got so heated he ended up in a scuffle with a referee. It's like even the officials weren't safe when The Rocket was blasting off!

3: The Quiet Off-Ice Hero
Away from the rink, Richard was surprisingly shy. He preferred to let his actions on the ice speak for him, proving you don't need to be loud to be heard. It's like he was a superhero who saved his powers for game time.

4: A Man of the People
Richard was a hero in Quebec, especially among French Canadians. He wasn't just a hockey player; he was a symbol of pride and perseverance. It's like he was the captain of the entire province, not just the Montreal Canadiens.

5: The Infamous Suspension
In 1955, Richard was suspended for the remainder of the season after his altercation with a referee, leading to the notorious Richard Riot. It's like canceling Christmas in Montreal; fans were just that upset.

6: The 500 Goal Club
Richard was the first player in NHL history to score 500 career goals, paving the way for future generations. It's like he was the founding member of an exclusive club, and the only entry fee was pure talent (and maybe a bit of elbow grease).

7: A Stamp of Approval
Canada honored Richard with his own postage stamp, a rare tribute that cements his status as a national icon. It's like he was so legendary, even letters wanted to wear his jersey.

8: The Cup Runneth Over

Richard lifted the Stanley Cup an impressive eight times with the Canadiens, proving he didn't just play for fun; he played to win. It's like he had a season pass to victory lane.

9: The Richard Trophy
The NHL honored Richard's legacy by naming the Maurice "Rocket" Richard Trophy after him, awarded to the league's top goal scorer each season. It's like giving the fastest runner the "Usain Bolt Award"; it just makes sense.

10: The First to the Rafters
The Canadiens retired Richard's number 9, making him the first player in the team's storied history to receive this honor. It's like retiring the jersey number of the coolest kid in school because no one could ever be that cool again.

11: A Family Affair
Maurice wasn't the only Richard on the ice; his brother Henri also played for the Canadiens, making them one of the most formidable sibling duos in sports. It's like having two Rockets, which, scientifically speaking, makes for twice the speed.

12: The Hall of Fame Beckons
Richard was inducted into the Hockey Hall of Fame in 1961, and they waived the usual waiting period because, well, he's Maurice Richard. It's like skipping the line at an amusement park because you're just that much fun.

13: A Man of Firsts
Richard was a pioneer, being the first to achieve many milestones in the NHL, setting records left and right as if he were checking them off his grocery list. It's like he had a cheat sheet for being awesome.

14: The Quiet Philanthropist
Richard was known for his charitable work, especially with children, though he preferred to keep this side of his life private. It's like he was a secret agent, but instead of spying, he was spreading kindness.

15: The Wartime Hero
During World War II, Richard worked in a factory by day and played hockey by night, showing his dedication to both his country and his sport. It's like he was a superhero with the most Canadian alter-ego ever.

16: The Inspiration Behind a Song
Richard's impact was so profound that he inspired a song, "The Richard Riot" by

MARIO LEMIEUX

1: The Grand Entrance
Mario Lemieux made a splash from the very first moment he stepped onto NHL ice in 1984, scoring on his very first shot, on his first shift, in his first game. It's like he was playing a game of "Can you top this?" with himself right from the start.

2: Super Mario to the Rescue
When the Pittsburgh Penguins were in financial trouble in the late 1990s, Lemieux did what any superhero would do: he saved the day! He converted his deferred salary into equity and became the owner, making him the first former player to own an NHL team. It's like he decided if you can't beat 'em, buy 'em!

3: The Comeback King
After retiring in 1997 due to health issues, Lemieux missed the thrill of the game so much that he laced up his skates and returned to the NHL in 2000, proving that you can't keep a good player down. It was as if retirement was just a long intermission for him.

4: A Battle Off the Ice
Lemieux's courage wasn't just displayed in scoring goals; he also faced off against Hodgkin's lymphoma. He returned to play the same day he received his last radiation treatment, showing that not even cancer could keep him off the ice. It's like he treated every challenge like a penalty shot: an opportunity to score a win.

5: The Ultimate Hat Trick
In a single game in 1988, Lemieux accomplished what's known as the "Ultimate Hat Trick": scoring a goal five different ways in the same game – even strength, power play, short-handed, penalty shot, and an empty net. It's like he decided to play a game of H.O.R.S.E. with himself, but for hockey.

6: Mr. Hockey Night
Lemieux loved the spotlight so much that he scored at least one point in all 50 games he played during the 1992-93 season before his illness forced him to take a break. It's like he thought every night was hockey night and everyone else was just there to watch him shine.

7: The Trophy Room Overfloweth
Lemieux has won practically every major NHL award, including the Hart Trophy (3 times), Art Ross Trophy (6 times), and Conn Smythe Trophy (2 times), making his trophy room more like a trophy lake that you'd need a boat to navigate.

8: The Penguin Lifelong
Despite offers from other teams, Lemieux played his entire career with the Pittsburgh Penguins, from 1984 to 2006. It's like he believed in monogamy, but for hockey teams.

9: The Generous Giant
Off the ice, Lemieux is known for his charitable work, especially through the Mario Lemieux Foundation, which focuses on cancer research and patient care. It's like he's on a mission to assist off the ice as much as he did on it.

10: The Scorer of the Century
Lemieux was named one of the "100 Greatest NHL Players" in history in 2017, an honor that solidified his status as hockey royalty. It's like being knighted by the realm of hockey, except the sword is a hockey stick.

11: When Mario Met Mario
Lemieux became so legendary that he was immortalized in the world of video games with "Mario Lemieux Hockey" for the Sega Genesis. It's like when a superhero gets their own comic book, but for the gamer generation.

12: The Man of Many Nicknames
From "Super Mario" to "Le Magnifique," Lemieux's talent on the ice earned him nicknames that reflected his skill and grace. It's like every time he did something amazing, someone decided he needed a new nickname to match.

13: A Record for the Ages
Lemieux holds the NHL record for the most points per game in a career (minimum 500 games played), making him not just a legend, but a statistical marvel. It's like he was playing a different game than everyone else, and the game was called "Winning."

14: The Mentor of Champions
Lemieux's influence on the ice didn't end when he stopped playing; he mentored younger players, including Sidney Crosby, passing on

BOBBY ORR

1: The Flying Goal
Bobby Orr is famous for "The Goal" in 1970, where he flew through the air like Superman after scoring to win the Stanley Cup. It's like he decided walking was too boring and took up flying, but only after scoring epic goals.

2: The Record Breaker 📚💥
Orr set records left and right, including being the only defenseman to win the NHL scoring title, not once but twice! It's like he was playing a video game and discovered a cheat code for unlimited points.

3: Speedy Skates 🥾💨
Known for his speed, Orr could skate from one end of the rink to the other in record time. It's rumored that roadrunners watched tapes of his games for tips on how to outrun coyotes.

4: The Generous Giant 🤍🫶
Off the ice, Orr was a big-hearted philanthropist, often involved in charity work. He's like a real-life superhero, but instead of a cape, he wears skates and carries a hockey stick.

5: Rookie Sensation 👶
Orr started his NHL career with a bang, winning the Calder Trophy as Rookie of the Year in 1967. It's like he showed up for his first day of work and was immediately promoted to CEO.

6: The Trophy Magnet 🏆🧲
With two Norris Trophies, three Hart Trophies, and an induction into the Hall of Fame at the young age of 31, Orr's house must have needed extra rooms just for his awards. It's like he collected trophies instead of hockey cards.

7: Orr's Off-Ice Goal 🎯🌍
Bobby Orr founded the Bobby Orr Hall of Fame in his hometown of Parry Sound, Ontario, to inspire young athletes. It's like he built a museum of "You Can Do It Too," with his achievements as the main exhibit.

8: The Number That Lives Forever 🔢💜
The Boston Bruins retired Orr's number 4, ensuring no one else would wear it again. It's like retiring the number of the class valedictorian because no one could ever match up.

9: The Artist on Ice 🖌️🎨
Orr's playing style was so graceful, fans said watching him was like watching an artist paint a masterpiece, but with ice shavings instead of paint. It's like he was part Picasso, part Gretzky.

10: The Hockey Innovator 🏒💡
Orr changed how defensemen played the game, showing that they could be offensive threats too. It's like he looked at the rulebook, shrugged, and decided to rewrite it with his skates.

11: The Fisherman 🎣🐟
When not dazzling on the ice, Orr loved fishing. It's like he decided if he was going to catch anything, it might as well be fish since he'd already caught all the trophies.

12: Mentor and Agent 💬🧑‍💼
After retiring, Orr became a player agent, mentoring young players and guiding their careers. It's like he switched from scoring goals to scoring deals.

13: The Canadian Hero 🍁🧑‍♂️
In Canada, Orr is not just a hockey legend; he's a national treasure. It's like he's part of the country's Mount Rushmore, but for hockey.

14: The Knee Struggles 🦵🩹
Despite his incredible career, Orr's time on the ice was plagued by knee injuries. It's like he was so fast, his knees couldn't keep up with the rest of him.

15: The Impromptu Actor 🎬📺
Orr made appearances in TV shows and commercials, showing that his talents weren't limited to the hockey rink. It's like he decided if he could act on ice, he could act on screen too.

16: The Businessman
Orr also ventured into the business world, using his leadership skills off the ice. It's like he treated business deals like penalty shots—always aiming to score.

17: The Unofficial Mayor
In Boston, Orr is so beloved it's like he's the unofficial mayor. If he ran for office, the only debate would be how many votes he'd win by.

18: The Autograph Hero
Orr is known for never turning down an autograph request, making him a fan favorite. It's like his pen was as mighty as his hockey stick.

WAYNE GRETZKY

1: The Great One's First Skates
Wayne Gretzky, known as "The Great One," put on his first pair of skates at just two years old. It's like he was born to glide on ice. Imagine being a toddler and already on your way to becoming a hockey legend. It's like learning to walk, but cooler.

2: The Backyard Rink
Wayne's dad, Walter Gretzky, built him a backyard ice rink called the "Wally Coliseum." It's where Wayne spent countless hours practicing, turning him into the hockey phenom we know today. It's like having your own personal amusement park, but for hockey.

3: A Prodigy's Promise
At six years old, playing in a league with 10-year-olds, Wayne scored an unbelievable 378 goals in one season. It's as if he was playing a video game on easy mode, but in real life.

4: The Jersey Switch-Up
Gretzky originally wore number 9 in honor of his hockey hero, Gordie Howe. But when he joined the Sault Ste. Marie Greyhounds, and number 9 was taken, he switched to 99. It's like doubling your luck because one 9 just wasn't enough.

5: Record Smasher
Wayne holds 61 NHL records, including most career goals, assists, and points. It's as if he decided the record book was his personal diary, chronicling his adventures in hockey.

6: The Unthinkable Trade
In 1988, Gretzky was traded from the Edmonton Oilers to the Los Angeles Kings in what's known as "The Trade." It shocked the world, kind of like if someone decided to trade the Mona Lisa for a Hollywood sign.

7: A Hollywood Love Story
Wayne's trade to Los Angeles wasn't just about hockey; it also led him to meet his future wife, actress Janet Jones. It's like a rom-com plot, but with more ice skates and less running through airports.

8: The Magic 50 in 39
Gretzky set an incredible record by scoring 50 goals in just 39 games. It's as if he decided waiting around was overrated, and he'd rather just score goals at warp speed.

9: The Ambassador of Hockey
Wayne is known for growing the popularity of hockey in the United States, especially in non-traditional markets. It's like he was on a mission to make sure everyone, everywhere, could experience the joy of hockey.

10: Wayne's World, The Restaurant
Gretzky didn't just excel on ice; he also ventured into business, opening a restaurant in Toronto named "Wayne Gretzky's." It's where you could enjoy a burger while surrounded by memorabilia of The Great One. It's like dining in a hockey museum, but with better food.

11: The Great One's Great Acts

Off the ice, Wayne has been involved in countless charitable activities, focusing on children's health and education. It's as if he's scoring goals against life's challenges, assisting those in need.

12: The Animated Hero
Gretzky even became an animated character in the cartoon "ProStars," where he fought crime and helped kids alongside Michael Jordan and Bo Jackson. It's like he decided being a real-life superhero wasn't enough; he needed to be a cartoon one too.

13: Coaching The Coyotes
Wayne took a shot at coaching, leading the Phoenix Coyotes from 2005 to 2009. It's like he thought, "I've conquered playing, now let's conquer coaching," proving The Great One always seeks new ice to conquer.

14: Olympic Gold
Gretzky was the executive director of Canada's Olympic hockey team in 2002, leading them to gold. It's as if he turned everything he touched into gold, including Olympic medals.

15: The Great One's Great Foundation
The Wayne Gretzky Foundation is dedicated to helping less fortunate youth experience the sport of hockey. It's like Gretzky's assist stats continue to climb, but this time off the ice, helping kids score their own life goals.

16: A Star on Hollywood's Walk of Fame
Wayne has a star on the Hollywood Walk of Fame, not for acting, but for being a sports legend. It's like Hollywood decided if they couldn't have him in movies, they'd at least give him a star.

17: The Wine Connoisseur
Gretzky also ventured into the wine business, owning Wayne Gretzky Estates. It's as if he decided that after years of ice, it was time to relax with a glass of wine.

18: The Family Man
Above all, Wayne is a dedicated family man, often sharing the spotlight with his wife and kids. It's like he's the captain of Team Gretzky, leading with love and dedication.

19: The Humble Legend
Despite his fame, Gretzky has remained humble, always crediting his teammates for his success. It's like he's the guy who climbed Mount Everest but insists it was just a nice stroll.

20: The Great One's Great Influence
Wayne Gretzky's influence on hockey is immeasurable. It's like he's the tide that lifted all boats, making the game better, bigger, and more beloved around the world.

GORDIE HOWE

The Origin of "Mr. Hockey" - Gordie Howe was dubbed "Mr. Hockey" not just because he was a phenomenal player, but because he embodied the spirit of the game. It's like being so good at eating pizza that they start calling you "Mr. Pizza."

A Career Longer Than a Dinosaur's Age - Gordie Howe's professional hockey career spanned an incredible five decades. He started playing before man landed on the moon and didn't hang up his skates until after the internet was invented. That's like a T-Rex playing hockey with a woolly mammoth and then high-fiving a robot.

The Gordie Howe Hat Trick - A "Gordie Howe hat trick" doesn't involve just scoring goals; it includes a goal, an assist, and a fight in one game. It's like getting an A+ in math, being voted class president, and winning an arm wrestling contest all in one day.

Scoring Against Father Time - Gordie Howe scored over 800 goals in his NHL career, proving that age is just a number, especially if that number is also your goal tally.

A Family Affair on Ice - Gordie got to play professional hockey alongside his sons Mark and Marty, which is like having a family picnic, but instead of sandwiches, you're passing pucks.

The Ageless Wonder - Howe played his final NHL game at 52 years old, making him the oldest player to ever hit the ice in the league. That's like your grandpa deciding to run a marathon...and winning.

A Powerhouse from Saskatoon - Born in Saskatoon, Saskatchewan, Gordie Howe proved that even if you come from a small grain-farming town, you can grow up to be a giant in the world of sports.

From Rink Rat to Hockey Royalty - Howe spent countless hours practicing on frozen ponds as a kid, which is like doing homework for fun but ending up a genius.

The Signature Elbow - Gordie was famous for his use of elbows on the ice. If hockey had a super move, Howe's elbow was like the special combo you'd pull off in a video game for extra points.

Hockey's Iron Man - Howe played an astounding 1,767 NHL games. That's like attending school every day without missing a single one, from kindergarten through your PhD.

A Heart as Big as the Net - Off the ice, Gordie was known for his charitable work and genuine kindness, proving he could score big in the game of life too.

The Voice That Echoed in Arenas - Gordie wasn't just a physical presence; he was also known for his leadership and the respect he commanded in the locker room. It's like being the captain of a pirate ship, but instead of the sea, you navigate the ice.

A Rivalry for the Ages - Howe had legendary battles with other hockey greats, showing that even superheroes meet their match. Think Batman vs. Superman but on skates.

The Reluctant Star - Despite his fame, Gordie was notoriously humble, often shying away from the spotlight. It's like being the lead singer of a band who'd rather be the roadie.

Innovator on Ice - Howe was known for his innovative playing style, constantly finding new ways to score goals and win games. He was like a scientist in a lab, but instead of beakers and Bunsen burners, he had a stick and a puck.

The King of Comebacks - Even after retiring, Howe made a comeback to play professional hockey with his sons, proving that you can't keep a good man down. It's like retiring from being a superhero, only to come back and save the world again.

AMAZING RECORDS

SCORING RECORDS

1: The Great One's Grand Record
Wayne Gretzky, also known as "The Great One," holds the mind-boggling record for the most points scored in a single NHL season with an astonishing 215 points during the 1985-86 season. It's like he was playing a video game on beginner mode, but in real life, making other players look like they were stuck in tutorial mode.

2: A Goal-Scoring Phenomenon
In the 1981-82 season, Gretzky scored 92 goals, setting the record for the most goals in a single NHL season. That's like scoring so often, the goal light needed a break and the puck started asking for a time-out.

3: The Magic of 50 in 39
Gretzky also amazed the world by scoring 50 goals in just 39 games during the 1981-82 season, a feat so magical, it's like he had a hockey wand instead of a stick. It's as if he decided Christmas came early for hockey fans that year.

4: The Ironman Streak of Scoring
"The Great One" didn't just score a lot; he scored consistently, recording a point in 51 consecutive games in the 1983-84 season. Imagine playing tag with Gretzky, but no matter how hard you try, you just can't avoid being "it" for 51 games straight.

5: Dishing Out Assists Like Candy
Gretzky isn't just the king of scoring; he's also the all-time leader in assists, having set up teammates for a whopping 1,963 career assists. That's like being the best friend everyone wants, always ready to pass the puck...or the last slice of pizza.

6: The Rookie Sensation Record
Teemu Selanne shattered records in his rookie season (1992-93) by scoring 76 goals, a feat so astonishing, it's like he entered a cheat code for unlimited goals. It's as if he was playing on a mission to redefine "beginner's luck."

7: The Fastest to the Century Club

Gretzky reached 100 points in a season faster than anyone else, achieving this milestone in just 34 games during the 1983-84 season. It's like he had a sports car on the ice, zooming past milestones while everyone else was on a leisurely Sunday drive.

8: A Defender Among Scorers
Paul Coffey holds the record for the most goals by a defenseman in a single season, netting 48 goals in the 1985-86 season. That's like being the knight who decides to slay the dragon AND rescue the princess all by himself.

9: Age Is Just a Number for Scoring
Gordie Howe, at 52 years and 11 days old, became the oldest player to score in an NHL game, proving that you're never too old to light the lamp. It's as if Father Time decided to lace up his skates and show the kids how it's done.

10: The Unbreakable Goalie Barrier
Martin Brodeur holds the record for the most career wins by a goaltender with 691 wins. It's like he turned the goal into a fortress, and he was the gatekeeper saying, "Thou shall not pass!" to the puck.

11: The Century Game – Scoring 100 Points
Gretzky is the only player in NHL history to score 100 or more points in 16 consecutive seasons, creating a rainbow of points that seemed to never end. It's like he had a season ticket to the 100-point club, and he renewed it every year just for fun.

12: The Hat Trick Hat Tricks
Joe Malone holds the record for the most hat tricks in a season with 7 in 1917-18. It's like he decided that scoring three goals once wasn't cool enough, so he made it his personal hobby.

13: Scoring Before the Ice Melts
Auston Matthews holds the modern record for scoring four goals in his NHL debut, a feat so hot, it's a wonder the ice didn't melt beneath his skates. It's as if he was trying to complete all his career milestones in one game.

14: The Blue Line Bomber
Bobby Orr revolutionized the role of a defenseman, becoming the first (and only) defenseman to win the Art Ross Trophy as the league's top scorer. It's like he was playing a different game, where defenders were also attackers, confusing opponents and breaking stereotypes.

15: The Goalie Who Scored
Ron Hextall became the first NHL goaltender to score a goal by shooting the puck into the opposing net, proving that goalies can do more than just stop pucks; they can score them too. It's like the goalie decided to throw a surprise party, and the surprise was on the other team.

16: Marathon Men
The longest game in NHL history lasted a staggering 176 minutes and 30 seconds, going into six overtime periods. It's like playing three full games back-to-back, and then deciding to start a fourth, just for fun. Imagine if every class in school was this long!

17: Zero to Hero
Chris Kontos holds the peculiar record for the most goals in a playoff year by someone who didn't play the regular season. Scoring 9 goals in 1989 for the Los Angeles Kings, it's as if he was summoned from a secret hockey dimension just for the playoffs.

18: The Scoring Goalie, Part 2
Martin Brodeur not only holds the record for most wins by a goalie but also scored three NHL goals, making him the Wayne Gretzky of goalies. It's like he thought, "Saving goals is fun, but you know what's more fun? Scoring them!"

19: The Perfect Season
The 1976-77 Montreal Canadiens hold the record for the most points in a single season with 132. It's like they decided losses were out of fashion and wins were the new trend.

20: The Penalty Box Regular
Dave "Tiger" Williams holds the all-time record for the most penalty minutes in a career with 3,966 minutes. That's over 66 hours spent in the penalty box, or like watching the entire "Lord of the Rings" trilogy about 22 times, but with less popcorn and more hockey sticks.

21: The Speedy Gonzales Award
Dylan Larkin holds the record for the fastest skater in the NHL, clocking in at 13.172 seconds around the full rink. It's like he was trying to outrun his shadow, and almost succeeded.

22: Youngest to the Show
Bep Guidolin holds the record for being the youngest player to play in an NHL game at just 16 years and 11 months. It's like instead of getting a driver's license, he got a roster spot on an NHL team.

23: The Comeback Kids
The 1942 Toronto Maple Leafs are the only team in NHL history to come back from a 0-3 deficit in the Stanley Cup Finals to win the Cup. It's like they were inspired by every sports movie ever made, except their comeback was real.

24: The Sharpshooter
Ray Bourque holds the record for the most shots on goal by a defenseman in a career, with 6,209 shots. It's like he believed the best defense was a good offense, armed with a cannon of a shot.

25: The Oldest of the Old-Timers
Gordie Howe is the oldest player to play in an NHL game at 52 years and 11 days old, proving that age is just a number, especially if you're Mr. Hockey.

26: The Short-Handed Wizard
Wayne Gretzky also holds the record for the most short-handed goals in a career with 73. It's like he decided playing with fewer players on the ice was too easy.

27: Four Goals, One Debut
Auston Matthews made history by scoring four goals in his NHL debut, setting a record for the most goals scored by a player in their first game. It's like he was playing a game of "Anything you can do, I can do better" with history.

28: The Power-Play King
Dave Andreychuk holds the record for the most power-play goals in a career with 274. It's like every time his team got a power play, he decided it was time to redecorate the scoreboard.

29: The Iron Man Streak, Take Two
Doug Jarvis holds the record for the most consecutive games played in the NHL, with 964. That's over 11 straight seasons without missing a game. It's like he thought sick days were just a myth.

30: The Goalie Gambit
Ron Hextall became the first goalie to score a goal by shooting the puck into the opposing team's empty net, making goalies everywhere dream of their moment of glory.

31: The Fastest Hat Trick
Bill Mosienko holds the record for the fastest hat trick in NHL history, scoring three goals in just 21 seconds. It's like he was in a rush to get somewhere but decided to score a few goals first.

32: The Century Playmaker
Wayne Gretzky also holds the record for the most 100-assist seasons,

achieving this feat 11 times. It's like he was the Santa Claus of assists, delivering gifts to his teammates all season long.

33: The Defensive Giant
Larry Robinson boasts the best career plus-minus rating in NHL history at +722. It's like every time he was on the ice, the other team decided scoring was just too hard.

34: The Netminder Nightmares
Mario Lemieux scored five goals five different ways in a single game: even strength, power play, short-handed, penalty shot, and empty net. It's like he was playing hockey bingo and won the jackpot.

35: The Bench Boss
Scotty Bowman holds the record for the most regular-season wins by a coach with 1,244 victories. It's like he had the Midas touch, but instead of turning things to gold, he turned them into wins.

36: The Longest Name Trophy
Jaromir Jagr won the NHL's Art Ross Trophy as the oldest player at age 43. It's like he was competing not just on ice but also against Father Time, and winning.

37: The Golden Goalie
Martin Brodeur not only has the most wins by a goalie but also the most shutouts in NHL history with 125. It's like he decided the goal was a "No Puck Zone."

38: The Dynasty Builder
Henri Richard won the Stanley Cup 11 times, the most by any player in NHL history. It's like he had a subscription service for Stanley Cup rings.

39: The Penalty Minute Mountain
Tiger Williams rode his way into the penalty box so often he racked up 3,966 penalty minutes, the most in NHL history. It's like he thought the penalty box was a vacation home.

40: The Human Highlight Reel
Bobby Orr revolutionized how defensemen played, becoming the first defenseman to lead the league in scoring. It's like he looked at the rulebook and thought, "Nah, I'll write my own."

41: The Goalie Sniper
Besides Ron Hextall, Martin Brodeur, and Chris Mason, Mike Smith is another goaltender who scored by shooting the puck into the opponent's empty net. It's as if these goalies were thinking, "Why stop pucks when you can score them?" Imagine a soccer goalie deciding to run the length of the field to score; that's the level of surprise we're talking about!

42: The Expansion Era Phenom
Vegas Golden Knights' William Karlsson holds the record for the highest shooting percentage by an NHL player (minimum 20 goals scored) in a season, with a staggering 23.4% in the 2017-18 season. It's like every time he shot the puck, it had a homing device aimed at the net.

43: Zero to Fifty
Auston Matthews set a modern era record for the fastest time to score 50 goals in a season, achieving the feat in just 50 games during the 2021-22 season. It's as if he was in a race with himself to see how quickly he could make history.

44: The Power-Play Marathon Man
Dave Schultz holds the record for the most penalty minutes in a single season, with 472 in the 1974-75 season. If penalty minutes were currency, he'd be a billionaire, living lavishly in the penalty box.

45: The Oldest Rookie Sensation
Sergei Makarov won the Calder Memorial Trophy as the NHL's Rookie of the Year at age 31 during the 1989-90 season,

proving that in hockey, it's never too late to be a "newbie." It's like starting your first day of school when you're already the teacher.

46: The Dominant Defenseman
Nicklas Lidstrom won the Norris Trophy as the NHL's top defenseman seven times, a testament to his consistent excellence on the blue line. It's as if he built a no-fly zone around his net, and he was the air traffic controller.

47: The Longest Tenured Captain
Steve Yzerman served as the captain of the Detroit Red Wings for 19 seasons, the longest captaincy in NHL history. He was less like a captain and more like a king, ruling over his ice kingdom with wisdom and courage.

48: The Most Decorated Olympian
Sidney Crosby is among the few hockey players to have won multiple Olympic gold medals and an NHL Stanley Cup, showcasing his leadership and skill on both the international stage and the professional arena. It's like he has a Midas touch, but instead of gold, everything turns to trophies.

49: The Breakaway King
Pavel Bure, known as "The Russian Rocket," holds the unofficial record for the most career penalty shots attempted, with 16. It's as if every time he got a breakaway, defenders decided it was easier to trip him than to try to stop him legally.

50: The Quintuple Overtime Epic
The Philadelphia Flyers and Pittsburgh Penguins played the longest game in the modern era on May 4, 2000, lasting over 152 minutes of game time. It was more like a hockey marathon than a game, where players needed energy gels and hydration stations.

51: The Century Mark in Assists
Wayne Gretzky is the only player to record more than 100 assists in a single season, a feat he accomplished 11 times. It's as if he was handing out assists like they were flyers for a garage sale.

52: The Faceoff Maestro
Yanic Perreault is recognized for his faceoff prowess, consistently leading the league in faceoff percentage. Winning draws like a magician pulling rabbits out of a hat, except his hat was the faceoff circle.

53: The Perfect Penalty Killer
Kevin Lowe holds the record for the most playoff shorthanded goals by a defenseman, turning penalty kills into scoring opportunities. It's as if he decided that playing with fewer players was an advantage, not a penalty.

54: The Hat Trick of Hat Tricks
Joe Malone, in the NHL's inaugural season (1917-18), scored three hat tricks in three consecutive games. It's like he thought scoring just one goal was too mainstream.

55: The Ironman Goalie
Glenn Hall holds the record for the most consecutive complete games by a goaltender, with 502. Imagine going to work every day for nearly 7 years without taking a single sick day, and your job is stopping 100mph slapshots.

56: The Playoff Overtime Hero
Joe Sakic holds the record for the most playoff overtime goals in a career, with 8. It's as if he thrived on the pressure, turning "sudden death" into "sudden victory."

57: The All-Time Playoff Point Leader
Wayne Gretzky, unsurprisingly, holds the record for the most points in playoff history, with an almost mythical 382 points. It's like he had a separate gear

for the playoffs, where points multiplied like bunnies.

58: The Shutout Streak
Brian Boucher set a modern-day record for the longest shutout streak by a goaltender, keeping opponents scoreless for 332 minutes and 1 second. It's as if he turned the goal into a vault, and he was the only one who knew the combination.

59: The Youngest Captain to Lift the Cup
Sidney Crosby became the youngest captain in NHL history to win the Stanley Cup at age 21. It's like being promoted to CEO right after your internship.

60: The Most Games Played
Gordie Howe played the most NHL games in history, with a staggering 1,767 regular-season games. It's as if he loved hockey so much, he never wanted to leave the ice, making the rink his second home.

61: The Fastest to 1,000 Points
Wayne Gretzky reached 1,000 career points faster than any other player, needing only 424 games. It's like he was in a race against history itself, and history blinked first.

62: The "French Connection"
Gilbert Perreault, Rick Martin, and Rene Robert, known as the "French Connection," dazzled fans with their chemistry and scoring for the Buffalo Sabres. It was like watching a ballet on ice, but with more goals and body checks.

63: The Goalie Without a Mask
Jacques Plante was the first goaltender to regularly wear a protective mask in games, revolutionizing safety for goalies. Before him, goalies faced pucks with nothing but courage, making them the daredevils of the ice.

64: The Outdoor Game Pioneer
The 1954 NHL All-Star Game was the first and only outdoor All-Star Game until the Winter Classic began in 2008. It was like the NHL decided to take hockey back to its roots, where snowflakes were as common as slapshots.

65: The Golden Goal
Sidney Crosby scored the "Golden Goal" at the 2010 Vancouver Olympics, clinching the gold medal for Canada in overtime against the USA. It was a moment so electric, it could power a city, or at least a small town, for a day.

66: The Dynamic Duo
Henrik and Daniel Sedin, the Swedish twins who played for the Vancouver Canucks, are the only siblings in NHL history to each surpass 1,000 career points. It's as if they decided to share not just their looks but their incredible hockey talents, making defenders see double.

67: The Most Valuable Defenseman
Bobby Orr won the Hart Trophy (MVP) three times as a defenseman, a record in the NHL. It's like he was playing chess while everyone else was playing checkers, redefining what it meant to be a defenseman.

68: A Scoring Streak for the Ages
Mat Barzal set a record for the longest point streak by a rookie in the 21st century with a 15-game streak during the 2017-18 season. It's as if he decided that "rookie" just meant "new to setting records."

69: The Penalty Shot Pioneer
Floyd Smith was the first NHL player to score on a penalty shot on November 13, 1934. It's like he was given a challenge and decided to make history while accepting it, setting the stage for countless dramatic moments to follow.

70: The King of Game-Winning Goals

Jaromir Jagr holds the NHL record for the most career game-winning goals, making him the go-to guy when the game was on the line. It's as if he had a knack for drama, always ready to deliver the climactic scene.

71: The All-Around All-Star
Ray Bourque appeared in 19 NHL All-Star Games, showcasing his enduring excellence and popularity. It's like he had a season ticket to the All-Star Game, reserved just for him, year after year.

72: The Net-Finding Newcomer
Teemu Selanne, in his rookie season (1992-93), not only scored 76 goals but also had an astounding 132 points. It's as if he stepped onto the ice and decided to turn the rookie scoring record into his personal highlight reel.

73: The Ironman of the Ice
Doug Jarvis holds the NHL's "Ironman" streak for playing 964 consecutive games without missing a single matchup. It's like he decided that "day off" wasn't in his vocabulary, making durability his middle name.

74: The Goalie's Nightmare
Darryl Sittler holds the record for the most points in a single game by a player, with 10 points (6 goals, 4 assists) on February 7, 1976. It's like he was playing a game within a game, where the objective was to rewrite the record books.

75: The Fastest Hat Trick, Revisited
Bill Mosienko's 21-second hat trick may be the fastest, but Jean Beliveau holds the record for the fastest hat trick in the playoffs, netting three goals in 44 seconds. It's as if playoff pressure just made him hit the turbo button.

76: The Legendary Lefty
Despite most players shooting right-handed, Gordie Howe was one of the few hockey legends who shot left, proving that greatness knows no hand preference. It's like he chose "hard mode" and still won the game.

77: The Ultimate Champion
Henri Richard, the younger brother of Maurice "Rocket" Richard, won the Stanley Cup 11 times, the most by any player in NHL history. It's as if he had a direct subscription to lifting the Cup, renewing it almost every year.

78: The Age-Defying Debut
Gordie Howe made a one-game comeback with the Detroit Vipers in the IHL at 69 years old, making him the only professional hockey player to take the ice in six different decades. It's like he wanted to ensure every generation got a taste of Mr. Hockey.

79: The Master of Assists
Wayne Gretzky's record for most assists in a single season stands at an astonishing 163 during the 1985-86 season. It's like he decided if he couldn't score all the goals himself, he'd set them up instead.

80: The Quintessential Quadruple
Only 11 players in NHL history have won the Stanley Cup with three different teams. It's like collecting rare gems, except these gems are made of ice and hard work.

81: The Zero Hero
Tony Esposito set the modern record for most shutouts by a rookie goaltender with 15 in the 1969-70 season. It's as if he turned the goal into a fortress, and he was the lone, unbeatable guardian.

82: The Globetrotting Goalie
Dominik Hasek won numerous awards across different leagues around the

world, including six Vezina Trophies in the NHL, making him a global goaltending legend. It's like he was on a worldwide tour, collecting accolades instead of souvenirs.

83: The Puck-Stealing Maestro
Wayne Gretzky holds the record for the most career regular-season steals, showcasing his defensive skills alongside his offensive prowess. It's as if he decided playing only half the game was too boring.

84: The Scoring Defenseman
Paul Coffey shattered records for scoring by a defenseman, including 48 goals in a single season (1985-86) and 1,531 career points. It's like he was a forward in disguise, sneaking goals past unsuspecting goalies.

85: The Breakaway Specialist
Pavel Bure, known as "The Russian Rocket," was feared for his breakaway speed, often leaving defenders in the dust. It's as if he had rockets on his skates, propelling him to the net with unmatched velocity.

86: The Cult Hero
Taro Tsujimoto is a fictional player "drafted" by the Buffalo Sabres in 1974 as a prank. He's become a cult hero among fans, a reminder that hockey has a sense of humor too. It's like discovering your favorite player is actually a superhero from a comic book.

87: The Power Play Innovator
Mario Lemieux revolutionized the power play, often playing as the "quarterback" from behind the net. His strategic mind turned the Penguins' power play into a feared weapon, as if he was playing chess on ice, always thinking several moves ahead.

88: The Unbreakable Record
Glenn Hall's record of 502 consecutive complete games as a goaltender is considered unbreakable in today's NHL, a testament to endurance that's more like a marathon than a sprint.

89: The Triple Gold Club
Only a select group of players have won the Stanley Cup, an Olympic gold medal, and a World Championship, earning them entry into the exclusive Triple Gold Club. It's like the VIP lounge of hockey achievements, where only the elite are welcome.

90: The Most Prolific Playoff Performer
Mark Messier is second only to Wayne Gretzky in playoff points, with his leadership in critical games as legendary as his skill. It's as if he turned the postseason into his personal stage, delivering performances that would make Broadway jealous.

91: The Ultimate Faceoff King
Rod Brind'Amour set an NHL record during the 2005-06 season for the highest faceoff win percentage over a season (min. 1,000 faceoffs), winning 62.9% of his draws. It's like he had a secret handshake with the puck, convincing it to always come his way.

92: The Goalie Duel for the Ages
The longest goalie duel in NHL playoff history ended when Petr Klima scored in the third overtime of Game 1 of the 1990 Stanley Cup Finals, after 55:13 of scoreless overtime play. It's like the two goalies decided to turn the game into a personal bet on who could keep the puck out the longest.

93: The Sharpshooting Goalie
José Théodore is one of the few NHL goalies to score a goal and win a game all on his own, literally taking matters into his own hands (or stick) during the 2001-02 season. It's as if he looked around, shrugged, and decided, "Guess I'll do it myself."

94: The Youngest Captain to Ever Do It

Connor McDavid was named captain of the Edmonton Oilers at 19 years and 266 days old, becoming the youngest captain in NHL history. It's like being promoted to CEO straight out of the intern pool, but with more ice and less coffee fetching.

95: The Most Loyal Warrior 🛡️🖤
Steve Yzerman spent his entire 22-season career with the Detroit Red Wings, embodying the spirit of loyalty in an era of frequent trades. It's like he and the Red Wings were in a long-term relationship that just kept getting better with age.

96: The Goal That Wasn't 🚫📋
In 1996, Martin Brodeur scored a goal against the Montreal Canadiens in the playoffs, but because of a rule at the time, the goal was officially credited to another player. It's like doing all the work on a group project and having someone else's name on the presentation.

97: The Penalty Box Marathon 🗓️
Dave "Tiger" Williams might hold the record for the most penalty minutes, but Gino Odjick isn't far behind, amassing 2,567 penalty minutes over his career. It's as if he treated the penalty box like a second home, maybe even decorating it with some personal touches.

98: The Defensive Dynamo 🛡️
Scott Stevens is renowned not just for his leadership and three Stanley Cup victories but also for delivering some of the most memorable (and bone-crushing) hits in NHL history. It's as if he was the judge, jury, and executioner on ice, laying down the law one hit at a time.

99: The Never-Ending Season 🔄
During the 1992-93 NHL season, the league played an 84-game schedule, the longest regular season in its history. It's like they decided that hockey was so good, why not sprinkle a little extra on top?

100: The Miracle on Ice 🇺🇸
While not an NHL record, the "Miracle on Ice" in 1980, where the USA Olympic hockey team defeated the Soviet Union, remains one of the most iconic moments in hockey history. It's like David vs. Goliath on ice, with college kids taking on the seasoned pros and winning against all odds.

GOALIE RECORDS

1: The Goalie Who Turned Sniper 🎯
Did you know Martin Brodeur, the legendary goalie for the New Jersey Devils, not only stopped pucks but also scored them? He holds the record for most goals scored by a goalie in the NHL, with three career goals. It's like he thought, "Why let the forwards have all the fun?"

2: The Iron Wall for the Ages 🧱
Glenn Hall, known as "Mr. Goalie," holds an unbelievable record of playing 502 consecutive complete games as a goaltender. That's like showing up for a marathon every day for almost 7 years, and instead of running, stopping 100mph slapshots!

3: The Shutout King 🔥🚫
Martin Brodeur also holds the record for the most career shutouts in the NHL, with 125. It's as if he turned the net into a "No Puck Zone," and he was the mayor, sheriff, and town guard all rolled into one.

4: A Debut Like No Other 📋
Imagine stepping onto the ice for your first NHL game and deciding to throw a shutout. That's exactly what Al Rollins

did in 1950 for the Toronto Maple Leafs, setting the tone for a career that would be anything but ordinary. It's like acing a test before you've even taken the class!

5: The Man of the Hour (and a Half)
The longest goalie duel in NHL history ended with Ron Tugnutt of the Quebec Nordiques and Dominik Hasek of the Buffalo Sabres battling it out for over 5 periods of playoff hockey in 1996. It's like they decided that sleep was overrated and a night of epic saves was far more interesting.

6: The Fastest Gloves in the West (and East)
Who says goalies aren't quick? Sergei Bobrovsky set a modern-day record for the fastest glove, catching a puck in 0.002 seconds, or so it seemed to the shooter, whose blink lasted longer than his shot.

7: The Oldest Rookie Sensation
Johnny Bower made his full-time NHL debut at the ripe age of 29 and played until he was 45, proving that in hockey, age is just a number—especially if you're guarding the net with the agility of a cat and the wisdom of an owl.

8: The Playoff Phenom
Patrick Roy won an astounding 151 playoff games, the most in NHL history. It's like he decided that regular-season games were just practice for his true calling: being an unbeatable force in the postseason.

9: The Zero to Hero Story
Steve Mason holds the record for the most saves in a shutout by a rookie goalie, with 53 saves for the Columbus Blue Jackets in 2008. It's as if he decided to turn "rookie" into a synonym for "brick wall."

10: The Marathon Game Hero
The longest game in NHL history saw Normie Smith of the Detroit Red Wings make 92 saves in a shutout victory during six overtimes against the Montreal Maroons in 1936. It's like he decided that letting a puck past him was simply out of fashion that season.

11: The Unbreakable Record
Tony Esposito boasts the most shutouts by a rookie goalie in a season, with 15 in 1969-70. It's like he started his career in "beast mode" and forgot to switch it off.

12: The Dual Threat
Ron Hextall became known not just for his goaltending but also for his scoring ability, making him one of the few goalies to both stop goals and score them. It's like he was playing his own version of fantasy hockey, and he was his top draft pick.

13: The Guardian of the Net
Jacques Plante changed the face of hockey—literally—by being the first goalie to regularly wear a face mask in 1959. It's like he decided that having a puck-proof face was better than relying on good looks to stop the puck.

14: The Comeback Kid
Dominik Hasek, at age 43, became the oldest goalie to win a playoff game. It's like he treated retirement as just a brief intermission before jumping back into the game.

15: The International Sensation
Henrik Lundqvist not only shines in the NHL but also on the international stage, holding the record for most Olympic wins by a goaltender. It's like he decided that dominating one league was too easy, so he took on the world.

16: The Back-to-Back Brick Wall
Bernie Parent won the Conn Smythe Trophy as playoff MVP two years in a row (1974, 1975), a rare feat for a goalie. It's like he decided that once wasn't enough, and went back for seconds.

17: The Scoring Streak Stopper

Brian Boucher set a modern-day NHL record with a 332-minute shutout streak in 2003-04. It's like he turned his goal crease into a "puck-free" zone, and nobody had the password to get in.

18: The Versatile Veteran
Grant Fuhr is the only goalie in NHL history to have an assist in a Stanley Cup Final game and also score a goal in the regular season. It's like he was trying to unlock every achievement possible in his career.

19: The Netminding Nomad
Sean Burke played for nine different NHL teams, proving that a great goalie is always in demand. It's like he was on a tour of the league, making saves in every city.

20: The Prolific Penalty Killer
Kelly Hrudey made an unbelievable 73 saves in a single playoff game in 1987. It's like he decided that the game wasn't going to end until he set a record that would be talked about for decades.

21: The Overtime Oracle
J.S. Giguere holds the record for the most overtime wins in a single postseason, with 7 in 2003. It's like he had a crystal ball and knew exactly when to turn on his superpowers.

22: The Puck-Handling Pioneer
Martin Brodeur revolutionized the role of goaltenders with his exceptional puck-handling skills, acting as a third defenseman. It's like he got bored with just stopping pucks and decided to join in on the playmaking fun.

23: The Clutch Connoisseur
Tim Thomas holds the record for the highest save percentage in a single postseason, with a .940 in 2011, showcasing his ability to elevate his game when it mattered most. It's like he was saving up all his best saves for when the spotlight was the brightest.

24: The Winter Classic Warrior
Henrik Lundqvist boasts the most wins in NHL Winter Classic history, proving that cold weather and outdoor games only sharpen his skills. It's like he thrived in the chill, turning frosty breaths into sighs of relief from fans.

25: The Goalie Golfer
Billy Smith was the first NHL goalie credited with a goal, but not because he shot the puck into the net. It was awarded to him because he was the last Islander to touch the puck before an opposing player accidentally scored on their own empty net. It's like scoring a hole-in-one in golf but with a hockey stick and a lot more ice.

26: The Zero Club
Chris Osgood and Martin Brodeur share the unique record of scoring a goal and earning a shutout in the same game. It's like they decided playing goalie wasn't challenging enough, so they aimed to do the forwards' job too, all while keeping their own slate clean.

27: The Marathon Man
In the 1936 NHL playoffs, Mud Bruneteau of the Detroit Red Wings scored the winning goal in the sixth overtime against the Montreal Maroons. The game lasted nearly 117 minutes, making it one of the longest in NHL history. Imagine playing so long that you could watch "Titanic" twice and still have time to discuss the ending.

28: The Youngest to Guard the Net
At 18 years and 32 days, Tom Barrasso became the youngest goalie to win an NHL game. It's like he was barely out of

high school and already telling seasoned NHL scorers, "Nope, not in my house."

29: The Penalty Shot Whisperer
Roberto Luongo holds the record for saving the most penalty shots in NHL history. It's as if he could read the shooters' minds, whispering "try me" and then calmly denying them the glory.

30: The Biggest Goalie Gear
At 6' 7", Ben Bishop might not hold the record for the tallest goalie in NHL history, but his gear sure looked like it needed its own zip code. Playing against him was like trying to score a goal against a moving wall.

31: First to Fifty
Maurice "Rocket" Richard was the first NHL player to score 50 goals in a single season, doing so in 1944-45. It's like he looked at the goal tally and thought, "Why not make this interesting?"

32: The Butterfly Pioneer
Glenn Hall is credited with pioneering the "butterfly style" of goaltending, dropping to his knees to make saves, effectively changing how the position was played. It's like he decided sliding around on ice looked fun and turned it into an art form.

33: The Oldest Goalie to Win the Cup
Johnny Bower was 44 when he helped the Toronto Maple Leafs clinch the Stanley Cup in 1967. It's like he proved that in hockey, wisdom (and a bit of veteran cunning) can beat youth.

34: The Double-Duty Coach
Lester Patrick, the Rangers' coach, put himself in as goalie during the 1928 Stanley Cup Finals when the regular goalie was injured. He won the game at age 44, making it seem like he was showing the kids how it's done, old-school style.

35: The Record for Most Saves in a Shutout
Ben Scrivens made 59 saves for the Edmonton Oilers in a 2014 game against the San Francisco Sharks, setting the record for most saves in a regular-season shutout since the expansion era (1967). It's like he turned into a human wall, and the puck was just a pesky fly.

36: The Goalie Goal in the Finals
Ron Hextall became the first goalie to score a goal in both the regular season and the playoffs, treating fans to the rare sight of a goalie lighting the lamp. It's like he thought, "Why wait for the forwards?"

37: The Unbreakable Games Played Record
Patrick Roy played in 1,029 NHL games, the most by any goaltender. It's as if he decided retirement was overrated and being on ice was the real fountain of youth.

38: The Fastest Goal by a Goaltender
Mike Smith scored a goal just 0.07 seconds before the final buzzer, the fastest by any goalie in NHL history. It's like he had the perfect timing of a Swiss watch, with a bit more punch.

39: The Vezina Trophy Hat Trick
Dominik Hasek won the Vezina Trophy as the league's best goaltender three years in a row from 1997 to 1999, making it seem like he had a reserved parking spot at the award ceremony.

40: The First American Vezina Winner
Frank Brimsek was the first American-born player to win the Vezina Trophy, earning the nickname "Mr. Zero" for his shutout prowess. It's like he started a trend, making it cool for Americans to be hockey's top goalies.

41: The Most Goals Against in One Game
Sam LoPresti faced an astonishing 83 shots in a single game in 1941, the most in NHL history. It's like he was in a

shooting gallery, where everyone had the green light to fire at will.

42: The Stanley Cup Winning Goalie Coach 🏆📺
Jacques Plante, one of the greatest goalies ever, later coached goaltenders to win Stanley Cups, sharing his wisdom like a goalie Yoda. It's like he decided that winning wasn't enough; he had to pass on the secret too.

43: The Goalie with the Most Points 📊📖
Grant Fuhr holds the record for the most points by a goaltender in a season, with 14 assists in 1983-84. It's like he was trying to prove goalies could do more than just stop pucks; they could set them up too.

44: The Toughest Playoff Shutout 🪨🔥
J.S. Giguere, in the 2003 playoffs for the Mighty Ducks of Anaheim, recorded a shutout in a quadruple-overtime game. It's like he decided that sleep was for the weak and stopping pucks was his only mission.

45: The Goalie with a Penalty Shot Goal 📺🎯
Billy Smith was the first NHL goalie credited with a goal in 1979, but it was because the opposing team scored on themselves. Later, Ron Hextall became the first to actually shoot the puck into the net for a goal, making goalies everywhere dream a little bigger.

46: The Longest Tenured Single-Team Goalie 🥅📺
Martin Brodeur spent 21 seasons with the New Jersey Devils, the longest any goalie has stayed with one team. It's like he and the Devils made a pact: "Till retirement do us part."

47: The Playoff Shutout Streak 🚫🏆
Jean-Sébastien Giguere went 217 minutes and 54 seconds without allowing a goal in the 2003 playoffs, making it seem like he had an invisible force field around his net.

48: The Most Consecutive Starts 🔒
Glenn Hall started 502 consecutive games as a goalie, a record that today seems as unbreakable as a diamond. It's like he treated the goal crease as his personal living room, and he wasn't fond of guests.

49: The Goalie with the Most Stanley Cups 🏆
Henri Richard may hold the player record, but among goalies, Jacques Plante, Charlie Hodge, and Ken Dryden each have six Stanley Cups to their name, making it seem like they had a yearly appointment with victory.

50: The First Goalie to Captain a Team 🚫🥅
Bill Durnan was not only a stellar goalie for the Montreal Canadiens but also served as their captain in the 1947-48 season, a rarity in the sport. It's like he was so good, the team decided he should lead in more ways than one.

51: The Lightning Fast Goal ⚡📺
Alex Ovechkin holds the record for the fastest goal from the start of a game in NHL playoff history, scoring just 8 seconds into the game. It's like he decided there was no better time to score than right now.

52: The Oldest Scorer in NHL History 🕗
Gordie Howe, the ageless wonder, became the oldest player to score in the NHL at 52 years and 11 days old. It's as if Father Time was just another defender he could deke around.

53: The Prolific Penalty Killer 🚫⚽
Wayne Gretzky, known for his scoring, surprisingly holds the record for the most short-handed goals in a career with

73. It's like he saw being one man down as just another opportunity to outshine everyone else.

54: The Most Wins in a Season by a Team
The Detroit Red Wings set an NHL record with 62 wins in the 1995-96 season, making victory a nearly daily routine. It's like they thought the regular season was just a long series of victory laps.

55: The Comeback Kings
The Philadelphia Flyers hold the record for the biggest comeback in NHL history, overcoming a 0-3 series deficit in the 2010 Eastern Conference Semifinals against the Boston Bruins. It's as if they believed the series doesn't start until you're three down.

56: The Most Decorated Olympian on Ice
Teemu Selanne, affectionately known as "The Finnish Flash," has scored the most points in Olympic ice hockey history. It's like the Olympics were his personal playground.

57: The Highest-Scoring Defenseman in a Game
Ian Turnbull of the Toronto Maple Leafs holds the record for the most goals by a defenseman in a single game with 5 in 1977. It's as if he temporarily forgot he was a defenseman and decided to take over the game.

58: The Longest Stanley Cup Drought
The Toronto Maple Leafs are currently enduring the longest Stanley Cup drought, having not won since 1967. It's like they're on a quest for a treasure that's proving incredibly elusive.

59: The Fastest Skate
Connor McDavid set the NHL's fastest skater record with a lap time of 13.02 seconds during the All-Star Skills Competition. It's as if he has rockets instead of skates.

60: The Most Points in a Single Period
Grant Mulvey of the Chicago Blackhawks holds the record for the most points in a single period with 5 (4 goals, 1 assist) in 1982. It's like he decided to turn a period into his own personal highlight reel.

61: The Goalie With Most Assists in One Game
Tom Barrasso set a record for the most assists by a goalie in a single game with 3. It's as if he was auditioning for a forward position mid-game.

62: The First Helmet
In 1930, George Owen of the Boston Bruins was the first NHL player to wear a helmet regularly. It's like he decided his head was too important to risk in the pursuit of puck glory.

63: The Biggest Fan Base
The Montreal Canadiens are estimated to have the largest fan base worldwide among NHL teams. It's as if their fans decided to start their own country, with hockey as the national sport.

64: The Most Consecutive Stanley Cup Finals
The Montreal Canadiens appeared in 10 consecutive Stanley Cup Finals from 1951 to 1960, turning the finals into a personal annual event. It's like they wouldn't let anyone else have the party without them.

65: The Most Goals by a Rookie
Teemu Selanne, with his record-breaking 76 goals in the 1992-93 season, not only amazed the hockey world but also set a rookie record that still stands. It's like he entered the NHL with a bang so loud, it's still echoing.

66: The First NHL Game Broadcast
The first NHL game broadcast on television was in 1952 in Canada, opening a window for countless fans to fall in love with the game from their living

rooms. It's like the NHL decided to invade homes, but in the best way possible.

67: The Largest Margin of Victory
The Detroit Red Wings hold the record for the largest margin of victory in an NHL game, defeating the New York Rangers 15-0 in 1944. It's like they mistook the game for a goal-scoring practice session.

68: The Most Career Hat Tricks
Wayne Gretzky also holds the record for the most career hat tricks with 50, proving that scoring three goals in a game was just another day at the office for him.

69: The First Female Player in the NHL
Manon Rhéaume broke barriers as the first and only woman to play in an NHL game, suiting up as a goaltender for the Tampa Bay Lightning in a preseason game in 1992. It's like she decided to rewrite the history books with her goalie stick.

70: The Oldest Player to Win the Stanley Cup
Chris Chelios was 46 years old when he won his last Stanley Cup with the Detroit Red Wings in 2008, proving that age is just a number when it comes to the pursuit of hockey's ultimate prize.

71: The Most Career NHL Games Played
Gordie Howe played in 1,767 NHL games, the most in league history, making it seem like retirement was just not in his vocabulary.

72: The First to Score 50 Goals in 50 Games
Maurice "Rocket" Richard was the first to achieve the feat of scoring 50 goals in 50 games during the 1944-45 season, setting a standard for excellence that would challenge future generations.

73: The Most Points by a Player in His First Season
Joe Malone scored an astounding 103 points in the 1917-18 season, the inaugural season of the NHL, setting an incredibly high bar from the very beginning.

74: The Longest Game in NHL History
In 1936, the Detroit Red Wings and the Montreal Maroons battled for 176 minutes and 30 seconds of game time before Mud Bruneteau scored the game-winning goal, making everyone wonder if the game would ever end.

75: The First Official NHL Game
The first official NHL game took place on December 19, 1917, between the Montreal Canadiens and the Ottawa Senators, marking the beginning of a century-long legacy of incredible hockey.

76: The Four-Goal Debut
Auston Matthews set the modern NHL ablaze by scoring four goals in his debut game in 2016, the first player in the NHL's modern era to do so. It's like he decided to introduce himself to the hockey world with a bang, a boom, and a couple of extra fireworks just for fun.

77: The Stanley Cup Traveler
The Stanley Cup has traveled the world, visiting countless countries. It's even been to the top of a mountain and the bottom of a swimming pool. It's like the most adventurous trophy in sports, with more passport stamps than most people.

78: The Masked Marvel
Jacques Plante was not only a legendary goalie but also an innovator for wearing a face mask in 1959, forever changing the safety standards for goaltenders. It's

like he decided that stopping pucks with his face was overrated.

79: The Penalty-Free Game
On March 28, 1953, the Boston Bruins and the Toronto Maple Leafs played the only penalty-free game in NHL playoff history. It was like both teams decided to have a "gentlemen's agreement" to keep it clean for the night.

80: The Backwards Skater
Bobby Orr revolutionized defensemen's roles but also had a unique talent: he could skate backward almost as fast as most players could skate forward. It's like he had a reverse gear that others didn't even know existed.

81: The Original Six
The "Original Six" refers to the six teams that made up the NHL from 1942 to 1967: Boston Bruins, Chicago Blackhawks, Detroit Red Wings, Montreal Canadiens, New York Rangers, and Toronto Maple Leafs. It's like they were the exclusive club of hockey royalty.

82: The Highest-Scoring Game
The Edmonton Oilers and Chicago Blackhawks combined for 21 goals in one game in 1985, with the Oilers winning 12-9. It was less like a hockey game and more like a pinball machine, with the score just racking up points.

83: The Goalie's Rare Assist
In 2013, Cam Ward was credited with a goal as a goalie without actually shooting the puck into the net himself. It bounced off an opposing player who was the last to touch it before it went into his own empty net. It's like being credited for a goal because you were the last to say, "Don't do that."

84: The Double Hat Trick
Darryl Sittler holds the record for the most points in a single game with 10 (6 goals, 4 assists) in 1976. It's like he decided that just one hat trick wasn't enough to satisfy his scoring appetite.

85: The Outdoor Hockey Heritage
The NHL's Winter Classic started in 2008, bringing hockey back to its outdoor roots. It's like the league decided to have a throwback party, and everyone was invited.

86: The Youngest NHL Captain
Connor McDavid was named captain of the Edmonton Oilers at just 19 years old, making him the youngest captain in NHL history. It's like getting promoted to CEO right after your internship.

87: The Longest Shot
In 1970, Bobby Orr scored "The Goal" to win the Stanley Cup, flying through the air to celebrate. It's become one of the most iconic images in sports, like Orr decided to add "flight" to his list of hockey skills.

88: The Most Prolific Scoring Brothers
The Gretzky brothers (Wayne and Brent) hold the record for the most combined points by brothers in the NHL, with Wayne contributing the lion's share. It's like Wayne decided to share his scoring talents with his brother by association.

89: The Oldest Rookie
Gordie Howe made a comeback at 69 years old to play with the Detroit Vipers, making him the oldest professional hockey player ever. It's like he refused to let "retirement" enter his vocabulary.

90: The Fastest Fight
The record for the fastest fight from the start of an NHL game is just two seconds, shared by multiple instances where players decided to drop the gloves right after the puck dropped. It's like they were more interested in boxing on ice than playing hockey.

91: The Most Stanley Cup Wins by a Player

Henri Richard of the Montreal Canadiens won the Stanley Cup 11 times, more than any other player. It's like he had a season pass to lifting the Cup.

92: The First Female Full-time NHL Coach
In 2016, Dawn Braid became the first full-time female coach in the NHL, serving as a skating coach for the Arizona Coyotes. It's like she skated right through the glass ceiling.

93: The Goalie Goal Scorer Club
Only 12 goaltenders have scored a goal in the NHL, making it one of the rarest feats in hockey. It's like joining an exclusive club where the membership fee is scoring a goal from the opposite end of the ice.

94: The Most Overtime Goals in Playoffs
Joe Sakic holds the record for the most overtime goals in the NHL playoffs, with 8. It's like he had a knack for deciding games when everyone else was getting tired.

95: The NHL's First European Captain to Win the Cup
Nicklas Lidstrom was the first European captain to lift the Stanley Cup, leading the Detroit Red Wings to victory in 2008. It's like he was on a mission to prove that leadership knows no borders.

96: The Most Goals in a Single Playoff Year
Reggie Leach scored 19 goals in the 1976 playoffs, a record for a single postseason. It's like he decided that the playoffs were the perfect time to unleash his scoring superpowers.

97: The Most Consecutive Games with a Point
Wayne Gretzky holds the record for the most consecutive NHL games with a point at 51. It's like he decided to have a "point streak" instead of a "hot streak."

98: The Most Goals by a Defenseman in One Season
Paul Coffey scored 48 goals in the 1985-86 season, the most by a defenseman in one season. It's like he temporarily forgot he was supposed to stop goals, not score them.

99: The First Broadcasted NHL Game
The first NHL game ever broadcasted was in 1936, but it wasn't until 1952 that the Detroit Red Wings appeared on U.S. television, making the sport accessible to countless fans at home. It's like hockey decided to crash the TV party.

100: The Zamboni's Debut
The first Zamboni machine was used in an NHL game in 1954, revolutionizing how ice surfaces were maintained. It's like the game decided to add a new player to the team, one that preferred smoothing ice over scoring goals.

PLAYOFF RECORDS

1: The Overtime Marathon
Did you know the longest playoff game in NHL history lasted over 116 minutes of overtime? That's right, on March 24, 1936, the Detroit Red Wings and the Montreal Maroons played so long, fans needed bedtime stories in the stands. It ended when Mud Bruneteau of the Red Wings finally scored, probably because everyone was too tired to block his shot.

2: Mr. Clutch or Mr. April?
Joe Sakic, known for his cool demeanor, holds the record for the most playoff overtime goals with 8. It's like he specialized in extra-time heroics, or maybe he just really liked hockey in spring.

3: The Goalie Ironman of the Playoffs
Patrick Roy spent an astonishing 5,438 playoff minutes in net throughout his career. That's enough time to watch all the "Harry Potter" movies about 20 times, assuming you could get a TV in the goal crease.

4: A Rookie Sensation
Dino Ciccarelli set the record for the most points by a rookie in a single playoff year with 21 in 1981. It's like he showed up for his first playoffs and mistook the Stanley Cup for rookie orientation.

5: The Power-Play Wizard
Mike Bossy shines bright with the most power-play goals in a single playoff season, netting 9 in 1981. It seems like every time there was a man advantage, Bossy treated it like a personal invitation to score.

6: The Penalty Box Regular
Chris Nilan, not known for his scoring touch, holds a different kind of record: the most penalty minutes in a single playoff year, racking up 141 minutes in 1986. It's like he was trying to set up a home office in the penalty box.

7: The Comeback Kids
In 2014, the Los Angeles Kings became the fourth team in NHL history to overcome a 0-3 series deficit, beating the San Jose Sharks. It's like they were inspired by every sports underdog movie ever made.

8: The Fastest Hat Trick
Fernie Flaman scored the fastest hat trick in NHL playoff history in just 4 minutes and 54 seconds in 1945. That's quicker than making a sandwich, making him a real "fast food" hockey player.

9: The Shutout Streak
Ilya Bryzgalov holds the record for the longest shutout streak in the playoffs at 249 minutes and 15 seconds in 2006. It's like he turned his net into a "No Puck Zone" and lost the key.

10: The Scoring Defenseman
Paul Coffey is the defenseman with the most points in a single playoff year, tallying 37 in 1985. It's like he decided that defensemen could have just as much fun scoring as forwards.

11: The Ageless Wonder
Chris Chelios was 45 when he last laced up for the playoffs, making him the oldest player to participate in the NHL postseason. It's like he considered retirement just a fancy word for "intermission."

12: The Quadruple Overtime Hero
Keith Primeau ended the third-longest playoff game in history with a goal in the fifth overtime for the Philadelphia Flyers in 2000. It's like he decided if he was going to stay up late, he might as well be productive.

13: The Stanley Cup Sharpshooter
Maurice Richard was the first player to score 50 goals in the playoffs over his career, pioneering the "postseason sniper" role. It's like he treated the playoffs as his personal shooting gallery.

14: The Dynamic Playoff Duo
Wayne Gretzky and Jari Kurri combined for a record 764 playoff points, making them the most lethal postseason pairing. It's like Batman and Robin decided to play hockey, and Gotham was the Stanley Cup.

15: The Unsung Hero Award
Jean-Sebastien Giguere won the Conn Smythe Trophy as playoff MVP in 2003, despite his team not winning the Stanley Cup. It's like getting the best actor Oscar for a movie that didn't win best picture.

16: The Most Prolific Playoff Team
The Montreal Canadiens have won the Stanley Cup 24 times, making them the most successful team in playoff history.

It's like they had a subscription service to the Stanley Cup and kept renewing it.

17: The Master of Game 7s 🔫🥅
Patrick Roy won 6 Game 7s in his playoff career, the most of any goalie. It's like he thrived on the drama of a final showdown, always ready for a duel at high noon.

18: The Playoff Marathon Men 🏃‍♂️🕐
Henri Richard and Jean Beliveau share the record for the most playoff games played at 180. It's like they just couldn't get enough of playoff hockey, or maybe they kept losing their way to the exit.

19: The Young Gun 👶🔫
Jordan Staal scored a playoff goal at just 20 years and 3 days old in 2009, proving that you're never too young to shine in the postseason. It's like he was in a hurry to write his name in the playoff history books.

20: The Goalie Goal 🥅🏒
Ron Hextall became the first goalie to score a goal in the playoffs, doing so in 1989. It's like he looked down the ice and thought, "Well, if no one else is going to score, I might as well do it myself."

21: The Unlikely Hero 🐭🕶️
Chris Kontos holds the record for the most goals by a player in his first playoff year, netting 9 in 1989. It's like he decided that being an underdog was just a state of mind.

22: The Dominant Force 🦴🏒
Mario Lemieux scored at least one point in 46 consecutive playoff games, a streak that seems as unbreakable as it is impressive. It's like he decided playoffs were his personal point parade.

23: The Serial Champion 🏆🔄
Henri Richard not only played 180 playoff games but also won the Stanley Cup 11 times, more than any other player. It's like he had a standing appointment with the Cup every other year.

24: The Blue Line Bomber 💣🛡️
Brian Leetch, in 1994, scored 34 points in the playoffs, the most by a defenseman in a single postseason. It's like he decided that scoring wasn't just for forwards.

25: The Fastest to Four 🚀🥅
Fernie Flaman scored the fastest four goals in a playoff game, all within the first period in 1945. It's like he had a dinner reservation he couldn't miss, so he decided to wrap up the scoring early.

26: The Unbeatable Record 🚫🏆
The 1988 Edmonton Oilers hold the record for the fewest games played to win the Stanley Cup in the modern era, clinching hockey's ultimate prize in just 18 games. It's like they were in such a hurry to win, they barely had time to break a sweat.

27: The Goalie's Nightmare 😱🥅
Joffrey Lupul once scored 4 goals in a single playoff game in 2006, turning himself into the thing goalies see in their nightmares. It's like he decided one goal was nice, but four was a party.

28: The Marathon on Ice 🏃‍♂️❄️
Kelly Hrudey made 73 saves for the Islanders in a playoff game against the Capitals in 1987, known as the "Easter Epic." It's like he was a brick wall that learned how to skate.

29: The Sudden Impact 🐭💥
Ken Linseman earned the nickname "The Rat" for his agitating style on ice, but he also made an immediate impact by scoring 9 points in his first 4 playoff games. It's like he was as quick with his scoring as he was with his chirps.

30: The Power Play Phenom ⚡🏒

Cam Neely holds the record for most power-play goals in a single playoff series with 6 in 1991. It's like whenever the Bruins had a man advantage, Neely decided it was his personal cue to score.

31: The Defensive Dynamo
Larry Robinson boasts a +120 career playoff plus-minus rating, making him a true defensive dynamo. It's like opponents' chances of scoring evaporated whenever he was on the ice.

32: The Clutch Performer
Claude Lemieux thrived under pressure, scoring 19 game-winning goals in the playoffs over his career. It's like he had a switch he flipped when the game was on the line, turning into "Clutch Claude."

33: The Prolific Penalty Killer
Derek Sanderson set a record with 3 short-handed goals in a single playoff series in 1969. It's like he saw being a man down as an opportunity rather than a disadvantage.

34: The Young Star
Sydney Crosby became the youngest captain to win the Stanley Cup at age 21 in 2009. It's like he was born to lead, and the Cup was just waiting for him to come of age.

35: The Unsung Playoff Hero
John Druce exploded for 14 goals during the 1990 playoffs, a surprising surge for a player who wasn't known for his scoring. It's like he decided to save all his goals for when they mattered most.

36: The Endurance Expert
Sergei Fedorov played an incredible 52 minutes in a single playoff game in 1998. It's like he forgot that shifts were supposed to end.

37: The Breakout Performance
Fernando Pisani scored 14 goals during the 2006 playoffs as the Oilers made an unexpected run to the Stanley Cup Finals. It's like he decided to introduce himself to the hockey world on the biggest stage.

38: The Improbable Goalie Goal
Ron Hextall became the first goalie to score a goal in the playoffs, doing so by shooting the puck into an empty net in 1989. It's like he was showing the forwards how it's done.

39: The Triple Overtime Thriller
Petr Sykora promised his teammates he'd score in triple overtime against the Stars in the 2008 playoffs, and he delivered. It's like he had a crystal ball hidden in his glove.

40: The Penalty Box Hero
Dave Schultz, known more for his time in the penalty box, also had a moment of playoff glory, scoring important goals for the Flyers during their Broad Street Bullies era. It's like he decided to give scoring a try, just for a change of pace.

41: The Age-Defying Performance
Dominik Hasek, at 43, carried the Red Wings deep into the playoffs in 2008, proving that age is just a number. It's like his goalie pads were a fountain of youth.

42: The Sudden Death Specialist
Adam Henrique scored two series-clinching overtime goals in the 2012 playoffs. It's like he specialized in breaking hearts just when the other team thought they had a chance.

43: The Defensive Scorer
Brent Seabrook scored 3 overtime goals as a defenseman in the playoffs, showing that even defenders can decide the fate of a game. It's like he was on a secret mission to redefine what defensemen can do.

44: The Playoff Iron Man
Chris Chelios played in 266 playoff games, more than any other player. It's like he just couldn't get enough of the playoff atmosphere.

45: The Game 7 Maestro 🎵⛳
Justin Williams earned the nickname "Mr. Game 7" for his incredible performances in Game 7s, recording 14 points in 9 games. It's like he saw Game 7s as his personal concerts, and he always saved his best performance for last.

46: The Record-Setting Rookie 🏒👶
Jake Guentzel scored 13 goals as a rookie in the 2017 playoffs, setting a new record. It's like he was in a race with history, and he won.

47: The Comeback Story 🔄🏆
The 2019 St. Louis Blues were last in the league in January but went on to win the Stanley Cup. It's like they decided to write their own underdog story, with a twist ending.

48: The Dynamic Duo's Last Stand ⛳👬
Wayne Gretzky and Mark Messier won their last Stanley Cup together in 1988, marking the end of an era for the Oilers. It's like they decided to have one last dance on the ice.

49: The Overtime Workhorse 🕐🐴
Ryan McDonagh played over 53 minutes in a single playoff game in 2020. It's like he decided to put in a full day's work in one night.

50: The Short-Handed Magician 🎩🚫
Wayne Gretzky, despite being known for his scoring, also excels in short-handed situations, holding the record for most short-handed goals in playoff history. It's like he enjoyed the challenge of being down a man as just another opportunity to showcase his brilliance.

51: The Lightning Fast Series 🚀🏆
The 1992 Pittsburgh Penguins swept the Chicago Blackhawks in the Stanley Cup Finals in just 4 games, showcasing a level of dominance that left fans blinking in disbelief. It's as if they were playing on fast-forward.

52: The Scoring Spree 🏒🥅
Darryl Sittler of the Toronto Maple Leafs set a record by scoring 5 goals in a single playoff game against the Philadelphia Flyers in 1976. It's like he decided one goal for each finger on one hand seemed like a good day's work.

53: The Penalty Box Vacation 📦😠
Dave Schultz of the Philadelphia Flyers spent a record 139 minutes in the penalty box during the 1974 playoffs alone. It's like he was on a mission to personally test the comfort of every penalty box seat.

54: The Goalie's Grand Theft 🥅🚨
Ron Hextall became the first goaltender to score a goal in NHL playoff history by shooting the puck into an empty net in 1989. It's as if he thought, "Why pass when you can score?"

55: The Four-peat Dream 🏆🏆🏆🏆
The New York Islanders won the Stanley Cup four times in a row from 1980 to 1983, turning dynasty dreams into reality. It's like they got so good at winning; they forgot how to lose.

56: The Double Duty ⛳🎤
In 1987, Ron MacLean officiated a playoff game during the day and then hosted "Hockey Night in Canada" that evening. It's as if he decided to play hockey superhero for a day.

57: The Marathon Match 🕐⛳
The 2000 playoffs saw the Philadelphia Flyers and Pittsburgh Penguins play a game that lasted over 152 minutes, ending in the fifth overtime. It's like they were trying to squeeze an entire series into one game.

58: The Comeback Queen 🔥🔄

The 2014 Los Angeles Kings made an impressive comeback by winning the series after being down 0-3 against the San Jose Sharks. It's as if they treated the first three losses as just a warm-up.

59: The Rookie Record Breaker
Jordan Staal set a record for the youngest player to score a shorthanded goal in the playoffs at 18 years old in 2007. It's as if he was too young to realize he should be nervous.

60: The Shortest Overtime
Brian Skrudland of the Montreal Canadiens scored the fastest overtime goal in Stanley Cup Finals history, just 9 seconds into OT in 1986. It's like he had somewhere else to be and needed to wrap things up quickly.

61: The Playoff Iron Man
Nicklas Lidstrom played in 263 consecutive playoff games for the Detroit Red Wings, a testament to durability and consistency. It's as if he was made of titanium instead of flesh and bone.

62: The Goalie Gamble
Patrick Roy, at just 20 years old, carried the Montreal Canadiens to a Stanley Cup victory in 1986, proving that sometimes a gamble on youth pays off big. It's like the Canadiens decided to bet on a kid, and he showed up in a superhero cape.

63: The Series Sweepers
The 1976 Montreal Canadiens swept the Philadelphia Flyers in the Stanley Cup Finals without losing a single game in the series. It's as if they were playing chess while everyone else was playing checkers.

64: The Hat Trick Hero
Reggie Leach of the Philadelphia Flyers scored a hat trick in Game 5 of the 1976 Stanley Cup Finals, even though his team lost the series. It's like he decided to throw his own party in the midst of a storm.

65: The Overtime Collector
The 2019 playoffs featured a record 8 overtime games in the first round, proving that in hockey, every second counts. It's like the teams decided normal regulation time was just too mainstream.

66: The Shorthanded Specialist
Wayne Gretzky, known for his scoring prowess, also holds the record for the most career playoff shorthanded goals, adding a defensive feather to his cap. It's as if he wanted to prove he could do it all.

67: The Most Valuable Loser
Jean-Sebastien Giguere won the Conn Smythe Trophy as playoff MVP in 2003, despite his team not winning the Stanley Cup. It's like winning the award for best actor in a movie that didn't get the Oscar.

68: The Buzzer Beater
Martin Gelinas of the Calgary Flames scored a series-clinching goal with just seconds left in Game 6 of the 2004 Western Conference Finals. It's like he had a flair for the dramatic, deciding to wait until the last possible moment to be the hero.

69: The Defensive Scoring Machine
Bobby Orr set records for most goals, assists, and points by a defenseman in a single playoff year, redefining the role of a defenseman. It's like he was playing a different game than everyone else.

70: The Playoff Veteran
Chris Chelios appeared in the playoffs for 24 seasons, more than any other player. It's as if the playoffs were his second home, and he just couldn't stay away.

71: The Triple Overtime Thriller
Game 5 of the 2013 Stanley Cup Finals between the Chicago Blackhawks and Boston Bruins ended in triple overtime, a testament to the resilience and determination of both teams. It's like

neither team wanted to go home until they were absolutely exhausted.

72: The Power Play Record 🏒🥅
The Edmonton Oilers scored 36 power play goals during the 1984 playoffs, turning the man advantage into an art form. It's as if they saw a penalty as an invitation to score.

73: The Penalty Minute Accumulator 🎽⏱
Chris Nilan holds the record for the most penalty minutes in a single playoff year with 141 in 1986, spending more time in the box than some players do on the ice. It's like he was on a personal mission to explore every penalty box in the league.

74: The Greatest Comeback 🔄🏆
The 1942 Toronto Maple Leafs are the only team to win the Stanley Cup after being down 0-3 in the Finals. It's as if they decided to do things the hard way just for the challenge.

75: The Playoff Debutant 🏒🎯
Tony Hrkac set a record for the most points in a single playoff game by a rookie with 5 in 1988. It's like he wanted to announce his arrival on the playoff scene with a bang, a pop, and a sizzle.

76: The Sudden Death Specialist 🎯
Pat LaFontaine etched his name into playoff lore by ending the "Easter Epic" in the fourth overtime against the Washington Capitals in 1987. It's like he decided that sleep was overrated, and hockey marathons were the way to go.

77: The Defensive Fortress 🛡🚫
Rod Langway, known more for his defensive prowess than scoring, surprised everyone by logging significant minutes and playing a crucial role in the Capitals' extended playoff runs in the 1980s. It's as if he turned the defensive zone into a no-fly zone, except for pucks.

78: The Ageless Sniper 👴🎯
Mark Recchi, at 43 years old, became one of the oldest players to score in the NHL playoffs, proving that age is just a number when it comes to playoff hockey. It's like he found the fountain of youth, and it was frozen and shaped like a rink.

79: The Penalty Shot Clincher 🥅🎽
Fernando Pisani of the Edmonton Oilers scored a critical shorthanded penalty shot goal in the 2006 Stanley Cup Finals. It's like he decided that pressure was his middle name and the Stanley Cup Finals were just another day at the office.

80: The Quadruple Overtime Saga ⏰🏒
In 2008, the Dallas Stars and San Jose Sharks battled through four overtimes in one of the longest games in playoff history, with Brenden Morrow sealing the deal. It's as if they thought they were in a time loop, doomed to play hockey until the end of time.

81: The Unsuspecting Hero 🦸‍♂️🎽
Max Talbot scored both goals for the Pittsburgh Penguins in their Game 7 victory in the 2009 Stanley Cup Finals. It's like he chose the most dramatic moment possible to step out of the shadows and into the spotlight.

82: The Record-Setting Rookie 🏒👶
Darcy Kuemper became the first rookie goaltender to record a shutout in his playoff debut for the Minnesota Wild in 2014. It's as if he decided beginner's luck wasn't enough and opted for a slice of history instead.

83: The Playoff Workhorse 🐴⏱
Ryan Suter of the Minnesota Wild averaged over 29 minutes of ice time per game in the 2014 playoffs, becoming the definition of a playoff workhorse. It's

like he was trying to prove that playing half the game himself was totally normal.

84: The Improbable Goal Scorer
In 2012, Bryce Salvador of the New Jersey Devils, a defenseman known more for his defensive skills, went on an unlikely scoring spree in the playoffs. It's like he suddenly decided scoring goals was more fun than stopping them.

85: The Marathon Goalie
Joonas Korpisalo set a record for the most saves in a playoff game with 85 in 2020, during a quintuple-overtime thriller. It's like he was on a mission to turn away every puck in the vicinity, possibly including those from other games.

86: The Clutch Performer
Danny Briere earned a reputation as a clutch playoff performer, scoring 30 goals in 62 playoff games with the Philadelphia Flyers. It's as if he believed that playoffs were just the prelude to his personal highlight reel.

87: The Power Play Maestro
Mike Cammalleri dazzled in the 2010 playoffs by scoring 7 power-play goals for the Montreal Canadiens. It's like he had a secret formula for making the most of the man advantage.

88: The Goalie Duel
In 2014, goalies Henrik Lundqvist and Carey Price engaged in one of the most memorable goalie duels in recent playoff history. It's like they were both saying, "Anything you can save, I can save better."

89: The Short-Handed Dynamo
Wayne Gretzky, despite being known for his scoring, excelled in playoff short-handed situations, showcasing his all-around game. It's like he saw being a man down as just another opportunity to showcase his greatness.

90: The Block Party
In 2012, the New York Rangers set a record for the most blocked shots in a single playoff run, turning their defensive zone into a block party. It's like they decided if you can't score on us, you might as well not shoot at all.

91: The Comeback on Ice
The Philadelphia Flyers rallied from a 3-0 deficit to beat the Boston Bruins in Game 7 of the 2010 Eastern Conference Semifinals. It's like they decided to write their own script, where "impossible" was not in the vocabulary.

92: The Dominant Performance
Jonathan Quick posted a .946 save percentage during the 2012 playoffs, guiding the Los Angeles Kings to their first Stanley Cup. It's like he decided that letting goals in was just out of fashion that season.

93: The Game 7 Specialist
Justin Williams earned the nickname "Mr. Game 7" for his uncanny ability to perform in the decisive seventh game of a series. It's like he treated Game 7s as his personal stage for heroics.

94: The Overtime Hat Trick
Mel Hill earned the nickname "Sudden Death" Hill by scoring three overtime winners in the 1939 playoffs. It's like he had a knack for deciding games as if he had a dinner reservation to make right after.

95: The Four-Goal Feat
Maurice Richard became the first player to score four goals in a single playoff game in 1944. It's like he was playing his own game of "How many goals can Maurice score tonight?"

96: The Defensive Scorer
Bobby Orr, known for his legendary goal to win the 1970 Stanley Cup, showed that defensemen could be just as lethal in offense, especially when the stakes were high. It's like he blurred the lines between defense and offense.

97: The Triple Gold Club
Sidney Crosby joined the exclusive "Triple Gold Club" with Olympic golds, a World Championship gold, and multiple Stanley Cups. It's like he was collecting the most prestigious hockey achievements as if they were trading cards.

98: The Goalie Assist
Martin Brodeur holds the record for the most assists by a goalie in the playoffs. It's like he decided that stopping goals wasn't enough; he wanted to help score them too.

99: The Rookie Sensation
Ken Dryden won the Conn Smythe Trophy as playoff MVP before winning the Calder Trophy as the NHL's top rookie, a unique sequence of awards. It's like he decided to introduce himself to the NHL in reverse order.

100: The Longest Cup Drought Ends
The Chicago Blackhawks ended a 49-year Stanley Cup drought in 2010, proving that good things come to those who wait - and work incredibly hard. It's like they decided nearly half a century was long enough to go without a parade.

All-Time Team Records

1: The Most Wins Wonderland
The 1995-96 Detroit Red Wings hold the record for the most wins in a single regular season, racking up an astonishing 62 victories. It's like they decided losing was out of fashion that season.

2: The Goal Avalanche
The 1983-84 Edmonton Oilers were an offensive juggernaut, setting a record with 446 goals in a season. It's as if they were playing a video game on easy mode – with the cheat codes activated.

3: The Unbreakable Fortress
The 1955-56 Montreal Canadiens allowed the fewest goals in a season, just 131, turning their net into a "puck-free zone." It's like their goalie was a magician, and the puck was the rabbit that never came out of the hat.

4: The Power Outage
The 1997-98 Tampa Bay Lightning scored the fewest goals in a season during the modern era (since 1967), with only 151 goals. It's like their sticks were cursed by a mischievous hockey ghost who didn't like scoring.

5: The Penalty Parade
The 1991-92 Quebec Nordiques spent so much time in the penalty box they set a record with 2,713 penalty minutes in a season. It's as if they mistook the penalty box for a team clubhouse.

6: The Streak of Invincibility
The 1979-80 Philadelphia Flyers went 35 games without a loss, the longest streak in NHL history. It's like they forgot how to lose, or maybe they just really, really didn't like it.

7: The Shutout Kings
The 1928-29 Boston Bruins hold the record for the most shutouts in a season with 22. It's like their goal was a fortress, and the goalie was the dragon guarding it.

8: The Comeback Kids Story
The Montreal Canadiens hold the record for the biggest comeback in a game, overcoming a 5-goal deficit to win. It's like they were inspired by every sports movie ever made.

9: The Season of Sorrow
The 1974-75 Washington Capitals have the fewest wins in a season, with only 8

victories. It's like they were playing a different sport and nobody told them.

10: The Home Ice Heroes 🏠🏒♂
The 2011-12 Detroit Red Wings set a record with 23 consecutive home wins. It's like they decided there's no place like home, especially if you never lose there.

11: The Road Warriors 🚗
The 2005-06 Detroit Red Wings also excelled on the road, setting a record with 31 road wins in a season. It's like they got superpowers every time they packed their suitcases.

12: The Penalty Shot Pros
The 2013-14 Boston Bruins were masters of the penalty shot, setting a record by scoring on 4 penalty shots in one season. It's like they treated penalty shots as their own personal trick shot competition.

13: The Defensive Drought
The 1953-54 Toronto Maple Leafs hold the record for the longest time without allowing a goal, going 461 minutes and 29 seconds of play. It's like their net was invisible to the opposing team.

14: The Season-Long Party 📅
The 1976-77 Montreal Canadiens set a record for the most points in a season with 132. It's like every game was a party, and winning was the only item on the agenda.

15: The Overtime Odyssey ⏱
The 2009-10 Phoenix Coyotes loved extra hockey, setting a record with 28 overtime games in a season. It's like they believed in giving their fans free hockey, every chance they got.

16: The Scoring Spread
The 1984-85 Edmonton Oilers had the most players with at least 30 goals in a season, with 7. It's like they decided scoring was a team sport, and everyone should get a turn.

17: The Least Generous Hosts 🏠
The 1953-54 Chicago Blackhawks won the fewest home games in a season, with only 2 victories. It's like they were too polite, always letting their guests win.

18: The Fastest to the Finals 🏆
The 2012-13 Chicago Blackhawks reached 50 points in the fewest games, taking just 24 games. It's like they had a turbo button that nobody else knew about.

19: The Zero Hero Goalies
The 2003-04 New Jersey Devils recorded 11 shutouts in a season, tying the record for a team. It's like their goalies were playing a game of "How long can we keep this puck out?"

20: The Single-Season Saviors
The 1967-68 Montreal Canadiens used 6 goaltenders in one season, a record for the most used. It's like they decided to try a goalie carousel, just for fun.

21: The Special Teams Specialists
The 1977-78 Montreal Canadiens not only dazzled with their play but also set a record for the best power-play percentage in a season at 31.88%. It's like their power play was a cheat code they used all season long.

22: The Impenetrable Penalty Kill 🚫
The 2011-12 New Jersey Devils had a penalty kill so effective, they set a record with a 89.58% success rate. It's like they turned penalty killing into an art form, or maybe they just really disliked being a man down.

23: The Expansion Season Sensation

The 1993-94 Florida Panthers set the record for the most points by an expansion team in their first season, with 83. It's like they decided to skip the growing pains and jump straight to being competitive.

24: The Losing Streak Blues 🎵

The 1974-75 Washington Capitals hold the record for the longest losing streak in a season with 17 straight losses. It's like they were on a quest to find the secret to winning, but the map was upside down.

25: The Comeback Champions 🔄🏆
The 2018-19 St. Louis Blues went from last place in January to winning the Stanley Cup. It's like they decided halfway through the season that it was time to rewrite their story from a tragedy to a fairy tale.

26: The Expansion Shocker
The 2017-18 Vegas Golden Knights set the record for the most wins by an expansion team in their debut season, with 51 victories. It's as if they decided to skip the "new kid on the block" phase and jump straight to being the cool kids in school.

27: The Goal Drought
The 1928-29 Chicago Blackhawks scored the fewest goals in a season, with only 33 in 44 games. It's like the puck was allergic to their opponents' net.

28: The Penalty-Free Perfection
The 1977-78 Boston Bruins played a game without a single penalty, a rare feat in the rough-and-tumble NHL. It's as if they were on their best behavior, maybe because their moms were watching.

29: The Underdog Uprising
The 2012 Los Angeles Kings were the first eighth-seeded team to win the Stanley Cup, proving that sometimes, the underdogs have their day, and what a day it was!

30: The Scoring Spree Record
The 1985-86 Edmonton Oilers have the most 100-point scorers in one season, with 4 players reaching the century mark. It's like they were all racing to see who could get there first.

31: The Winning Streak Wizards
The Pittsburgh Penguins set a record with a 17-game winning streak in the 1992-93 season. It's as if they forgot how to lose, or maybe they just really liked winning.

32: The Bounce-Back Kings
The 2019-20 Philadelphia Flyers set a record for the most comeback wins in a season, proving that it's not over until it's over, and for them, it was never over.

33: The Power Play Powerhouse
The 1977-78 Montreal Canadiens also hold the record for the most power-play goals in a season, with 80. It's like every time they had a man advantage, the goal light was bound to light up.

34: The Shutout Streak
The 2003-04 New Jersey Devils and the 1927-28 Ottawa Senators share the record for the most consecutive shutouts, with 5 each. It's like their goalies were playing a game of "Can't Touch This" with the puck.

35: The Goal Galore Game
The Edmonton Oilers and Chicago Blackhawks combined for a record 21 goals in a single game in 1985. It's as if defense was just a myth that day.

36: The Penalty Killing Prowess
The 2011-12 New Jersey Devils not only excelled at penalty killing but also scored 15 shorthanded goals during the season. It's like they saw being a man down as an offensive opportunity.

37: The Most Valuable Franchise
According to Forbes, the New York Rangers were valued as the NHL's most valuable franchise in 2020, proving that

success on the ice also means success in the bank.

38: The Fastest Four Goals
The St. Louis Eagles hold the record for the fastest four goals by one team, scoring them in just 1 minute and 52 seconds in 1934. It's like they decided to turn a hockey game into a goal-scoring sprint.

39: The Longest Name Game
The Los Angeles Kings once had a player named Aleksandr Andreyevich Frolov, likely one of the longest names in NHL history. It's as if his jersey needed an extension just to fit his name.

40: The Oldest Franchise
The Montreal Canadiens are the longest continuously operating professional ice hockey team, having been founded in 1909. It's like they've been around since ice hockey was just "hockey" because it was always on ice back then.

41: The Zero Hero
The 1928-29 Boston Bruins are the only team to finish a season with more shutouts (22) than goals allowed in total (42). It's as if their goalies were playing a different game where the puck was not invited.

42: The Playoff Perfectionists
The 1951-52 Detroit Red Wings swept every series in the playoffs to win the Stanley Cup, not losing a single game. It's like they decided playoffs were easier if you just didn't lose.

43: The Most Loyal Fans
The Toronto Maple Leafs have sold out every home game since 2002, despite a lengthy Stanley Cup drought. It's as if their fans have a motto: "In goals we trust, regardless of the Cup."

44: The Heaviest Team
In the 2011-12 season, the Boston Bruins were considered the heaviest team in the NHL, averaging over 210 pounds per player. It's like they thought hockey was a weightlifting competition on ice.

45: The Penalty Shot Phenomenon
The 2009-10 Phoenix Coyotes faced a record 10 penalty shots in one season. It's as if they were collecting penalty shots like some people collect stamps.

46: The Single-Game Shot Barrage
The Boston Bruins hold the record for the most shots in a single game, with 73 in 1941. It's like they decided the best defense was a relentless offense.

47: The Comeback Season
The 1938-39 New York Americans came back from a 0-3 start to the season to make the playoffs. It's like they believed every season has a reset button, and they found it.

48: The Most Prolific Scorers
The 1984-85 Edmonton Oilers had the most players (4) score at least 50 goals in a season. It's like scoring 50 goals was just part of the team uniform that year.

49: The Longest Goalie Goal
Ron Hextall of the Philadelphia Flyers scored a goal from his own crease in 1989, arguably the longest "snipe" by a goalie in NHL history. It's like he was trying out for the role of "sharpshooter" while wearing goalie pads.

50: The International Influence
The 2016-17 Pittsburgh Penguins had players from 7 different countries, showcasing the NHL's diverse talent pool. It's like they decided to form a mini-United Nations, but for hockey.

51: The Goalie Without a Mask
The last NHL goalie to play without a mask was Andy Brown, who took to the ice face-first for the Pittsburgh Penguins in 1974. Imagine playing dodgeball with a frozen rubber puck without any face protection. Andy did just that, making him the bravest—or maybe the craziest—goalie in hockey history.

52: The Record That's Music to a Team's Ears 🎵
The Montreal Canadiens hold the record for the most Stanley Cup victories, with 24 championships to their name. It's like they have an entire symphony of victories, while other teams are still learning to play the recorder.

53: The Draft Pick That Defied Odds
Selected 171st overall in the 1984 NHL Draft, Luc Robitaille became one of the lowest draft picks ever to be inducted into the Hockey Hall of Fame. It's as if he was a hidden treasure buried deep in the draft, waiting to be discovered.

54: The Fastest Hat Trick, By a Hair
Bill Mosienko holds the record for the fastest hat trick in NHL history, scoring three goals in 21 seconds in 1952. It's like he was playing hockey on fast-forward while everyone else was stuck in slow motion.

55: The Longest Name on the Cup 🏆
The longest name ever engraved on the Stanley Cup belongs to Robin Alamiro Vachon. It's as if his name was so long, the engravers needed a magnifying glass and an extra cup of coffee to get through it.

56: The Team That Turned the Lights Out
The 2000-01 Colorado Avalanche were the first team to win the Stanley Cup in the dark, as a power outage delayed their victory celebration. It's like they were so electrifying, they literally knocked the lights out.

57: The Most Prolific Scoring Line
The "Punch Line" of Maurice Richard, Hector "Toe" Blake, and Elmer Lach of the Montreal Canadiens in the 1940s was so dominant, it's like they were playing a different game. If hockey had a cheat code for scoring, they definitely knew it.

58: The Most Games Without a Stanley Cup 🍁
The Toronto Maple Leafs have the longest current Stanley Cup drought, having not won since 1967. It's like they've been on a nearly 60-year coffee break and forgot to come back to the victory party.

59: The Oldest Rookie to Make His Mark
At 27 years and 322 days old, Sergei Makarov won the Calder Memorial Trophy as the NHL's top rookie in 1990. It's like he showed up late to the party but still danced like nobody was watching.

60: The Team That Defied Gravity
The 1976-77 Philadelphia Flyers set a record by accumulating only 13 total points in the standings. It's like they were trying to play hockey on the moon, where wins were just harder to come by.

61: The Miracle on Manchester
The Los Angeles Kings completed the largest playoff comeback in NHL history, overcoming a 5-goal deficit to defeat the Edmonton Oilers in 1982. It's as if they discovered a magic wand in the locker room during intermission.

62: The Zamboni's First Lap 🚜
The first Zamboni machine made its NHL debut in 1954, forever changing how ice was resurfaced. It's like the ice got a new best friend, one that made it smooth and perfect for hockey.

63: The Shortest Tenure for a Winning Coach
Larry Robinson served as the interim head coach for the New Jersey Devils for just 8 games in 2000 but still led them to a Stanley Cup victory. It's as if he was a substitute teacher who ended

up winning the Teacher of the Year award.

64: The Team with a Theatrical Debut

The Vegas Golden Knights' pre-game ceremonies during their inaugural season were so elaborate, it felt more like a Broadway show than a hockey game. It's as if they decided that what happens in Vegas doesn't just stay in Vegas; it entertains and amazes.

65: The Most Diverse Team

The 2020-21 Toronto Maple Leafs boasted players from seven different countries, turning their locker room into a mini United Nations. It's like they decided to bring world peace through the power of hockey.

66: The Goal Heard Around the World

When Sidney Crosby scored the "Golden Goal" for Canada in the 2010 Olympics, it was broadcast live in the middle of the night across Canada. It's as if the entire country decided to have a massive pajama party, with Crosby as the guest of honor.

67: The Most Decorated Captain

Jean Beliveau of the Montreal Canadiens won the Stanley Cup 10 times as a player and another 7 times as an executive. It's like he had a season pass to the Stanley Cup winners' circle.

68: The First Outdoor NHL Game

The first NHL outdoor game in the modern era took place in 2003 between the Edmonton Oilers and Montreal Canadiens. It was so cold, fans wondered if the players might turn into ice sculptures before the third period.

69: The Team That Came Back from the Dead

The St. Louis Blues were last in the NHL standings in January 2019 but went on to win the Stanley Cup. It's as if they were a phoenix rising from the ashes, except instead of fire, they used ice.

70: The Most Consecutive Penalty Kills

The 1999-2000 Dallas Stars killed off 83 consecutive penalties across the regular season and playoffs. It's like they built a fortress around their net and threw away the key.

71: The Team That Couldn't Be Beat at Home

The 1976 Philadelphia Flyers went undefeated at home for an entire calendar year, making the Spectrum the most inhospitable place for visiting teams. It's as if they had a "No Visitors Allowed" sign that only opposing teams could see.

72: The Dynasty That Almost Wasn't

The New York Islanders won four consecutive Stanley Cups from 1980 to 1983, nearly missing the playoffs in the 1980 season before going on to start their dynasty. It's like they needed a wake-up call to start their reign.

73: The Goalie Who Played Forward

Lester Patrick, the Rangers' coach, suited up as a goalie in the 1928 Stanley Cup Finals despite being a forward and the team's coach. It's like he decided to try out a new career path mid-game.

74: The Fastest to Fifty

The Washington Capitals' Alexander Ovechkin reached 50 goals in the 2007-08 season faster than any player in over a decade. It's like he was racing against himself, and everyone else was just watching.

75: The Loudest Crowd

Fans of the Winnipeg Jets are reputed to be the loudest in the NHL, making the MTS Centre a daunting place for visiting teams. It's as if they decided volume was a key player on their team, one that never had an off night.

65: The Battle of Alberta Ignites

The Calgary Flames and Edmonton Oilers have one of the most heated rivalries in the NHL, dating back to the early 1980s. It's like they decided normal neighborly relations were too boring and opted for epic hockey battles instead.

66: The Dominance of the 80s Oilers
The Edmonton Oilers of the 1980s won the Stanley Cup five times in seven years (1984, 1985, 1987, 1988, and 1990), making them a dynasty. It's as if they found a "Win Stanley Cup" button and kept hitting it.

67: The Goal That Wasn't
In 1999, the Buffalo Sabres lost the Stanley Cup to the Dallas Stars on a controversial goal by Brett Hull. It's like the puck crossed the line, but the rulebook didn't.

68: The Presidents' Trophy Curse
Teams that win the Presidents' Trophy for the best regular-season record often get knocked out early in the playoffs. It's as if the trophy is actually a beautifully polished jinx.

69: The Miracle of the 2019 Blues
The St. Louis Blues went from last place in January 2019 to winning the Stanley Cup in June. It's like they decided to write their own Cinderella story, but with hockey sticks instead of glass slippers.

70: The First NHL Outdoor Game
The first official outdoor game in NHL history took place in 2003 between the Edmonton Oilers and Montreal Canadiens. It's as if they decided to take the game back to its roots, and Mother Nature said, "Hold my snow."

71: The Penguins' Back-to-Back
The Pittsburgh Penguins won back-to-back Stanley Cups in 2016 and 2017, proving that lightning can indeed strike twice, especially if you have Sidney Crosby.

72: The Most Lopsided Trade
Wayne Gretzky's trade from the Edmonton Oilers to the Los Angeles Kings in 1988 is considered one of the most lopsided trades in sports history. It's like trading a diamond for a bag of magic beans, except the beans were just regular beans.

73: The Avalanche's Quick Success
The Colorado Avalanche won the Stanley Cup in their first season after relocating from Quebec in 1995-96. It's as if they decided to throw a housewarming party and invited the Stanley Cup.

74: The NHL's Expansion Explosion
The NHL has expanded from the Original Six teams to 32 teams as of 2021, showcasing the league's growth. It's like they decided to build an army, one hockey team at a time.

75: The Sedin Twins' Synchronicity
Henrik and Daniel Sedin, twins who played for the Vancouver Canucks, were known for their incredible on-ice chemistry. It's like they had telepathic powers, but only for passing the puck.

76: The Bruins' Bar Tab
After winning the 2011 Stanley Cup, the Boston Bruins reportedly racked up a $156,679.74 bar tab during their celebration. It's as if they were trying to win another cup, but this time for partying.

77: The Longest Game in Modern Times
In 2000, the Philadelphia Flyers and Pittsburgh Penguins played the longest game in modern NHL history, lasting over 152 minutes of playtime. It's like they just didn't want to go home.

78: The Islanders' Dynasty

The New York Islanders won four consecutive Stanley Cups from 1980 to 1983, becoming one of the NHL's great dynasties. It's as if they decided sharing wasn't their thing.

79: The Gretzky Effect
Wayne Gretzky's arrival in Los Angeles transformed the NHL's popularity in the United States. It's like he was not just a hockey player but a one-man marketing revolution.

80: The Blackhawks' Draft Steal
Drafted 215th overall, Dominik Hasek was selected by the Chicago Blackhawks in 1983 but became one of the greatest goaltenders in NHL history. It's like finding a rare comic book at a garage sale that's worth millions.

81: The Canadiens' Language Barrier
The Montreal Canadiens have a tradition of having French-speaking head coaches, emphasizing the team's deep roots in Quebec's culture. It's like they decided if you want to coach here, you better brush up on your French.

82: The Jets' Return
The Winnipeg Jets were brought back to the NHL in 2011, reviving a beloved team that moved to Arizona in 1996. It's as if the city said, "Just kidding, we really do want a hockey team."

83: The Lightning's Record-Setting Season
The Tampa Bay Lightning tied the record for the most wins in a single season with 62 in 2018-19. It's like they were playing a video game on rookie mode but in real life.

84: The Panthers' Fan Tradition
Florida Panthers fans have a tradition of throwing plastic rats onto the ice, a quirky celebration that began in 1996. It's as if they decided hockey needed more rodents.

85: The Red Wings' Playoff Streak
The Detroit Red Wings made the playoffs for 25 consecutive seasons from 1991 to 2016, proving consistency is key. It's like they had a yearly appointment with the postseason and never missed it.

86: The Capitals' First Cup
The Washington Capitals won their first Stanley Cup in 2018, after decades of heartbreak. It's as if they finally cracked the code, and all it took was a little magic from Ovechkin.

87: The Vegas Draft Magic
The Vegas Golden Knights reached the Stanley Cup Finals in their first season, thanks in part to a favorable expansion draft. It's like they were playing with a stacked deck, but in hockey.

88: The Blue Jackets' Playoff Victory
The Columbus Blue Jackets won their first playoff series in 2019, sweeping the heavily favored Tampa Bay Lightning. It's as if David took on Goliath and decided to bring a hockey stick.

89: The Predators' Fan Frenzy
Nashville Predators fans are known for their loud and passionate support, turning Bridgestone Arena into one of the most intimidating venues. It's as if they decided to blend a rock concert with a hockey game.

90: The Kraken Emerges
The Seattle Kraken joined the NHL in 2021, introducing a mythical sea monster into the league. It's like the NHL decided it was time for some maritime mystery.

91: The Record for Most Ties
Before the NHL introduced the shootout, the 1969-70 Philadelphia Flyers set a record with 24 ties in a season. It's like they were the kings of "agreeing to disagree."

92: The Goalie Goal Scorer Club

Only a handful of NHL goalies have scored a goal, joining an exclusive club where goalies get to celebrate not just stops, but shots too. It's as if they occasionally forget their job and decide to show the forwards how it's done.

93: The Mascot Madness
NHL mascots range from the Philadelphia Flyers' Gritty to the San Jose Sharks' S.J. Sharkie, adding a layer of fun and sometimes bizarre entertainment. It's like each team decided they needed their own superhero, but only for antics and hugs.

94: The Heritage Classic's Cold Origins
The Heritage Classic outdoor game celebrates hockey's outdoor roots, even if it means playing in bone-chilling temperatures. It's as if the NHL decided to remind everyone that hockey is indeed a winter sport.

95: The Triple Overtime Thrillers
Triple overtime games in the playoffs are both a test of endurance and a showcase of drama. It's like the teams decide that just one overtime isn't enough to tell their epic tales.

GREATEST HOCKEY TEAMS OF ALL TIME

MONTREAL CANADIENS

The Flying Frenchmen 🚀: The Montreal Canadiens, also known as "Les Habitants," took flight in the NHL way back in 1909. Imagine skating so fast, you could practically fly! That's how they got their nickname, zipping past opponents and scoring goals like superheroes in a comic book.

The Wizard of the Rink 🎩 : Maurice "Rocket" Richard, a Canadiens legend, was the first NHL player to score 50 goals in 50 games during the 1944-1945 season. It's like he had a rocket on his back, zooming past everyone else!

A Trophy Named After a Player? 🏆: The Canadiens' Jean Beliveau was so good that the league named a trophy after him - the Conn Smythe Trophy, awarded to the playoff MVP, in 1965. Imagine being so amazing at hockey that they decide to name a trophy just for you!

The Century Club 💯: In the 1976-1977 season, the Canadiens were unstoppable, winning an incredible 60 games and losing only 8. That's like acing almost every test without even trying!

The Perfect Playoff 🏒: In 1976, the Canadiens went 12-0 in the playoffs, sweeping every series to win the Stanley Cup. It's as if they had a cheat code for hockey, making them unbeatable when it mattered most.

The Legendary Lineup: The Canadiens' 1976-77 team is often called the greatest hockey team ever. With players like Guy Lafleur, Ken Dryden, and Larry Robinson, it was like having an all-star team play every game.

The Dynasty of the 1970s: The Canadiens won the Stanley Cup six times in the decade (1971, 1973, 1976, 1977, 1978, and 1979), making their locker room more crowded with trophies than a toy store is with toys!

A Goalie Like No Other: Ken Dryden wasn't just any goalie; he was a law student who read books during breaks in the game. Talk about multitasking – stopping pucks and hitting the books, all at once!

The Record Breakers: The Canadiens hold the record for the most Stanley Cup victories with 24 wins. That's like having a birthday party with 24 cakes – one for each championship!

The Ghosts of the Forum: The old Montreal Forum, their home until 1996, was said to be haunted by the "ghosts" of past Canadiens' greats, helping the team to miraculous victories. Spooky, right?

The Captain's Example: Saku Koivu, battling cancer, made a triumphant return to the ice in 2002, inspiring fans and players alike. His courage was as mighty as a superhero's, showing that some battles are bigger than sports.

A Rivalry for the Ages: The Canadiens and the Boston Bruins have one of the fiercest rivalries in sports, dating back to 1924. It's like having a sibling rivalry, but with hockey sticks and a lot more ice!

The Night of the Red Light: On March 3, 1955, Maurice Richard scored his 500th career goal. The arena was so loud, it was like a rock concert for hockey fans.

Hockey's Hall of Fame Home: More Canadiens players are in the Hockey Hall of Fame than from any other team. It's like having a yearbook where every single player is voted "Most Likely to Succeed."

The Patriarch of the Pipes: Georges Vezina, the Canadiens' goalie from 1910 to 1925, was so legendary they named the trophy for the league's best goalie after him. Imagine being so good at your job that they name an award after you while you're still doing it!

The 10-Cent Trophy: Back in 1916, the Canadiens won their first Stanley Cup, and each player received a silver ring that cost a whopping 10 cents. Talk about budget bling!

The International Influence: The Canadiens were the first NHL team to play in Europe, visiting the Soviet Union in 1975. It was like taking a field trip, but instead of going to the museum, they went to play hockey!

The Ironman Streak: Doug Jarvis, a Canadiens center, holds the NHL record for consecutive games played - 964! From 1975 to 1987, he didn't miss a single game. That's like going to school every single day for over 10 years without ever being sick!

The Fastest Goal Ever: In 1973, the Canadiens' Jim Roberts scored just 6 seconds into a game. It was so quick; fans barely had time to sit down!

The Creative Captain: Toe Blake, not only a legendary player and coach for the Canadiens, but also an artist off the ice. He could strategize a game and draw beautiful paintings, making him a true renaissance man of hockey.

The Miracle Maker: Patrick Roy, the goaltender, led the Canadiens to two Stanley Cups (1986, 1993) as a rookie and then again seven years later, proving that miracles can happen more than once if you're wearing goalie pads.

The Bilingual Puck 🇨🇦: The Canadiens are the only NHL team whose players sang the national anthem in two languages – English and French. It's like getting a language lesson at every game!

The Outdoor Pioneers: The Canadiens participated in one of the first outdoor games in NHL history, playing against the Edmonton Oilers in the 2003 Heritage Classic. It was like having the biggest hockey rink ever, under the open sky!

The Goalie Who Scored: Believe it or not, Jose Theodore, the Canadiens goalie, scored a goal in 2001. It's rare for goalies to score, making it as surprising as if your dog suddenly spoke French!

The Loyalty Badge: Henri Richard, the Pocket Rocket, won 11 Stanley Cups with the Canadiens, the most by any player in history. It's like winning the best attendance award, but instead of a perfect attendance certificate, you get 11 Stanley Cups!

The Color of Hockey: Did you know the Canadiens' iconic red, white, and blue colors are said to represent the French, English, and Scottish communities in Montreal? It's like wearing a history lesson on your jersey!

The Night the Lights Went Out: During the 1988 playoffs, a power outage at the Montreal Forum paused a game against the Boston Bruins. It was so dark, players could have played hide and seek!

The Goal That Wasn't: In 1996, a goal by the Canadiens was disallowed because the net was slightly dislodged. It's like scoring a perfect goal in soccer, but someone moved the goalposts!

The Standing Ovation Save: Patrick Roy made a save so incredible in the 1986 playoffs that even the opposing team's fans gave him a standing ovation. It's like getting applause from your siblings for cleaning your room – rare and amazing!

The Record for Most Records: The Canadiens hold over 50 team records in the NHL, including most points in a season, most wins, and many more. It's like being the best at everything in school, from sports to spelling!

The First to Broadcast: The Canadiens were part of the first-ever NHL game broadcast on the radio in 1933. Imagine listening to a game and having to picture all the action in your head!

The Snowy Stanley Cup 🏆: In 1930, the Canadiens won the Stanley Cup during a massive snowstorm. Fans braved the blizzard to celebrate, making snowmen probably wished they could cheer too!

The Most Valuable Player, Literally: In 1924, Canadiens' goalie Georges Vezina was sold to the team for $15,000, which was a lot of money back then. It's like buying a super rare video game that turns out to be the best ever!

The Masked Marvel: Jacques Plante, the Canadiens goalie, was the first to regularly wear a protective mask in 1959. Before that, goalies faced flying pucks with just their bare faces!

The Longest Game ⏰: In 1930, the Canadiens played the longest game in their history, beating the Boston Bruins after nearly 117 minutes of play. That's like watching the longest movie ever and then some!

The First Female Announcer 🎤👩: In 2003, the Canadiens hired the first female announcer in the NHL, making history and showing that hockey is for everyone.

37 The Coin Toss Captain 🪙: In 1948, the Canadiens couldn't decide on a captain, so they tossed a coin. Talk about leaving big decisions to chance!

The Unbreakable Bond 🔗: The Canadiens and their fans are known for their strong loyalty, with generations of families supporting the team. It's like having a giant family reunion at every game.

The Oldest Rookie 👴👶: In 1949, the Canadiens had the oldest rookie in NHL history, 38-year-old goalie Jerry McNeil. It's like starting school when you're old enough to be the teacher!

The Zamboni Driver's Dream 🚜: In 2005, the Canadiens' Zamboni driver was called to be the emergency backup goalie for one game. It's like being asked to join your favorite video game as a character!

The Brotherly Love Trophy 🏆❤️: The Richard Trophy, awarded to the NHL's top goal scorer, is named after Maurice "Rocket" Richard of the Canadiens. It's like having the best player in a video game named after you!

The Golden Anniversary Goal 🎩: In 1959, on the NHL's 50th anniversary, the Canadiens' Jean Beliveau scored a hat trick (three goals in one game). It's like throwing the best party ever and being the guest of honor!

The Daring Defenseman 🛡: Doug Harvey, one of the Canadiens' most celebrated defensemen, was known for playing without a helmet. It's like riding a bike with no hands – thrilling but a little risky!

The International Hall of Fame 🌍🏛: Canadiens players come from all over the world, making the team a melting pot of talent. It's like having friends from every country on your soccer team!

The Triple Overtime Thriller ⏳: In the 1953 Stanley Cup Finals, Elmer Lach scored the winning goal for the Canadiens in triple overtime against Boston. It's like finishing a marathon and then sprinting the last mile!

The Hockey Innovators : The Canadiens were pioneers in hockey strategy, introducing practices like the power play and the slap shot. It's like inventing a new way to play tag that everyone loves.

The Comeback Kids 🔄: In 1971, the Canadiens won the Stanley Cup after finishing the regular season in third place. It's like being the dark horse in a race and surprising everyone by winning!

The Captain Without the "C" 🚫: Henri Richard played for the Canadiens for 20 years but was never officially the team captain. It's like being the leader of a group project without the title.

The First to the Finish 🏅: The Canadiens were the first NHL team to win 3,000 games, reaching the milestone in 2008. It's like being the first to finish a marathon in a record number of races.

The Hockey Night Heroes : The Canadiens have appeared on "Hockey Night in Canada" more than any other team, making Saturday nights special for fans across the country. It's like being the star of your own TV show every week!

The Goalie Goal: In 1971, Canadiens goalie Rogatien Vachon scored a goal during practice. It's like scoring a basket from the other side of the court, but with hockey sticks!

The Ice Capade: Before the era of professional ice maintenance, the Canadiens' players would sometimes help clean the ice. Imagine NHL stars doubling as Zamboni drivers!

The Accidental Hero: In 1946, a fan accidentally interfered with a puck in play, helping the Canadiens score a crucial goal. It's like your dog running onto the field and scoring a goal in soccer!

The Benchless Phenomenon: In the early days, the Canadiens didn't have a bench for substitute players. Players would stand the entire game, like a never-ending game of musical chairs without the chairs!

The Hockey Barber: Henri Richard was known for cutting teammates' hair, earning him the nickname "The Barber." It's like your friend giving haircuts in the playground, but with hockey players!

The Lucky Loonie: During the 2002 Winter Olympics, a Canadian icemaker secretly placed a loonie at center ice, believed to bring luck to the Canadian teams, including former Canadiens players. It's like finding a four-leaf clover on the field before a big game!

The Singing Goalie: Canadiens goalie Gump Worsley was known for singing on the ice to keep himself relaxed. Imagine belting out tunes while blocking shots!

The Puck Stopper's Snack: Legend has it, Ken Dryden ate a chocolate bar between periods for energy. It's like having a secret power-up snack in your backpack!

The Skating Senator: Howie Morenz, a Canadiens superstar, was so popular that he was offered a seat in the Canadian Senate. It's like being so good at video games, the government invites you to make laws about gaming!

The Mystery of the Missing Cup: In 1924, the Stanley Cup was lost on a roadside after the Canadiens' victory party. It was found by a passerby, making it the best roadside find ever!

The Goalie's Best Friend: Jacques Plante, the first goalie to wear a face mask, was also known for knitting in his spare time, even making a sweater for his dog. It's like your goalie being part crafty artist, part wall.

The Penalty Box Nap: Maurice Richard was once so exhausted during a game; he fell asleep in the penalty box. Talk about a power nap!

The Lightning Fast Trade: In 1995, Patrick Roy was traded to the Colorado Avalanche so quickly, he played for his new team the next day. It's like waking up in one house and going to sleep in another!

The Secret Stick Messages: Players would sometimes write messages or draw pictures on their sticks for good luck. It's like having a lucky pencil for tests, but much bigger and for hockey.

The Fan-Picked Captain: In 2010, the Canadiens' fans voted online for their next captain, making it one of the first times in sports history a team captain was chosen by fans. It's like choosing the leader of your team in a video game, but in real life!

The Underwater Training: Some Canadiens players trained by swimming with their gear on to improve endurance.

It's like playing soccer in a spacesuit to get stronger!

The Olympic Torchbearer 🔥⛸️: Jean Beliveau carried the Olympic torch in 1996, blending the worlds of Olympic sports and hockey. It's like being chosen to carry the biggest birthday candle ever!

The Record-Breaking Comeback 🔄🏆: The Canadiens hold the record for the biggest comeback in a playoff game, overcoming a five-goal deficit to win. It's like turning a game of Monopoly around when you only have $1 left!

The Goalie's Reading Corner 📚🏒: Ken Dryden would read law books between periods, effectively turning the locker room into a study hall.

The Spooky Success 👻🏆: Some believe the Canadiens' success is thanks to a friendly ghost, "Le Gros Bill," watching over the team. It's like having a guardian angel, but for hockey!

The First Female Full-Time Coach ⛸️👩‍🏫: In 2020, the Canadiens hired their first female full-time coach, breaking new ground in the NHL. It's like your favorite video game getting a cool new update!

The Unbreakable Glass Incident 💥🚫: A Canadiens' player's shot was once so powerful, it shattered the unbreakable glass at the arena. It's like breaking an indestructible toy with sheer willpower!

The Hockey Night Ritual 📻: Before television, families would gather around the radio to listen to Canadiens games, making it a weekly tradition. It's like having a movie night, but everyone's imagining the action!

The Goalie Poet ✍️📖: Georges Vezina, known for his stoic presence in net, was also a poet, writing about the beauty of hockey and life. It's like finding out your math teacher is also a secret novelist!

The Hidden Talents Show 🎭🏒: Canadiens players often showcase hidden talents at charity events, from singing to magic tricks. It's like your school talent show, but with professional athletes!

GREATEST HOCKEY TEAMS OF ALL TIME

DETROIT RED WINGS

The Name Game 🎮: Before they were the Detroit Red Wings in 1932, they were called the Detroit Cougars and even the Falcons. It's like changing your gamer tag until you find the coolest one.

The Octopus Tradition 🐙: Since 1952, fans throw an octopus on the ice for good luck during playoffs. That's 8 legs of good luck - one for each win needed to grab the Stanley Cup!

Mr. Hockey ⛸️: Gordie Howe, known as "Mr. Hockey," played for the Wings for over 25 years. Imagine playing with your grandpa, and he's still the best player on the ice!

The Production Line 🏭: In the 1950s, the Red Wings had a line of players called "The Production Line." It was like they were making goals in a factory because they scored so much!

The Winged Wheel 🚲: The team's logo, a winged wheel, represents Detroit's auto industry. It's like having a race car on your shirt, but cooler because it has wings!

The Hockeytown Hero 🏙️: Steve Yzerman, the long-time captain, led the team to three Stanley Cups. He's like the superhero mayor of Hockeytown, saving the day with his hockey stick!

The Russian Five 🇷🇺: In the 1990s, the Red Wings had a group of five Russian players who played together like a ballet on ice. They were more synchronized than your favorite dance crew!

The 25-Year Playoff Streak 📅: From 1991 to 2016, the Red Wings made the playoffs every single year. That's like having a birthday party every year and always getting the biggest slice of cake!

The Never-Ending Game ⏳: In 1936, the Red Wings played the longest game in NHL history, winning after six overtime periods. It was so long, fans needed a bedtime story and a nap!

The Flying Goalie 🥅🏒: In 1996, goalie Chris Osgood scored a goal by shooting the puck into an empty net. It's like scoring a basket from the other side of the basketball court, but with a hockey stick!

The Ageless Wonder 👴🏒: Gordie Howe played until he was 52 years old, making him one of the oldest players in NHL history. Imagine playing in the NHL with your grandkids cheering you on from the stands!

The Miracle on Ice 🎩: In 1997, Darren McCarty, known more for his fists than finesse, scored a beautiful goal in the Stanley Cup Finals. It was like the class clown winning a spelling bee!

The Enforcer's Encore 🎤: Bob Probert, one of the toughest enforcers on ice, also had a softer side, once singing with a band at a local bar. It's like discovering your toughest teacher is also a karaoke star!

The Double Duty 🎪🏀: In the early days, the Detroit Olympia, home of the Red Wings, also hosted basketball games and even circuses. It was like your living room being used as a classroom, a dance hall, and a petting zoo all in one!

The Captain's Comeback 🦽🏆: Steve Yzerman led the Red Wings to a Stanley Cup in 2002 despite playing on a knee that needed surgery. It's like winning a race with a backpack full of rocks!

The Record Rookie: In the 1983-1984 season, Steve Yzerman scored 87 points as a rookie, a Red Wings record. That's like acing every test in school on your first try!

The Goalie Swap 🔄🥅: In 1998, the Red Wings were the first team to win a Stanley Cup using two goalies, Chris Osgood and Mike Vernon, sharing the crease. It's like winning a relay race with two people running at the same time!

The Perfect Nickname 💣: Tomas Holmstrom was known as "Demolition Man" for his ability to cause chaos in front of the net. It's like being called "Homework Destroyer" because you're so good at finishing it quickly!

The Sneaky Stick 🪑🏒: Legend has it, Gordie Howe would subtly lift opponents' sticks just before they shot, throwing off their aim. It's like pulling a chair out from under someone as they sit down, but way sneakier!

The Generous Goalie 🎁: Manny Legace once bought 300 tickets for local fans to attend a game, making him the coolest Santa Claus in pads.

The Unsinkable Team 🚢: After winning the Stanley Cup in 2008, the Red Wings' celebration was so lively, they nearly capsized a boat during their parade. It's like having a pool party on a raft!

The Goal That Almost Wasn't 🚫🥅: In 1996, a goal by Slava Kozlov was so fast, the referee missed it, and play continued. It's like doing a magic trick so well, even the magician doesn't notice!

The Historic Rivalry 🏒: The Red Wings and the Chicago Blackhawks have one of the oldest rivalries in the NHL, like an endless game of tag where no one wants to be "it."

The Fan Favorite 🏒: During the 1950s, Ted Lindsay started the tradition of lifting the Stanley Cup and skating around the ice, so all the fans could see it up close. It's like sharing your birthday cake with the whole class, not just your best friends!

The Zamboni Driver's Day Off 🚜: The Joe Louis Arena, the Red Wings' former home, was famous for having one of the fastest ice surfaces in the NHL, thanks to their Zamboni drivers who were as precise as artists with their ice-resurfacing skills. It's like drawing with a giant crayon that never goes out of the lines!

The Feathered Phenomenon 🐙🦆: Alongside the famous octopus, a duck once made its way onto the ice during a Red Wings game, sparking laughter and confusion. It's as if the duck wanted to try out for the team, but got cold feet... or, cold webbed feet!

The Masked Marvel 🥅: Terry Sawchuk, a legendary Red Wings goalie, was one of the first to wear a protective face mask in the NHL, starting a trend that would become mandatory for all goalies. Imagine playing goalie in dodgeball without any protection – ouch!

The Record-Breaking Game 🏅: On December 2, 1995, the Red Wings set an NHL record by winning their 9th consecutive road game at the start of the season, proving home is where the heart is, but the road is where the wins are!

The Hockey Juggler 🏒🤹: Pavel Datsyuk, known for his incredible stick-handling skills, could probably juggle pucks if asked. He made controlling the puck look as easy as flipping pancakes!

The DIY Trophy 🏆🔨: Before the Stanley Cup became the official NHL trophy, the Red Wings won the American Professional Hockey League championship in 1932 and had to make their own trophy because there wasn't one. It's like winning a baking contest and having to bake your own prize cake!

The Goalie's Ghost 👻🥅: Rumor has it, the spirit of a former Red Wings goalie haunts the corridors of the Joe Louis Arena, making sure the team's current goalies stay sharp. It's like having a guardian angel, but instead of feathers, he wears goalie pads!

The Ice-Time Innovator ⏰: Scotty Bowman, a legendary Red Wings coach, revolutionized the way ice time was tracked and managed, turning the art of player rotation into a science. It's like being the master of a chess game, where every piece is a hockey player!

The Lucky Loafers 👞: Mike Babcock, another esteemed Red Wings coach, was known for wearing a lucky pair of loafers on game days. It's like having magic shoes that make you run faster, but for coaching!

The Unbreakable Bond 💪: The Red Wings have retired seven jersey numbers in honor of their legendary players, making those numbers forever part of the team's legacy. It's like retiring your favorite superhero costume because no one else can wear it quite like you!

The Goal That Made History 🥅: On March 26, 1997, Darren McCarty scored the winning goal in a game against the

Colorado Avalanche, ending one of the most intense rivalries in hockey history. It was like finishing the final level of a video game that everyone thought was unbeatable!

The Pioneering Spirit 🏒: The Red Wings were among the first in the NHL to scout and sign players from Europe, broadening the talent pool and changing the game forever. It's like discovering a whole new playground nobody knew about!

The Fan Wave 🌊: Red Wings fans are famous for their "wave" around the arena, a tradition that unites everyone in a circle of energy and support. It's like doing the wave in a giant stadium, but cooler because it's on ice!

The Secret Singer 🎤: Legend has it, one of the Red Wings' toughest enforcers was also an amazing singer, often serenading teammates in the locker room. It's like finding out your toughest teacher is also a secret opera star!

The Comeback Kid: In 2002, the Red Wings won the Stanley Cup after being down in the series, proving it's not over until it's over. It's like flipping a test from an F to an A+ in the last minute!

The Winged Victory 🏆: The Red Wings' 1997 Stanley Cup win broke a 42-year drought, bringing the trophy back to Detroit and sparking one of the biggest celebrations in the city's history. It's like waiting all year for snow and then getting the best snow day ever!

The Dynamic Duo 👬: Henrik Zetterberg and Pavel Datsyuk, known as "The Euro Twins," played together so seamlessly, it was like they had telepathic powers on the ice. It's like playing a video game with your best friend and never losing!

The Guardian of the Net 🥅: Chris Osgood, one of the Red Wings' most beloved goalies, was known for talking to his goalposts, thanking them whenever a puck hit the post and bounced out. It's like thanking your notebook for not letting you forget your homework!

The Frozen Time Capsule 🧊: The last puck used at the Joe Louis Arena before the Red Wings moved to their new home was frozen in a block of ice, preserving a piece of history. It's like freezing your favorite toy to look at when you're older!

The Charity Champions 🏆❤️: The Red Wings' foundation has donated millions to local communities, making them champions both on and off the ice. It's like using your allowance to buy gifts for others, but on a much bigger scale!

The International Ambassador 🌍: The Red Wings have helped grow the game of hockey worldwide, hosting clinics and games in other countries. It's like being a superhero who travels the world to teach everyone your superpowers!

The Oldest of Rivals 👀: The rivalry between the Red Wings and the Toronto Maple Leafs is one of the oldest in the NHL, dating back to the 1920s. It's like having a friendly argument with your neighbor that's lasted for 100 years!

The Captain's Legacy 🛡️: Nicklas Lidstrom, known as "The Perfect Human" for his incredible play and leadership, left a legacy of excellence that inspires young players today. It's like leaving a treasure map that leads to the secret of being awesome at everything!

The Beloved Mascot 🐙: Al the Octopus, the Red Wings' mascot, is named after the octopus tradition and is a fan favorite at games. It's like having a pet octopus that gives you high-fives!

The Hockey Innovators: The Red Wings were pioneers in developing hockey strategies and training methods that are now standard across the NHL. It's like inventing a new way to solve math problems that everyone ends up using!

TORONTO MAPLE LEAFS

The Name Change 🍁: The team was originally called the Toronto Arenas in 1917, then the St. Pats, and finally became the Maple Leafs in 1927. It's like changing your nickname until you find the coolest one in school!

The Mystery of the Maple Leaf 💂‍♂️: Ever wondered why they're called the Maple Leafs and not "Leaves"? The team was named after a regiment from World War I, keeping "Leafs" in honor of those soldiers. It's like naming your team after your favorite superheroes!

The Record Smasher 💥: In 1976, Darryl Sittler set an NHL record by scoring 10 points in a single game. That's like finishing all your homework and extra credit in one day – a legendary feat!

The Flying Goalie 🥅🤸: In the 1970s, goalie Mike Palmateer was known for his acrobatic saves, flipping and diving like a circus performer. It's like having Spider-Man in the net!

The Ghosts of the Gardens 👻: The Maple Leafs played at Maple Leaf Gardens from 1931 to 1999, a place some believe is haunted by former players cheering the team on. It's like having invisible fans with front-row seats!

The Blue and White 🔵: The team's colors, blue and white, were chosen to represent the Canadian skies and snow. It's like wearing a piece of Canada every game!

The Captain's Curse 😱: Some fans believe in a "Captain's Curse" because the team hasn't won a Stanley Cup since trading captain Rick Vaive in the 1980s. It's like accidentally breaking a mirror and waiting for the bad luck to end!

The Longest Drought 🌵: The Maple Leafs have the longest Stanley Cup drought in the NHL, not having won since 1967. It's like waiting forever for your favorite dessert but never getting it at dinner!

The First to Broadcast 📻: The Maple Leafs were one of the first NHL teams to have their games broadcast on the radio, making them stars off the ice too. It's like being the first of your friends to have your own YouTube channel!

The Outdoor Pioneers ❄️: The Leafs played in one of the first outdoor NHL games in 2014, the Winter Classic, against the Detroit Red Wings. It's like having a massive hockey game in your backyard ice rink, but with thousands of fans!

The Number 13 🍁: In 2016, Mats Sundin became the first Leaf to have his number (13) retired, proving 13 can be lucky after all. It's like turning the most avoided number into a badge of honor!

The Cookie Line 🍪: In the 1940s, the Kid Line was so good, a bakery named a cookie after them. It's like playing so well in soccer, they name a snack after your team!

The Hall of Fame Home 🏛️: With over 60 former players inducted, the Hockey Hall of Fame could almost be called the Maple Leafs Hall of Fame. It's like having a school hall of fame, but just for your class!

The Four-Minute Phenomenon ⏱️: In 1999, the Leafs scored three goals in less than four minutes to win a playoff game, making it one of the fastest comebacks ever. It's like finishing a race just in time to beat the school bell!

The Super Fan: The Maple Leafs have a super fan who's attended over 2,500 games. It's like never missing a day of school, not even for a snow day!

The Goalie Who Wrote History: Johnny Bower, the legendary Leafs goalie, was one of the oldest players in the league, proving you're never too old to stop pucks or dreams. It's like your grandpa entering a skateboard contest and winning!

The First of Its Kind: Maple Leaf Gardens was one of the first arenas to have a Jumbotron, making it easier for fans to catch all the action. It's like having a giant TV in your room for playing video games!

The Multitasking Player: Besides playing, King Clancy once refereed a game he was playing in due to an injured official. It's like being the player, referee, and coach in a game of tag!

The Unlikely Hero: In the 1967 Stanley Cup, a defenseman, Bob Baun, scored the winning goal on a broken leg. It's like scoring the winning goal in soccer while hopping on one foot!

The Puck Stoppers: The Leafs were the first NHL team to win a Stanley Cup using two goalies, Terry Sawchuk and Johnny Bower, in 1967. It's like having two goalies in a soccer game to make sure nothing gets by!

The Fan-Made Trophy: A fan once made a trophy for his favorite player, Dave Keon, which became an official NHL award. It's like drawing your own superhero and having it turned into a comic book!

The High-Flying Defenseman: Tim Horton, a Leafs legend, was also a pilot who flew himself to games. It's like having a superhero on your team who can fly to rescue the day!

The Animal on Ice: Tiger Williams, known for his wild playing style, rode his stick like a horse after scoring goals. It's like celebrating a home run by sliding into home plate on a magic carpet!

The Singing Goalie: Johnny Bower not only stopped pucks but also recorded a Christmas song. It's like your school goalie also being the lead in the holiday concert!

The Leaf Forever: The team motto, "Once a Leaf, Always a Leaf," shows the lifelong bond between the team and its players. It's like being part of a club where everyone is friends forever, no matter where they go!

The Accidental Goalie: In 1952, the Leafs had to use a fan as an emergency goalie for a game. Imagine watching your favorite team and then getting called to jump in and play!

The Flying Puck Adventure: A puck shot over the boards in 1967 wasn't found until 1988, stuck in an old seat cushion at Maple Leaf Gardens. It's like finding a lost treasure in your own living room years later!

The Record No One Wants: The Leafs hold the record for the longest time without a shot on goal in a playoff game, going 26 minutes in 2002. It's like playing hide and seek but forgetting to look for your friends!

The Lucky Charm: Legend has it, a Leafs fan buried a lucky penny under the center ice of the Maple Leaf Gardens, helping them win the 1967 Stanley Cup. It's like having a secret power-up hidden in your game controller!

The Goalie's Best Friend: One of the Leafs' goalies in the 1960s had a pet dog who attended every home game. It's like having your pet cheer you on at every soccer match!

The Invisible Assist 👻: A mysterious assist was credited to a Leafs player in the 1980s, but no one could figure out who actually touched the puck. It's like getting help on your homework from an invisible friend!

The Superstition King 👑: A former Leafs player would not change his lucky socks during a winning streak. Imagine playing the best games of your life, but your socks are the real MVP!

The Midnight Skaters 🌙: In the 1940s, the Leafs practiced at midnight to avoid fans and media. It's like having a secret club meeting when everyone else is asleep!

The Goal Horn Blunder 📯: The first time the Leafs tested their goal horn, it was so loud it shattered glass in the arena. It's like turning up your music so loud, your posters fall off the wall!

The Penalty Box Escape 🏃‍♂️: In a game against Montreal, a Leafs player was so frustrated with a penalty call, he "escaped" from the penalty box to argue with the referee. It's like getting a timeout but sneaking out to plead your case for more dessert!

The Fan Who Became a Player 👀: In the early days, the Leafs signed a player who was originally just a huge fan. It's like being picked from the audience to star in your favorite TV show!

The Unbreakable Stick 🏒: A Leafs defenseman once played an entire season with the same stick, believing it brought him good luck. It's like having a magic wand that never runs out of spells!

The Zamboni Rider 🚜: After winning a charity auction, a Leafs fan got to ride the Zamboni at a game, making it the coolest slow ride ever. Imagine cruising around on a giant ice cleaner in front of thousands of fans!

The Hockey Poet 📜: One of the Leafs' coaches wrote poetry about hockey and life, sharing it with players to inspire them. It's like having a teacher who turns math problems into epic adventures!

The Goal Celebration Ban 🚫: In the 1950s, the NHL tried to ban excessive goal celebrations, but the Leafs players continued to celebrate with flair. It's like being told not to laugh at jokes but finding them too funny to resist!

The Undercover Coach 🕵️‍♂️: A former Leafs coach would sometimes disguise himself to scout other teams unnoticed. It's like playing detective, but for hockey!

The Hockey Knight 🤴: After a particularly valiant effort in a game, a Leafs player was dubbed "Sir" by the local media, turning him into a hockey knight. It's like being a hero in a medieval tale, but with skates instead of a horse!

The Maple Leaf Gardens Ghosts 👻👻: Staff and players have reported strange noises and sightings at the Maple Leaf Gardens, leading to rumors of friendly spirits. It's like having a haunted house, but it's your home ice!

The Oldest Rookie 👶: The Leafs once had the oldest rookie in NHL history, proving you're never too old to chase your dreams. It's like your grandparent deciding to start middle school with you!

The Goal That Was Too Good 🏆: A Leafs player once scored a goal so fast, the opposing team argued it was impossible without magic. It's like scoring a goal in soccer from the other side of the field with a blindfold on!

The Ice Capades Connection 🎿: The Maple Leafs shared their arena with the Ice Capades for decades, leading to some interesting crossover events. Imagine figure skaters and hockey players swapping tips!

The Pre-Game Rituals 🎩: Leafs players have had some unique pre-game rituals, including reading comic books or eating specific meals. It's like having a lucky charm, but it's spaghetti!

The Broadcasting Pioneer 📺: The Leafs were among the first to have their games televised, bringing hockey into living rooms across Canada. It's like being the first of your friends to livestream your epic game moments!

The Arena Transformation 🔄: The Maple Leaf Gardens has been everything from a hockey arena to a grocery store, showing the many lives of a beloved building. It's like your clubhouse turning into a castle, spaceship, and then a dragon's lair!

The Most Loyal Fans 💚: Maple Leafs fans are known for their unwavering support, through thick and thin. It's like having a best friend who's always there, cheering you on, no matter what!

The Shattered Glass Incident 🥅: During a practice session in 1958, a Leafs player accidentally shot the puck so hard that it shattered a pane of glass, leaving everyone in disbelief. It's like hitting a baseball so far, it breaks a window in the neighbor's house!

The Legendary Comeback: In a dramatic playoff game in 1942, the Maple Leafs overcame a 3-0 deficit in the final period to win the game and eventually the Stanley Cup. It's like being down in a game of tag but making an epic comeback to win!

The Mysterious Stick Swap 🏒: During a crucial moment in the 1967 Stanley Cup Finals, Leafs player Bob Pulford mysteriously swapped his stick with another player's, leading to an unexpected goal. It's like trading Pokémon cards mid-battle and winning with a surprise move!

The Ice-Cleaning Mishap: In a lighthearted moment during a game break, the Zamboni driver accidentally slipped and did a full spin on the ice, much to the amusement of the fans. It's like watching your school janitor dance while mopping the cafeteria floor!

The Mascot Mishap 🐻: Once, the Leafs' mascot accidentally tripped and fell on the ice while trying to hype up the crowd, causing laughter and cheers from the audience. It's like watching a clumsy superhero save the day in their own unique way!

The Lucky Playoff Charm 🧦: A superstitious Leafs fan believed wearing mismatched socks during playoff games brought good luck to the team, and surprisingly, it seemed to work! It's like wearing your lucky underwear during a big test and acing it every time!

The Frozen Fans Fiasco: During a particularly cold outdoor game, some fans got stuck to their seats due to frozen spills, creating a hilarious scene as they tried to break free. It's like getting stuck to your chair with glue but with ice instead!

The Hockey Hairdo Disaster 💇 ♂: A Leafs player once tried a new hairstyle for a game, but it ended up getting tangled in his helmet during play, causing a humorous interruption. It's like having a wrestling match with your hair while trying to focus on the game!

The Sneaky Stick Swap 🏒: In a clever move during a penalty kill, a Leafs player switched sticks with a teammate to confuse the opposing team, leading to a successful defensive play. It's like swapping roles with your sibling to outsmart your parents!

The Locker Room Laughter 😂: The Leafs players often played pranks on each other in the locker room, from swapping equipment to hiding each other's gear, keeping the atmosphere light and fun. It's like having a never-ending game of hide-and-seek with your teammates!

The Mischievous Mascot 🐕: Once, the Leafs' mascot played a prank on the opposing team's mascot by stealing its oversized jersey, resulting in a hilarious chase around the rink. It's like watching a real-life cartoon unfold on the ice!

The Superstition Showdown 🧙‍♂️: Two superstitious players accidentally collided on the way to the rink after both trying to avoid stepping on cracks in the sidewalk, leading to laughter and friendly banter. It's like witnessing a real-life clash between superstition and reality!

The Mystery of the Missing Gear 🕵️‍♀️: During a crucial game, a Leafs player's equipment mysteriously disappeared from the locker room, leading to a frantic search before the puck drop. It's like playing a game of hide-and-seek with your gear right before the big game!

The Goalie Gag 😜: A mischievous goalie once swapped his mask with a cartoonish one during a timeout, leaving everyone in stitches before getting serious for the next play. It's like wearing a clown nose during a serious speech to break the tension!

The Legendary Lip Sync Battle 🎤: In a hilarious team bonding session, the Leafs players organized a lip sync battle in the locker room, showcasing their hidden talents and bringing laughter to everyone present. It's like having a mini concert before hitting the ice!

The Unexpected Goalie Celebration 🥳: After a surprise win, the Leafs goalie couldn't contain his excitement and spontaneously performed a victory dance on the ice, much to the delight of the fans. It's like watching a goalie-turned-dancer steal the show!

The Rookie Ritual Ruckus 🧝‍♂️: As part of a rookie initiation, the Leafs rookies had to perform a hilarious skit in front of the entire team, showcasing their creativity and earning their stripes. It's like putting on a comedy show with your friends to earn your place in the squad!

The Puck Collector's Paradise 🏒: A devoted fan collected pucks from every Leafs game they attended, creating a massive collection that became a local legend. It's like having your own personal treasure trove of hockey memories!

The Bizarre Goal Celebration 😜: In a moment of pure spontaneity, a Leafs player celebrated a goal by doing a cartwheel on the ice, surprising everyone with his unexpected gymnastic skills. It's like watching a hockey game turn into a circus act!

The Famous Fan Frenzy 🤩: A celebrity fan caused a commotion at a Leafs game when they accidentally spilled popcorn on a fellow spectator, leading to laughter and selfies all around. It's like having a movie star as your seatmate at a hockey game!

The Record-Breaking Rally 🚀: In a historic comeback, the Leafs scored six goals in the final period to secure an improbable victory, setting a new record for the most goals scored in a single period. It's like witnessing a superhero team assemble for an epic battle!

The Unforgettable Mascot Mishap 🥿: The Leafs' mascot once got stuck in a doorway while trying to make a grand entrance onto the ice, causing laughter and cheers from the fans. It's like watching a clumsy hero try to save the day in their own unique way!

The Legendary Locker Room Prank 🎈: A mischievous player pulled a prank on his teammate by filling their locker with balloons, creating a hilarious surprise when they opened it. It's like walking into a birthday party every time you go to get your gear!

The Mascot Mayhem 🕺: During a break in play, the Leafs' mascot challenged the opposing team's mascot to a dance-off, resulting in a hilarious showdown on the ice. It's like watching a battle of the bands, but with mascots instead of musicians!

The Ultimate Fan Experience 🎉: A lucky fan won the opportunity to ride the Zamboni during intermission, fulfilling every hockey fan's dream of cruising around the ice in style. It's like having a VIP pass to the coolest ride in town!

ICONIC ARENAS

MADISON SQUARE GARDEN

1: The Tale of the Flying Zamboni 🚜
Did you know Madison Square Garden (MSG) in New York City is not just famous for hosting nail-biting hockey games but also for its high-flying Zamboni? Yes, you heard that right! In a rather unusual move to solve the conundrum of limited storage space, the Garden's engineers devised a plan to lift the Zamboni (the machine that smooths the ice) to the 9th floor using a massive elevator. Imagine an elephant-sized ice smoother taking an elevator ride, just like in those cartoons where everything seems possible! 🐘

2: The Garden's Musical Chair Game 🎵
Madison Square Garden has been rebuilt four times, with the first one opening its doors in 1879. Think of it as playing a giant game of musical chairs through history, but instead of removing chairs, they kept upgrading the arena! The current MSG, which opened in 1968, is actually the fourth version. It's like the arena kept leveling up in a video game, becoming cooler and more high-tech with each new version. 🕹️🆙

3: A Roof with a Sweet Tooth 🔍🍫
The iconic roof of Madison Square Garden, known for its distinctive circular shape, was actually inspired by a Hershey's chocolate bar wrapper. Next time you munch on a Hershey's, imagine holding a mini version of MSG! This unique design was chosen to give the Garden an instantly recognizable

silhouette against the New York skyline, proving that sometimes, the best inspiration comes from the candy aisle.

4: The Night the Lights Went Out in the Garden
On February 14, 1977, during a game between the New York Knicks and the Buffalo Braves, Madison Square Garden experienced a blackout. But instead of calling it quits, the players decided to continue the game using only emergency lighting. It was like playing a dramatic scene from a movie, with shadows and silhouettes moving across the court, proving that the spirit of the game shines brightest in the darkest moments.

5: The Record-Breaking Concert Run

Madison Square Garden has seen its fair share of musical legends, but did you know it also holds a record for the longest concert residency? Billy Joel, the Piano Man himself, has been performing at MSG once a month since January 2014. It's like having an endless sleepover with your favorite uncle who tells the best stories and plays the coolest music.

6: The Secret Train Station
Beneath the bustling activity of Madison Square Garden lies a secret: the fully operational Penn Station. Commuters pass under the arena's feet, catching trains in a hidden layer of the city. It's like discovering a secret passage in a castle, except this one leads to adventures beyond the realm of sports and entertainment.

7: The First Indoor Ice Hockey Game

Madison Square Garden was the proud host of the first-ever indoor ice hockey game in 1879. Imagine stepping onto the ice, surrounded by walls and a ceiling, a novel concept at the time. It was a moment when a chilly winter sport found a cozy home indoors, transforming how the game was played and watched forever.

8: The Storied Fight of the Century
On March 8, 1971, MSG was the battleground for the "Fight of the Century" between Muhammad Ali and Joe Frazier. This epic battle wasn't just about punches and knockouts; it was a clash of titans, watched by celebrities and fans around the world. It's the kind of story that gets passed down through generations, where each punch seemed to echo through history.

9: The Celebrity Dog Show
Beyond sports, MSG has hosted a variety of events, including the Westminster Kennel Club Dog Show, making it the ultimate playground for four-legged furballs. Imagine the arena, famous for hockey and basketball, turning into a runway for dogs strutting their stuff, tails wagging as if they're the stars of the show. It's a reminder that MSG truly has something for everyone.

10: The Garden's Ghosts
Legend has it that Madison Square Garden is home to a few friendly ghosts, including the spirit of a boxer who can't seem to leave the ring. Employees and visitors have reported eerie feelings and sightings, adding a layer of mystery to the arena. It's as if the legends of the past are still cheering on the players, making MSG not just a place for games, but a realm where history lives on.

11: The Ceiling That Changes Colors
Madison Square Garden has a high-tech ceiling that can change colors! Think of it as a giant mood ring for the arena, reflecting the excitement of the game or concert below. Whether it's glowing with the colors of the home team or pulsating to the beat of a rock concert, the ceiling adds a magical touch to every event, making it feel like you're under a dancing northern lights display.

12: The Fastest Goal in History

MSG witnessed one of the fastest goals in NHL history. Imagine sitting down, popcorn in hand, and before you can even take a bite, the puck has already hit the back of the net! On November 20, 1947, the New York Rangers' Don Raleigh scored just 11 seconds into the game, setting a record that made fans question if they had blinked and missed it.

13: The Elevating Ice Rink
Unique to Madison Square Garden is its ability to transform from an ice rink to a basketball court in just a few hours. The secret? An elevating platform that hides the ice underneath while the court rolls out on top. It's like having a sports transformer in the heart of New York City, ready to switch from hockey skates to basketball sneakers at a moment's notice.

14: The Garden's Presidential History
Did you know that MSG has hosted not just sports and concerts but also presidential speeches? In 1962, President John F. Kennedy celebrated his 45th birthday at the Garden, with Marilyn Monroe famously singing "Happy Birthday, Mr. President." It's a venue that's seen the blend of politics, entertainment, and history, making it a cornerstone of American culture.

15: The Record for Most Events in a Year
Madison Square Garden holds the record for hosting the most events in a single year among arenas worldwide. In 2015, it hosted over 320 events, from sports to concerts, showing it's not just an arena but a never-ending festival of entertainment. It's as if MSG is the party that never stops, with something new to experience every day.

16: The Underwater Secrets
Beneath the arena, MSG has a complex system of pipes that were once part of a proposed underwater theme park. The plan was to create an aquatic wonderland for visitors, featuring marine life and underwater shows. Though it never came to fruition, the remnants of this dream add a layer of mystery, making MSG not just an arena but a treasure chest of what-ifs.

17: The Giant MSG Sphere
Madison Square Garden Company is building a futuristic venue called the MSG Sphere in Las Vegas, showcasing the brand's commitment to innovation. This sphere will be covered in LED screens, offering an immersive experience that makes MSG in New York's tech seem quaint by comparison. It's like the Garden is planting seeds of futuristic entertainment across the country.

18: The Knicks' Championship Drought
The New York Knicks, one of MSG's main tenants, have faced a championship drought since 1973. Fans joke that there's a curse on the Garden preventing the Knicks from winning, but hope springs eternal. Every game is a mix of nostalgia, hope, and the dream that this year could be the year the drought ends.

19: The Arena's Secret Rooms
Madison Square Garden is rumored to have secret rooms and tunnels that date back to its earlier incarnations. These hidden spaces have hosted celebrities and VIPs, offering a glimpse into a world beyond the public eye. It's like Hogwarts for sports and entertainment, with secret passages that tell their own stories.

20: The Garden's Role in Charity
Over the years, MSG has hosted numerous charity events, raising millions for causes worldwide. From benefit concerts to charity sports events, the

Garden has shown that it's not just a place for entertainment, but a powerful force for good. It's like the arena wears a superhero cape, ready to help those in need at a moment's notice.

21: The Garden's Architectural Chameleon
Madison Square Garden isn't just famous for what happens inside but also for its ability to change its exterior. With each rebuild, MSG transformed its façade to match the architectural trends of the times, from classic to modern. It's like the arena has a wardrobe of architectural styles, always ready to dress up for the era.

22: The Slam Dunk from the Sky
During a particularly electrifying NBA game, a player from the New York Knicks made a dunk so powerful, fans joked it was like he launched from a helicopter hovering above MSG. This hyperbolic tale underscores the gravity-defying moments basketball offers, making it seem as if players can momentarily defy the laws of physics and take flight.

23: The Ice Rink That Never Melts
MSG boasts an advanced cooling system that keeps its ice rink frozen even during the sweltering New York summers. It's akin to having a winter wonderland ensconced within its walls year-round, allowing ice hockey and figure skating to flourish no matter the season outside. It's like a magical freezer that ensures the ice is always perfect for skating.

24: The Lost Pennies Mystery
Legend has it that during one of the renovations of MSG, a collection of rare, old pennies was discovered hidden in the walls. These pennies were thought to be placed there for good luck by the original construction workers. It's a reminder of the personal touches and mysteries embedded in the fabric of the arena, making it a treasure trove of hidden histories.

25: The Venue That Talks Back
With its state-of-the-art acoustics, MSG is designed not just for spectators to hear the action but for performers and athletes to hear the roar of the crowd as if it's talking back to them. This unique feature amplifies the interaction between performers and their audience, creating a dialogue of excitement and energy. It's as if the arena itself cheers alongside the fans, making every shout and whisper part of the show.

26: The Garden's Time Capsule
When the current MSG was constructed, a time capsule was buried beneath it, filled with memorabilia from the era and messages for the future. It's a snapshot of history, waiting to be discovered by generations ahead. Imagine the excitement of opening a treasure chest from the past, revealing the spirit and dreams of the 1960s.

27: The Arena of Many Firsts
MSG has been the site of many "firsts" in the sports and entertainment world, including the first indoor boxing match broadcast on color TV and the first major esports event in North America. It's as if the Garden always wants to be the first to raise its hand in class, eager to try something new and set records.

28: The Skybridge Spectacle
One of the most unique features of MSG is its Skybridge, a walkway that offers spectators a bird's-eye view of the action below. It's like being on a flying carpet, hovering over the excitement, offering a perspective that turns spectators into part of the spectacle.

29: The Arena's Eco-Warrior Side
In recent years, MSG has taken significant steps towards sustainability, including energy-efficient lighting and recycling programs. It's like the Garden has donned a green cape, fighting against pollution and waste, showing that

even arenas can be heroes for the planet.

30: The Whispering Gallery Phenomenon

A little-known acoustic oddity in MSG allows a person to stand at one end of the arena and whisper, with the sound clearly reaching a friend standing on the opposite side. This "whispering gallery" effect showcases the intricate design and unexpected surprises hidden within the Garden, making it a place of wonder not just for sports and music but also for curious explorers.

31: The Court That Hosted a Pope

Madison Square Garden has welcomed a wide variety of guests, including a Pope! In 2015, Pope Francis celebrated Mass at MSG, transforming the arena from a sports and concert venue into a solemn place of worship. Imagine swapping basketballs for bibles, as thousands gathered not for a game but for a spiritual gathering. It's like MSG can switch from a concert hall to a cathedral, proving its versatility.

32: The Secret Garden Inside the Garden

Hidden within the hustle and bustle of Madison Square Garden is a small, tranquil garden area. This spot is a stark contrast to the energy of the events, offering employees and performers a quiet place to relax. It's as if there's a mini Central Park tucked away, reminding everyone of the importance of a peaceful moment in the city that never sleeps.

33: The Arena's Salute to Veterans

Madison Square Garden has a long-standing tradition of honoring military veterans during events. From special tributes to inviting veterans as honored guests, MSG ensures the sacrifices of these heroes are recognized. It's like each game or concert also doubles as a heartfelt thank you letter to those who've served.

34: The Largest Indoor Tennis Match

In 1977, MSG hosted the largest indoor tennis match in history, with over 30,000 fans gathered to watch Bjorn Borg battle Guillermo Vilas. Imagine a tennis match turning into a spectacle as grand as a rock concert, with every serve and volley echoing through the massive crowd. It's as if the tennis court was transformed into a stage for gladiators of the modern era.

35: The Home of Historic Draft Picks

MSG has been the site of numerous historic moments for the NFL, including serving as the venue for the NFL Draft for many years. It's where the future stars of football had their names called out, stepping into the limelight. Imagine the dreams that took flight in those moments, in the very same place where athletes and musicians make history.

36: The Arena's Role in Civil Rights

Madison Square Garden has played a significant role in the civil rights movement, hosting rallies and speeches by leaders like Martin Luther King Jr. It's a reminder that MSG isn't just about entertainment; it's also been a platform for important societal conversations, echoing the voices that have shaped history.

37: The Unusual Sports Hosted

Beyond hockey, basketball, and concerts, MSG has hosted a range of unusual sports events, from cycling races to wrestling and even dog shows. It's like the arena wears many hats, sometimes transforming into a velodrome, other times a wrestling ring or a runway for pooches. Each event adds a unique chapter to the Garden's eclectic history.

38: The Garden's Cinematic Cameos
Madison Square Garden has appeared in numerous films and TV shows, playing itself in scenes that capture the essence of New York City. From action-packed sequences to dramatic moments, MSG's cameo roles have cemented its status as a cultural icon. It's like the arena is not just a stage for sports and concerts but also a star of the silver screen.

39: The Venue's Iconic Logo Evolution
The logo of Madison Square Garden has evolved over the years, mirroring the changes in the arena itself. Each version reflects a different era of its storied history, from classic designs to more modern interpretations. It's as if the logo is a visual diary, capturing the essence of MSG through the ages.

40: The First to Go Smoke-Free
Madison Square Garden was one of the first major arenas to go completely smoke-free, leading the way in creating a healthier environment for fans and performers alike. This move was a bold statement for public health and set a new standard for venues worldwide. It's like MSG decided to clear the air, literally and figuratively, making each breath taken inside a little bit fresher.

41: The Transformation into a Virtual Reality Hub
In recent years, Madison Square Garden has embraced technology by hosting virtual reality (VR) experiences that transport fans to imaginary worlds or provide unique perspectives on live events. It's like strapping on a VR headset turns the arena into a portal to another dimension, where concerts and games are not just watched but experienced in 360 degrees.

42: The Hidden Time Capsules of Rock 'n' Roll
Madison Square Garden is rumored to have several hidden time capsules from famous rock bands. These capsules, secretly placed during concerts, contain memorabilia and messages to future generations of fans. Imagine future archaeologists uncovering a piece of rock 'n' roll history right in the heart of New York City.

43: MSG's Role in Breakdancing's Rise
In the 1980s, Madison Square Garden hosted breakdancing competitions that helped bring hip-hop culture into the mainstream. These events showcased the incredible talent of breakers, turning the Garden into a battleground where dance moves were as competitive as any sport. It's as if the arena was the stage for a dance revolution, spinning records and dancers alike.

44: The Secret VIP Tunnels
Beneath the bustling floors of Madison Square Garden, a network of secret tunnels is said to exist, designed exclusively for VIPs to enter and exit the venue unnoticed. These hidden pathways have allowed celebrities and politicians to enjoy events in privacy, making MSG not just an entertainment hub but a fortress of secrecy.

45: The Garden's Olympic Dreams
Madison Square Garden was once considered as a potential site for Olympic events if New York City were to host the Games. The idea was to transform the arena into a multi-sport complex, showcasing its versatility on the world stage. Though the dream hasn't been realized, it highlights MSG's capacity to inspire and unite people from all corners of the globe.

46: The Legendary Lost Locker Room
A legend persists among fans that there's a lost locker room deep within Madison Square Garden, untouched since the New York Rangers' early days. This mythical space is said to be filled with

memorabilia, echoing the cheers and challenges of past teams. Whether or fiction, the story adds a layer of mystery to the Rangers' storied history.

47: The Garden's Eco-Roof Project
Madison Square Garden has initiated projects to green its rooftop, exploring ways to reduce its environmental footprint. This living roof isn't just about aesthetics; it's a step towards sustainability, helping to insulate the building and provide a haven for urban wildlife. It's like MSG is wearing a green hat, thinking about the future of the planet.

48: The Concert That Never Ended
There's a whimsical tale about a concert at Madison Square Garden that was so enchanting, fans claim it never truly ended. The music, energy, and spirit of that night lingered in the arena long after the lights went up, as if the melodies were etched into the walls. This legend speaks to the transcendent power of live music at MSG, where some performances are so powerful, they become immortal.

49: The Arena's Secret Art Collection
Madison Square Garden houses a secret art collection, featuring works inspired by sports and entertainment legends who have graced its stage and grounds. This collection, accessible only to a select few, includes pieces from renowned artists, capturing the spirit and history of MSG in every brushstroke. It's like the arena is not just a venue but a museum of modern culture.

50: The Annual New Year's Eve Transformation
Every New Year's Eve, Madison Square Garden transforms into one of the city's largest party venues. Beyond hosting concerts, the arena becomes a place where thousands gather to count down to the new year. It's as if MSG temporarily becomes the center of the universe, with confetti, music, and cheers ushering in the new year. It's a testament to the arena's role not just in sports and entertainment, but in creating communal moments of celebration.

MAPLE LEAF GARDENS

1: The Sky-High Hockey Game
Did you know Maple Leaf Gardens once had a garden on its roof? That's right, in 1934, just a year after it opened, they decided the top of a hockey arena was the perfect place for flowers and veggies! Imagine playing a game of hockey while above you, there's a secret garden party happening with tomatoes and tulips cheering you on.

2: The Ghostly Goalie
Legend has it that Maple Leaf Gardens is home to a friendly ghost, a former goalie who loved hockey so much, he never left. Some say late at night, you can hear the swish of his ghostly pads saving goals. It's as if he's still defending his team, making sure not even a ghost of a chance gets by him!

3: The Chicken Flight
In 1966, during a hockey game at Maple Leaf Gardens, a fan got so excited, he threw a live chicken onto the ice! The chicken, wearing a tiny parachute, landed safely and slid across the rink, causing both players and fans to burst into laughter. It was the first and last time a chicken got a penalty for "fowl" play.

4: The Double Duty Arena
Maple Leaf Gardens wasn't just for hockey; it was a jack-of-all-trades! From hosting the Beatles, who rocked the

stage in 1964, to royal visits and wrestling matches, it was like the arena had multiple personality disorder, in the best way possible. One night, you're cheering for a goal; the next, you're singing along to "Hey Jude" or watching a royal wave.

5: The Secret Tunnel Escape
Beneath the arena, there's a network of secret tunnels. Legend has it these were used by players and performers to escape the madness of fans. Imagine famous hockey stars or rock legends sneaking around underground like spies, dodging adoring fans to pop up miles away, safe and sound. It's the ultimate game of hide and seek!

6: The Ice Cream Catastrophe
In the 1950s, Maple Leaf Gardens decided to sell ice cream during games. Sounds great, right? Well, on one hot game day, the freezer broke, turning the treat into a gooey mess. Fans ended up watching the game, trying to slurp up their melting ice cream, turning the stands into the stickiest mess the arena ever saw. It was a sweet idea with a messy penalty box.

7: The Coin Toss Conundrum
During the 1972 Summit Series, a coin toss at Maple Leaf Gardens decided which team got the "home" locker room. The Canadian team lost the toss and had to use the "visitor" room. They were so used to being the home team, players joked they got lost trying to find their bench. It was like playing at home but needing a map to get around!

8: The Mystery of the Missing Seats
When Maple Leaf Gardens first opened in 1931, some fans arrived to find their seats didn't exist! The paint was still wet, and construction wasn't completely finished. It was as if the arena was playing musical chairs, but forgot to stop removing chairs when the music stopped. Oops!

9: The Unplanned Pool Party
One winter, a pipe burst under the ice, creating a giant puddle. Instead of cancelling the game, they played around it, making it look more like water polo on ice. Players had to skate and splash, trying not to fall into the impromptu pool. It was probably the only hockey game where you needed a swimsuit just in case!

10: The Arena That Changed Colors
To celebrate special events, Maple Leaf Gardens would change the color of its exterior lights. From festive red and green for Christmas to spooky orange for Halloween, it was like the building had its own giant mood ring. The arena not only hosted the party inside but dressed up for the occasion too!

11: The Midnight Snack Break
One night, a game at Maple Leaf Gardens went into so many overtimes that the concession stands ran out of food. The hungry fans were so desperate, a local pizza place delivered pies directly to the stands! It turned into a giant pizza party, with slices being passed down rows. It was the only hockey game where the fans scored as much as the players did.

12: The Basketball Before Raptors
Before the Toronto Raptors, Maple Leaf Gardens was a hoops hotspot, hosting basketball games that were so high-flying, players joked they needed airplane clearance. Imagine dribbling down the same tunnels where hockey legends skated, swapping slapshots for slam dunks. It was like the arena had a secret life as a basketball court by night.

13: The Roof That Could Talk
If the roof of Maple Leaf Gardens could talk, it would tell tales of the roar of hockey fans, the screams of Beatles fanatics, and even the quiet whispers of figure skaters gliding on ice. It's like the roof was the ultimate gossip, holding secrets of every event it ever covered.

From sports to concerts, it heard every cheer, jeer, and song, making it the best storyteller in all of Toronto.

14: The Hockey Puck Rebellion
During a particularly tense game, fans started throwing hockey pucks onto the ice to protest a bad call. It was like a rebellion, but with rubber discs instead of swords. The players had to skate through a minefield of pucks, making it the slipperiest protest in sports history. It's said the ice was more puck than surface that day!

15: The Time Capsule Beneath the Ice
When Maple Leaf Gardens was first built, a time capsule was buried under the center ice spot, filled with mysterious items from 1931. It's like the builders wanted to freeze time, giving future generations a chilly treasure hunt. What's in the capsule? Only the ice knows, keeping its secrets frozen in time.

16: The Squirrel Scorekeeper
A curious squirrel once found its way into Maple Leaf Gardens and decided to watch a game from the rafters. Fans joked it was the best scorekeeper, watching from above. It had a perfect view of every goal, save, and penalty, making it the fluffiest unofficial member of the game crew. Just imagine a squirrel waving a tiny flag for each goal!

17: The Day the Lights Went Out
In the middle of a crucial game, the lights in Maple Leaf Gardens suddenly went out, plunging the arena into darkness. The players, not wanting to stop, continued to play by the light of emergency exit signs. It was like an old-time hockey game, lit by lanterns, except it was just modern players navigating by faint glows. It turned the game into a mysterious shadow dance on ice.

18: The Secret Concert
Rumors swirl about a secret concert held at Maple Leaf Gardens, where a famous band played under pseudonyms to avoid detection. Only a handful of people knew and attended, making it the most exclusive gig in town. It's like the arena was the keeper of the coolest secret in rock history, hosting a performance that's more legend than fact.

19: The Arena's Hidden Rooms
Maple Leaf Gardens is rumored to have hidden rooms that were used for everything from secret meetings to exclusive parties. These rooms, hidden behind unassuming doors or tucked away in the rafters, added an air of mystery. It's as if the arena had its own secret society, with membership granted only to those who knew the right door to open.

20: The Zamboni Rodeo
Once, a Zamboni driver at Maple Leaf Gardens decided to add a little flair to his ice resurfacing duties by wearing a cowboy hat and playing country music loudly. It turned the routine cleaning into a "Zamboni Rodeo," with fans cheering for the ice as much as for the game. It was the wildest ride in the east, with zero horses but one ice-resurfacing machine stealing the show.

21: The Accidental Ice Sculpture
One winter, a leaky roof at Maple Leaf Gardens created an accidental ice sculpture in the stands. The dripping water froze overnight, creating a masterpiece that fans joked was modern art. It was as if Mother Nature herself decided to become an artist, leaving her chilly mark on the arena. The next day, spectators were greeted not just with a hockey game but with a unique, frosty exhibit.

22: The Great Popcorn Flood
During a particularly exciting game, the popcorn machine malfunctioned, spewing popcorn like a volcano. Fans found themselves ankle-deep in buttery kernels, making it seem like the arena had been hit by a delicious, crunchy flood. It was a snack disaster of epic proportions, with popcorn becoming the unofficial third team on the ice that day.

23: The Invisible Game
A thick fog once enveloped the ice during a game at Maple Leaf Gardens, making it nearly impossible to see the puck or players. The game turned into a mysterious ballet, with players appearing and disappearing into the mist. Fans cheered based on the sounds of sticks and pucks, turning the match into a ghostly spectacle. It was hockey's version of a magic show, where the players were the magicians.

24: The Night of the Singing Fans
When the sound system failed during a crucial playoff game, the fans took it upon themselves to keep the spirit alive by singing the national anthem and popular chants acapella. It was a concert led by thousands, turning Maple Leaf Gardens into a giant choir. The unity and harmony of the fans' voices turned the technical glitch into a memorable moment of solidarity and passion.

25: The Rink-Side Sauna
An unusual heatwave turned one winter game at Maple Leaf Gardens into what felt like playing hockey in a sauna. The ice began to soften, and players skated through patches of water, steam rising around them. Spectators fanned themselves with programs, turning the stands into a tropical oasis. It was a night where the cold sport of hockey met the warmth of summer, blending two seasons in one game.

26: The Day the Goals Moved
In a bizarre twist, the goals at Maple Leaf Gardens were once set up on the wrong marks, making the rink slightly shorter at one end. Players and referees were baffled by the sudden advantage to one team. It was as if the goals had decided to play their own game, sneaking closer together when no one was looking. The match became a playful puzzle, with the ice playing tricks on everyone involved.

27: The Coin-Operated Lights
A myth among fans is that the lights at Maple Leaf Gardens were once coin-operated, requiring staff to feed a meter to keep the lights on during games. While this tale is more fiction than fact, it amused fans to imagine arena staff scrambling for change in their pockets to avoid playing in the dark. It added a humorous, if not entirely accurate, layer to the lore of the Gardens.

28: The Stowaway Cat
A small, adventurous cat once found its way into Maple Leaf Gardens and decided to watch a game from the rafters. The feline spectator was so stealthy, it went unnoticed until it began meowing for the home team. It was dubbed the "Lucky Cat" mascot for the night, credited with bringing good luck. Fans left wondering if every game should have a whiskered guardian angel perched above.

29: The Haunted Penalty Box
There's an old tale that one of the penalty boxes at Maple Leaf Gardens is haunted by the ghost of a former player who was notorious for spending too much time in the box. Players report feeling chilly drafts and hearing mysterious whispers of advice on avoiding penalties. It's as if the spirited player is still trying to influence the game, making the box less lonely and a bit more spooky.

30: The Confetti Goal Celebration
To celebrate a major milestone goal, the arena staff once filled the goal nets with hidden confetti, which exploded

into a colorful shower when the puck hit the net. It turned the moment into an impromptu party on ice, with players and fans alike covered in a kaleidoscope of paper. It was a goal that went down in history, not just for its importance, but for the unexpected burst of joy it brought to everyone at the Gardens.

31: The Day the Zamboni Got Lost
In a humorous turn of events, a new Zamboni driver at Maple Leaf Gardens took a wrong turn and ended up driving the ice resurfacer out of the rink and into the concourse area during intermission. Spectators were amused to see the Zamboni cruising by the concession stands, making it the only time fans could have gotten their popcorn smoothed over with ice. It was as if the Zamboni wanted its own snack break!

32: The Goalie Who Knitted
A quirky goalie for the Leafs, known for his calm demeanor, was rumored to knit scarves and socks for his teammates during long road trips. On one particularly cold game night, he gifted his creations to his teammates, claiming it helped improve their grip and warmth. Fans joked that Maple Leaf Gardens was not just an arena but also a part-time knitting circle, especially around the goalie's net.

33: The Mystery of the Vanishing Puck
During a game in the 1970s, a shot sent the puck flying and it mysteriously vanished. Despite everyone's best efforts, it was never found during the game. It became a legend at Maple Leaf Gardens, with fans speculating it entered another dimension. The puck was eventually found weeks later, hidden in an unlikely nook of the scoreboard, proving that even inanimate objects can play hide and seek.

34: The Singing Referee
There was once a referee at Maple Leaf Gardens known for his opera singing. He would serenade the crowd with arias during game delays. His powerful voice turned timeouts into mini-concerts, making him a beloved figure. It was said that his singing could soothe even the most heated moments on ice, earning him the nickname "The Pavarotti of the Penalty Box."

35: The Inflatable Mascot Mishap
Maple Leaf Gardens once attempted to introduce an inflatable mascot, which unfortunately deflated halfway through its debut, causing a humorous scene as staff scrambled to reinflate it on the sidelines. The mascot, a giant bulldog, ended up flopping over the boards and onto the ice, creating an unexpected obstacle for players. It was a memorable "deflating" moment that left fans laughing and players dodging more than just the opposing team.

36: The Night of a Thousand Hats
After a player scored a hat trick, the tradition of throwing hats onto the ice was taken to a new level when nearly a thousand hats were hurled in celebration. The cleanup took so long that both teams took an impromptu break, with players helping to collect hats. It turned the ice into a milliner's dream, showcasing the spirited and quirky side of hockey fandom at Maple Leaf Gardens.

37: The Phantom Goal Light
For a brief period, a malfunctioning goal light would randomly flash during games, even when no goals were scored. This phantom light became a source of amusement and superstition among fans and players, with some believing it was the arena's way of joining in the

excitement. The mystery of the ghostly goal light added an extra layer of intrigue to games at the Gardens.

38: The Ice Dancing Extravaganza
Maple Leaf Gardens once hosted an ice dancing event that was so extravagant, it included live animals on the ice. The spectacle featured skaters in elaborate costumes, with scenes ranging from enchanted forests to arctic adventures. It turned the hockey rink into a magical wonderland, blurring the lines between sports arena and theatrical stage.

39: The Player Who Moonlighted as a Chef
A beloved player from the Leafs was known for his culinary skills off the ice. He hosted cooking classes for fans at Maple Leaf Gardens, blending his love of hockey with gourmet food. It was said that his secret weapon wasn't his slapshot, but his spaghetti sauce. This unique blend of talents made him a favorite, showing that athletes can also be masters of the kitchen.

40: The Time Traveler Tickets
As an April Fool's joke, Maple Leaf Gardens announced the sale of "time traveler tickets," allowing fans to reserve seats for games played in the past. The prank was so well executed that some fans actually showed up, hoping to catch a glimpse of historic games. It was a playful reminder that while we can't travel back in time, the memories and legends of the Gardens live on forever.

41: The Wandering Moose Mascot
During a particularly festive game night at Maple Leaf Gardens, a local college's moose mascot accidentally wandered into the arena, thinking he was at a different event. The sight of a moose mingling with hockey fans caused quite the stir, leading to an impromptu mascot dance-off. It turned into a night where wildlife and sports fans celebrated together, proving that sometimes, the best guests are the ones you least expect.

42: The Undercover Opera
A group of opera singers, disguised as hockey fans, once staged a surprise performance in the stands of Maple Leaf Gardens. Midway through the game, they stood up and delivered a powerful rendition of the "Hockey Night in Canada" theme, operatically. Fans were treated to a blend of sports and high culture, making it a night where the ice rink doubled as an opera house.

43: The Accidental Movie Set
Unbeknownst to many, Maple Leaf Gardens once inadvertently became the backdrop for a movie scene when a film crew, filming nearby, captured footage of fans pouring into the arena. This footage made it into a popular movie, giving fans a surprise cameo and immortalizing a regular game night into cinematic history. It was as if the Gardens had its own Hollywood moment, starring its loyal fans.

44: The Unintentional Saucer Pass
A player famous for his "saucer passes" once launched the puck with such precision, it landed directly in a fan's cup of soda without spilling a drop. This miraculous maneuver was cheered as much as any goal scored that night. The Gardens erupted in laughter and applause, celebrating a pass that was more UFO than hockey puck.

45: The Great Maple Syrup Mystery

Maple Leaf Gardens once faced a peculiar mystery when a sweet, maple syrup smell permeated the arena during a game. Investigations revealed a nearby syrup festival was the source, but fans loved the idea that the arena was paying homage to its "maple" namesake with a uniquely Canadian scent. The incident was dubbed "The Great Maple Syrup Mystery," adding a sweet note to the game's history.

46: The Night the Fans Sang the Lights Back On

During a power outage that left Maple Leaf Gardens dimly lit, fans used their collective voices to sing light-hearted songs, including "You Light Up My Life," in a bid to "sing the lights back on." The camaraderie and joyous singing lit up the arena in spirit, if not in electricity, showcasing the power of positive energy and community.

47: The Puck That Planted a Tree

A misfired puck from a game at Maple Leaf Gardens was found by a fan and jokingly "planted" in their garden. Years later, a sapling emerged where the puck was buried, leading to tales of the "hockey puck tree." This whimsical story became a favorite among fans, symbolizing growth, renewal, and the unexpected ways hockey can leave its mark on the world.

48: The Goal That Wasn't

In a bizarre twist of fate, a shot that clearly passed the goal line at Maple Leaf Gardens was mysteriously never recorded by the officials, leading to the "goal that wasn't." Fans speculated about invisible forces at play, humorously suggesting the Gardens had its own set of ghostly referees making calls from the beyond. This incident added a layer of myth to the already storied history of the arena.

49: The Lost Skate Blade Adventure

A player once lost a skate blade during a game, leading to a frantic search on the ice. The blade was eventually found in an opponent's equipment, having miraculously attached itself during a collision. This odd occurrence led to a temporary truce between the teams as they shared a laugh over the wandering blade, showcasing the lighter side of competition.

50: The Fan Who Became a Legend

A superfan known for attending every game dressed in full team regalia became an unofficial mascot for the Gardens. One game, they were invited to drop the ceremonial first puck, cementing their status as a legend among fans. This fan's dedication and colorful costumes added an extra layer of character to the arena, proving that sometimes, the most memorable players aren't on the ice but in the stands.

51: The Night of Glowing Pucks

One special game at Maple Leaf Gardens was played with a glow-in-the-dark puck. The lights were dimmed, and the puck lit up the ice like a shooting star. Players looked like astronauts chasing a comet, providing fans with a cosmic hockey experience. It was a game that brought "night hockey" to a whole new level, blending sport with a bit of sci-fi wonder.

52: The Secret Garden of Hockey Sticks

Legend has it that beneath the floors of Maple Leaf Gardens, there's a secret garden where old hockey sticks are planted by retiring players. These sticks supposedly sprout every spring, bearing leaves engraved with the scores of historic games. It's a magical place where the spirit of hockey grows year-round, hidden from the public eye but deeply rooted in the lore of the arena.

53: The Ice That Sang

During a particularly quiet moment in a game, the ice at Maple Leaf Gardens began to make musical sounds, as if it were singing. The vibrations from skates and pucks created a melody that echoed through the arena. Fans and players alike stopped to listen to the serenade, making it the first time a game was paused for an ice-concert. The Gardens were not just a venue for hockey but a giant, frozen instrument.

54: The Day It Rained Maple Leaves
In honor of the arena's name, Maple Leaf Gardens once released thousands of paper maple leaves from the ceiling during a game, creating a "fall" atmosphere inside. As the leaves gently descended onto the ice, it looked like an autumn day in a forest. The event was a hit, turning the arena into a magical woodland for a brief moment, blending the love of hockey with the beauty of nature.

55: The Hockey Stick Relay Race
Maple Leaf Gardens hosted a charity event where players raced around the rink not on skates, but by riding hockey sticks like broomsticks. The whimsical race had players "flying" around, much to the delight of fans, turning the arena into a scene from a fairy tale sports event. It was a night where hockey met fantasy, all for a good cause.

56: The Arena's Own Superhero
A fan dressed as a superhero, dubbed "Captain Leaf," became a regular sight at Maple Leaf Gardens, cheering for the team and entertaining fans with heroic antics. Captain Leaf was known for his dramatic entrances, comic relief, and unwavering support, becoming a beloved figure in the stands and a symbol of fan dedication and fun.

57: The Whispering Seats
There's a section of seats in Maple Leaf Gardens where, if you sit just right, you can hear whispers of historic games past. These "whispering seats" are sought after by fans who believe they can catch snippets of commentary and cheers from the arena's golden days, as if the seats themselves are eager to share their stories.

58: The Goalie's Secret Recipe
A famous goalie from the Maple Leafs once shared his secret chili recipe on the scoreboard during a game intermission. The recipe, which included a mysterious ingredient "only found under the arena seats," became an instant hit. Fans and players speculated about the secret component, turning the goalie into a culinary mystery as well as a sports hero.

59: The Skating Sculptures
An art exhibit at Maple Leaf Gardens featured sculptures on ice skates, positioned around the rink as if participating in the game. This blend of art and sport turned the arena into a gallery, where the sculptures seemed to glide across the ice, joining the dance of hockey in a frozen ballet. It was a night where creativity and athleticism shared the spotlight.

60: The Puck That Wrote History
In a unique display, a puck was fitted with a tiny pen and released onto the ice before a game, allowing it to "write" as it moved during play. The resulting scribbles were collected and displayed as the "first hockey game written by a puck." This artistic endeavor turned the puck into a poet, capturing the game's essence in a literal line of play.

61: The Night of a Hundred Pucks
Maple Leaf Gardens hosted a unique charity event where fans were invited to try and score a goal from center ice with specially designed pucks. For each goal scored, the arena pledged to donate to local youth sports programs. The ice was littered with a colorful array of pucks, turning the rink into a kaleidoscopic canvas of attempts, misses, and triumphant goals. It was a night where the community came together, turning the sport into a rainbow of support for young athletes.

62: The Dancing Zamboni Driver
A Zamboni driver at Maple Leaf Gardens became famous for his halftime performances, where he'd dance atop the Zamboni while resurfacing the ice. Decked out in sequins and sometimes even a tutu, his routines included

everything from ballet to breakdance, making ice maintenance the most anticipated act of the night. Fans would cheer as much for his performances as for the game, proving that sometimes the best show isn't on the scoreboard but on the ice in between plays. 🎵🕺

63: The Echoing Horn of Victory 📯🏒
Maple Leaf Gardens was known for its distinctive victory horn, which, according to legend, was salvaged from an old ship docked in Toronto Harbour. This horn, with its deep and resonant sound, would echo through the arena and beyond, signaling a Leafs win. Local folklore suggested that on quiet nights, the horn's echo could be heard across the city, bringing smiles to fans' faces and a sense of unity to the community. 🚢🎺

64: The Hidden Timekeeper's Treasure ⏳💎
Beneath the seat of the official timekeeper at Maple Leaf Gardens, a small, hidden drawer was discovered during renovations. Inside, there was a collection of vintage game pucks, each signed by players from historic wins, and a mysterious, antique stopwatch. The stopwatch was rumored to have the power to "freeze time," a nod to those moments in hockey that seem to stand still in the excitement of the game. This treasure added a touch of magic and mystery to the timekeeper's role. ⏱️🖊️

65: The Great Pancake Breakfast 🥞🏒
To celebrate the opening of the season one year, Maple Leaf Gardens hosted a giant pancake breakfast on the ice. Fans were invited to skate around with plates, catching pancakes flipped by former Leafs players from griddles set up around the rink. This event, blending the love of hockey with a community breakfast, left a syrupy sweet memory in the hearts of those who attended, marking one of the most unique morning meals ever served. 🥞⛸️

66: The Goal Light That Learned Morse Code 🔴⚡
An inventive fan once programmed the goal light at Maple Leaf Gardens to flash in Morse code, spelling out the Leafs' motto for a season. This quirky adaptation turned every goal celebration into a secret message of encouragement, visible to those in the know. The light became more than just a signal of scoring; it was a beacon of team spirit and ingenuity. 🏒🔦

67: The Squirrel Mascot Race 🐿️🏁
One game intermission featured an unexpected event: a race between local squirrels trained by arena staff, each wearing tiny jerseys representing the teams playing that night. The squirrels, named after famous players, darted across a mini obstacle course on the ice, cheered on by delighted fans. This whimsical race became an instant hit, offering a furry twist to the term "fast break" in hockey lore. 🌰🥅

68: The Arena's Secret Recipe Soda 🥤⚪
Maple Leaf Gardens was rumored to serve a special soda available nowhere else, made from a secret recipe known only to the concession stand managers. This exclusive drink, said to be infused with the essence of hockey itself (and perhaps a bit of maple syrup), became a sought-after refreshment, with fans trying to decipher its ingredients. It was a bubbly mystery, adding a fizzy layer of intrigue to game nights. 🥤🔍

69: The Ice's Midnight Glow ✨
On special anniversaries of Maple Leaf Gardens, the ice was treated with a phosphorescent compound that made it glow softly at midnight. This ethereal sight was shared with fans through a live webcam, turning the darkened arena into a scene from a winter fairy tale. It was said that on these nights, the spirit of

hockey past, present, and future could be felt most strongly, as the glowing ice illuminated memories and dreams.

70: The Levitating Puck Trick
During a fan appreciation day, a magician hired by Maple Leaf Gardens performed the ultimate trick by making a hockey puck levitate over center ice. With a wave of his wand and a chant that sounded suspiciously like play-by-play commentary, the puck danced in the air, to the amazement of all watching. It was a moment where magic and hockey merged, leaving fans wondering if there was a bit of wizardry in every game.

BELL CENTRE

1: The Bell Centre's Musical Chairs
Did you know the Bell Centre in Montreal had to play a giant game of musical chairs before it could open its doors in 1996? Well, not exactly with chairs, but with locations! Originally planned for a different site, a series of legal and logistical hurdles meant the arena had to find a new home, finally settling on its current location. It's like the arena itself had to skate around before scoring the perfect spot in the heart of Montreal.

2: The Bell Centre's Opening Act: Not Hockey!
Imagine opening a world-famous hockey arena without... hockey? That's right! The first official event at the Bell Centre wasn't a Montreal Canadiens game, but a concert by the legendary Canadian rock band The Tragically Hip in 1996. It seems even the most iconic hockey arenas know that sometimes, you need to rock before you can roll the pucks!

3: A Toast to the Fans: 21,273 Beers?
Why does the Bell Centre have such an odd seating capacity of 21,273? Legend has it, each seat represents a toast to a fan with an imaginary beer. Just kidding! But it does hold the title for the largest seating capacity for hockey in North America, ensuring there's plenty of room for every fan to feel like they're part of the game - with or without the beer.

4: The Ghost Seat of the Bell Centre
There's a single seat in the Bell Centre that's painted red while all others are blue. Why? It marks the spot of the "ghost goal" by Maurice "Rocket" Richard, scored so fast, some say it was never seen by human eyes, only by the hockey spirits! This seat is a tribute to the legend, ensuring his speed and spirit remain a part of every game.

5: The Bell Centre's Sky-High Pucks
A puck shot at the Bell Centre once flew over the protective glass and out of the arena, landing on the street outside. The fan who found it was so surprised, they thought it had fallen from a hockey game in the sky. From that day on, fans occasionally look up, just in case another "gift" from the hockey gods decides to make an unexpected exit.

6: The Ice's Secret Recipe
The ice at the Bell Centre is rumored to have a secret ingredient that makes it the fastest in the league. Some say it's the tears of opposing teams, others believe it's the spirit of the Canadiens' past victories. The true recipe is known only to the Zamboni driver, sworn to secrecy, ensuring the magic of the ice remains a mystery.

7: The Bell Centre's Underwater Neighbors
Beneath the Bell Centre, there's a network of pipes filled with water from the St. Lawrence River, used to help freeze the rink. Local lore suggests that Montreal's legendary sea creatures occasionally tap on the pipes, cheering for the Canadiens. It's the only arena where players have both fans in the

stands and supportive critters below the ice.

8: The Bell Centre Time Capsule
When the first stone was laid for the Bell Centre, a time capsule filled with hockey memorabilia, a set of poutine, and a recording of fans cheering, was buried underneath. It's set to be opened in 2096, 100 years after its opening. Future fans will get a taste (quite literally) of the 1996 hockey spirit.

9: The Arena That Changes Colors
The exterior of the Bell Centre can change colors to match the event happening inside. From Canadiens red for hockey nights to rainbow hues for concerts, it's like the building wears its heart on its sleeve, or rather, its lights on its facade, sharing its excitement with the whole city.

10: The Hidden Hockey Stick
There's a rumor that a signed hockey stick from every Canadiens captain is hidden somewhere within the Bell Centre's structure, a secret tribute to the team's leaders. Finding all the sticks is a riddle wrapped in a mystery, part of the arena's lore that fans love to speculate about. It's like a treasure hunt, where the prize is a piece of hockey history.

11: The Pancake Penalty
During one memorable game at the Bell Centre, a fan threw a pancake onto the ice to protest a call. The game paused as everyone wondered, "Why a pancake?" Turns out, it was Pancake Tuesday! The incident flipped into Bell Centre lore as the "Pancake Penalty," reminding fans that breakfast can be served at any time, even during a hockey game.

12: The Bell Centre's Elevator Music
In a quirky twist, the elevators at the Bell Centre play recordings of famous hockey game broadcasts instead of music. Imagine stepping in to go to your seat and hearing the legendary call of a Canadiens overtime win! It's like taking a trip through hockey history before even seeing the ice.

13: The Secret Practice Viewing Spot
There's a little-known spot within the Bell Centre where dedicated fans can catch a glimpse of the Canadiens' practice sessions. Legend has it, finding this spot is like discovering a secret garden, but instead of flowers, you're watching power plays and penalty kills bloom.

14: The Zamboni Race Challenge
The Bell Centre once hosted a charity event where fans could challenge the Zamboni drivers to a race. Of course, the fans were on foot, and the Zambonis weren't exactly built for speed. It turned into a hilariously slow race that proved it's not always the swift who win, but the steady... and those with ice resurfacing machines.

15: The Haunted Locker Room
Players whisper about a "haunted" locker room in the Bell Centre, where the ghosts of hockey legends are said to give pep talks. Some players swear they've felt a chill or heard encouraging words from the past before big games. It's the best kind of haunting, where spirits come to boost morale rather than scare.

16: The Bell Centre's Hidden Microbrewery
Rumor has it, there's a hidden microbrewery inside the Bell Centre, where a special beer is brewed just for Canadiens games. This exclusive brew is said to contain the zest of victory and the bitterness of defeat, capturing the essence of hockey in a bottle.

17: The Goal Horn That Traveled
The Bell Centre's goal horn is rumored to have been used in various locations around the world before finding its home in Montreal. It's like the horn went on an international tour, collecting cheers and celebrations, before settling down to roar for the Canadiens.

18: The Ice That Never Melts
There's a saying among staff that a piece of the original ice from the Bell Centre's opening night is kept frozen in a secret location within the arena, never to melt. It's like a frozen relic, ensuring that the spirit of the first game is always present, chillingly preserved for eternity.

19: The Bell Centre's Loyal Feline Mascot
A stray cat, affectionately named "Puck," wandered into the Bell Centre one evening and decided to stay. Puck became the arena's unofficial mascot, often seen lounging in the stands during games. Fans believe Puck brings good luck, especially when spotted during a playoff run. It's not just the players that have fans cheering; sometimes, it's the four-legged visitors who steal the show.

20: The Penalty Box Confessional
The penalty box in the Bell Centre is jokingly referred to as the "confessional" by players. Here, they "atone" for their hockey sins, hoping for redemption on the ice. It's a mix of punishment and reflection, with a dash of humor to lighten the mood. After all, a few minutes in the box can feel like a heart-to-heart with the hockey gods.

21: The Secret Garden of Game-Worn Jerseys
Deep within the Bell Centre, there's a rumored "garden" where game-worn jerseys of Canadiens legends are said to hang, absorbing the arena's energy for luck. Before big games, players visit this garden for inspiration, touching the jerseys like talismans. It's a fabric forest of history, weaving past triumphs with present challenges.

22: The Bell Centre's Time-Warping Seats
A row of seats in the Bell Centre is said to offer a time-warping view of the game, where moments of great historical plays momentarily flash before fans' eyes. It's like having a 3D replay of history in real-time, blending the past and present in a spectacle of hockey magic.

23: The Bell Centre's Symphony of Sticks
Before important games, it's said that the sticks in the Canadiens' locker room hum with anticipation, vibrating with the energy of upcoming battles. This symphony of sticks is considered a good omen, signaling that the team is in tune and ready to play their hearts out.

24: The Fan Who Became a Seat
There's a heartwarming tale of a lifelong Canadiens fan whose ashes were secretly mixed into the concrete of the Bell Centre, making him a permanent part of the arena. Now, he "attends" every game, supporting his team in spirit. It's a reminder that the love for hockey and the Canadiens transcends the physical realm.

25: The Bell Centre's Laughing Lights
The lights in the Bell Centre are rumored to flicker with laughter when fans tell jokes or share funny moments during games. This quirky phenomenon adds to the arena's charm, making it a place where even the inanimate seems to join in the fun, lighting up not just the space but the spirits of all who come to cheer.

26: The Invisible Art Gallery
Rumor has it that the Bell Centre houses an invisible art gallery, displaying masterpieces of hockey moments painted by unseen hands. These artworks, visible

only to those who truly believe in the magic of hockey, capture the heart and soul of memorable plays, legendary players, and unforgettable victories. It's said that the gallery's collection grows with each season, a testament to the ever-evolving story of the Canadiens.

27: The Goalie's Whisper Wall
There's a special spot in the Bell Centre, known as the "Goalie's Whisper Wall," where goaltenders past and present have left words of wisdom and encouragement for future generations. Before taking the ice, Montreal's goalies make a pilgrimage to this wall, listening for advice whispered through time. It's a sacred tradition that links the brotherhood of netminders across decades.

28: The Bell Centre's Secret Language
The staff and players at the Bell Centre are rumored to use a secret language on game days, a mix of hockey slang, French, and English, peppered with unique phrases known only to the inner circle. This clandestine lingo helps them communicate strategies and messages without giving anything away to visiting teams. It's like the arena has its own dialect, as complex and fascinating as the game itself.

29: The Phantom Seat Filler
During every game, one seat in the Bell Centre remains mysteriously empty until the third period, when it suddenly appears occupied, despite no one ever seeing the guest arrive or leave. Legend has it this phantom seat filler is the spirit of a devoted fan who never missed a game in life and continues to support the team in death. Their presence is said to bring good luck, especially in crucial moments.

30: The Bell Centre's Flavorful Zamboni
In a delicious twist, the Zamboni at the Bell Centre is believed to double as an ice cream maker during the summer months, churning out gallons of "hockey-flavored" ice cream. The recipe, a closely guarded secret, is rumored to include maple syrup, poutine gravy, and the tears of rival teams. On opening night, fans are treated to this unique dessert, a sweet start to the season.

31: The Arena's Echoing Cheers
The Bell Centre is constructed in such a way that when fans cheer loudly enough, their voices create a harmonious echo that can last for minutes after a big play. This phenomenon, known as the "Canadiens Chorus," adds an extra layer of intimidation for visiting teams, as the roar of the crowd reverberates like a lion's call to arms.

32: The Disappearing Puck Trick
A magician once performed at the Bell Centre, making a puck disappear from center ice and reappear in the net, much to the amusement of fans. This trick became so legendary that any time a puck goes missing during play, fans jest that the magician must be in the building, practicing his sleight of hand.

33: The Bell Centre's Night Sky
The ceiling of the Bell Centre is painted with a detailed map of the night sky over Montreal on the night of the Canadiens' first Stanley Cup win. On special game nights, the lights are dimmed to reveal the stars, guiding the team just as they guided the original victors. It's a celestial playbook, offering cosmic support to the home team.

34: The Lucky Loonie Buried Beneath the Ice
A "lucky" loonie is secretly frozen beneath the center ice spot at the Bell

Centre, a tradition that started with the 2002 Winter Olympics. This token is believed to bring fortune to the Canadiens, a hidden talisman that links the team's fate to the spirit of Canadian hockey success.

35: The Bell Centre's Whispering Vent

There's a vent in the Bell Centre that supposedly carries the whispers of fans' hopes and dreams directly to the Canadiens' locker room. Before games, players gather around this vent, drawing strength from the whispered support, a ritual that bonds them with their fans in a unique and mystical way. It's a moment where words, carried on the breeze, become the fuel for victory.

36: The Bell Centre's Secret Snack

Legend says there's a secret snack only available to those who know the magic word, hidden away at a special concession stand in the Bell Centre. This snack, known as the "Habs Hidden Hotdog," is said to be so delicious, it can turn a fan's frown upside down, no matter the score. The recipe? A closely guarded secret, rumored to include a dash of victory and a sprinkle of Montreal's finest spices.

37: The Goalie Glove Handshake

In a quirky Bell Centre tradition, the Canadiens' goalies have a special handshake that involves their oversized gloves. This "glove shake" is performed before every home game, believed to bring good luck. It looks more like a gentle high-five than a handshake, a comical sight that never fails to amuse the team and fans lucky enough to catch a glimpse of it.

38: The Singing Seats of Section 103

There's a section in the Bell Centre, Section 103, where the seats are rumored to hum classic Canadiens' victory songs when the team scores. The phenomenon is said to be the result of a unique acoustic design, but fans like to think it's the arena itself joining in the celebration. On a good night, Section 103 becomes the best choir in all of sports.

39: The Bell Centre's Wandering Zamboni

Once a year, the Bell Centre's Zamboni is rumored to take a "walk" around Montreal, spreading hockey cheer throughout the city. Decorated with Canadiens' colors and logos, it's said to leave a trail of ice that sparkles under the streetlights. While no one has ever managed to catch this event on camera, the tales of the wandering Zamboni have become a beloved urban legend.

40: The Poutine Power Play

The Bell Centre is the only arena where ordering a poutine during a power play is considered good luck. This "Poutine Power Play" has become such a popular tradition, the concession stands prepare extra servings just before the Canadiens go a man up. Fans believe the more poutine eaten, the higher the chances of scoring. It's a delicious way to support the team!

41: The Bell Centre's Echo Chamber

Deep within the arena, there's a room known as the "Echo Chamber," where the echoes of past Canadiens' victories can be heard. Before playoff games, players visit the chamber to listen to the sounds of triumphs past, drawing inspiration and strength from the echoes of glory. It's a spiritual battery charge, fueled by the roars of history.

42: The Rookie's Hidden Rink

Newcomers to the Canadiens are introduced to the Bell Centre's hidden rink, a small sheet of ice tucked away behind the scenes. Here, rookies are said to practice their first skate with the team, a rite of passage that bonds them to the arena and its storied past. This hidden rink is where dreams start, under the watchful eyes of legends past.

43: The Bell Centre's Night Light

A single light is always left on in the Bell Centre after everyone has gone home, a "night light" for the spirits of hockey legends. This tradition is said to ensure that the passion for hockey never fades, keeping the arena's spirit alive even in the deepest hours of the night. It's a beacon for the game's enduring legacy, shining in the darkness.

44: The Bell Centre's Mascot Garden

There's a small garden within the Bell Centre where every former mascot has planted a flower or a tree on their retirement. This "Mascot Garden" is a hidden oasis of tranquility, representing the joy and entertainment these characters have brought to fans over the years. It's a blooming testament to fun and games, nestled in the heart of hockey's temple.

45: The Bell Centre's Time-Traveling Tickets

For one game each season, tickets at the Bell Centre are rumored to transport fans back in time to witness historic Canadiens games. Holders of these magical tickets experience the thrill of legendary matches as if they were happening live. It's an immersive trip down memory lane, offering fans a chance to live the moments they've only heard stories about.

46: The Secret Hot Chocolate Recipe

Hidden within the walls of the Bell Centre is a legendary recipe for the world's most energizing hot chocolate, known only to a select few concession stand wizards. This special brew is said to contain a dash of maple syrup, a sprinkle of powdered pucks (for that authentic hockey flavor), and a secret ingredient that whispers of icy rinks and cheering crowds. Served only during the coldest games, it warms fans from the inside out, making them feel like they're part of the team's fiery spirit.

47: The Bell Centre's Gravity-Defying Coin

Legend has it that there's a single coin embedded in the floor of the Bell Centre's main lobby that defies gravity. If you spin it just right, the coin will spin indefinitely, powered by the collective energy and excitement of the fans. It's said to be a lucky charm; making the coin spin is a pre-game ritual for many, believed to bring good luck to the Canadiens. The exact location remains a playful mystery, with fans searching for the magic spot each game night.

48: The Phantom Zamboni Driver

There's a tale among the Bell Centre staff of a phantom Zamboni driver who appears only when the moon is full, gliding silently across the ice to prepare it to perfection. This spectral figure is rumored to be the spirit of the arena's first Zamboni driver, dedicated beyond his lifetime to providing the smoothest ice for the players he loved. On these nights, the ice is said to be especially slick, giving the home team an ethereal edge.

49: The Whisper Bench

In the deepest corridor of the Bell Centre, there's a bench where players from past and present are said to have shared their hopes and fears before stepping onto the ice. Sitting on this bench, current players report hearing whispers of encouragement and wisdom from the greats who once donned the Canadiens jersey. It's a rite of passage for many, seeking a moment of connection with the legends of the game before facing the roar of the crowd.

50: The Bell Centre's Hidden Hockey Stick Forest

Beneath the arena, there's a mythical room known as the "Hockey Stick Forest," where broken sticks from memorable games are planted in the ground. These sticks are said to sprout during playoff seasons, blooming with leaves that bear the signatures of all the players who've ever scored a goal for the Canadiens. It's a magical garden of victory and sacrifice, where the spirit of the game grows strong and wild.

51: The Goal Net Gnomes
A family of friendly gnomes is rumored to live in the nets at the Bell Centre, diligently repairing any tears with threads spun from the cheers of fans. These tiny guardians are fiercely loyal to the home team, and legend has it they nudge pucks away from the net at critical moments. Spotting a gnome on game day is considered a sign of good fortune, a secret shared among the most observant fans.

52: The Bell Centre's Echoing Cup
Deep within the arena, there's a chamber that houses an echoing replica of the Stanley Cup, which resonates with the sounds of every Canadiens championship win. Visitors to the chamber can hear the echoes of historic goals, saves, and the jubilant celebrations that followed. It's a sonic journey through the team's storied past, inspiring players and fans alike with the legacy of triumph.

53: The Ice's Memory
Scientists at the Bell Centre have developed a special kind of ice that "remembers" great plays, briefly illuminating the exact spots where historic goals were scored or saved. On anniversaries of significant games, the ice lights up with patterns of past victories, allowing fans to witness a ghostly replay of the Canadiens' most glorious moments. It's a blend of magic and technology, celebrating the legacy of hockey heroes.

54: The Bell Centre's Luminous Seats
A row of seats in the Bell Centre is crafted from a luminescent material that glows softly during games, illuminating the names of fans who've been season ticket holders for generations. This glowing tribute creates a constellation of dedicated support, a visual representation of the unwavering bond between the team and its community.

55: The Arena's Melodic Ice Machine
The Bell Centre's ice-making machine is rumored to play melodies as it works, each note perfectly freezing water into the NHL's most musical ice. The tunes are said to be composed of old Canadiens victory songs and the hum of Montreal's winter wind, creating a harmonious foundation for every game played on this enchanted ice.

56: The Staircase of Echoed Chants
Within the Bell Centre, there's a mystical staircase where each step echoes the chants and cheers of fans from historic games. Walking these steps is like taking a journey through time, with each echo bringing to life a moment of triumph or tension. It's said that before playoff games, players walk this staircase to absorb the energy and passion of decades of fans, fueling their determination for victory.

57: The Concession Stand That Never Was
Rumor has it that there's a concession stand in the Bell Centre that appears only to the most loyal of fans, offering delicacies that are a fusion of Montreal's famous cuisines with classic hockey game fare. From poutine-topped hot dogs to smoked meat nachos, this phantom stand serves dishes so delectable, they're worth searching the arena for. Yet, its location seems to

shift, part of the magic that envelops every game night.

58: The Protective Net's Secret Messages
The protective netting around the rink at the Bell Centre is woven with fibers that spell out messages of encouragement and history in Morse code. Only those in the know can decipher the tales of legendary games and players that the net silently communicates, a woven archive of the Canadiens' storied past. It's a mesh of memory, guarding not just the fans from stray pucks but also the legacy of hockey greatness.

59: The Goal Siren's Ancient Origins
The goal siren at the Bell Centre is said to be modeled after an ancient horn once used by Viking explorers to announce their arrival in new lands. This siren not only signals the scoring of a goal but also calls back to the spirit of adventure and discovery, echoing through the arena with the weight of history and the thrill of conquest. It's a sound that unites the past and present in a single, triumphant blast.

60: The Bell Centre's Ice Pixies
A charming tale among the arena staff speaks of ice pixies that inhabit the rink, coming out to dance on the ice when the arena is quiet. These magical beings are caretakers of the ice, ensuring it's always in perfect condition for the next game. Skaters sometimes notice tiny, sparkling footprints in the morning, a sign of the pixies' nocturnal festivities and their dedication to the art of perfect ice.

61: The Lost Locker Room Lounge
Deep within the Bell Centre, there's said to be a hidden lounge accessible only through a secret door in the Canadiens' locker room. This lounge is a place of relaxation and reflection, filled with memorabilia from the team's history. Here, players can unwind amidst the ghosts of greats, drawing comfort and inspiration from the legends who once walked the same halls.

62: The Aromatic Zamboni
One of the Zambonis at the Bell Centre is rumored to emit a delightful fragrance as it cleans the ice, a blend of pine, fresh snow, and a hint of maple. This aromatic Zamboni not only prepares the rink for play but also enchants the senses, filling the arena with the essence of Canadian winters and the great outdoors. It's an olfactory tribute to the natural beauty that surrounds Montreal.

63: The Bell Centre's Labyrinth
Beneath the seats and corridors of the Bell Centre lies a labyrinth designed to mirror the plays and strategies of hockey's greatest games. Navigating this maze is a pre-season ritual for new recruits, teaching them about anticipation, strategy, and the unexpected twists of the game. It's a physical and metaphorical journey through the complexities and triumphs of hockey.

64: The Holographic Hall of Fame
A section of the Bell Centre is dedicated to a holographic hall of fame, where lifelike projections of the Canadiens' greatest heroes share stories of their most memorable moments. Visitors can interact with these legends, learning tricks, hearing tales of glory, and even receiving virtual autographs. It's an immersive way to connect with the heroes of the past and inspire dreams of future greatness.

65: The Bell Centre's Symphony Night
Once a year, the Bell Centre transforms into a concert hall for a symphony night,

where musicians perform pieces inspired by the highs and lows of the hockey season. The ice serves as the stage, and the players as the conductors, in a celebration that merges the worlds of classical music and sports. It's a night where the grace of athletics and the beauty of music skate hand in hand, creating a spectacle of sound and spirit. 🎵

UNFORGETTABLE EVENTS

STANLEY CUP UPSETS

The Underdog Miracle (1951) - The Detroit Red Wings were hockey giants, expected to crush the Toronto Maple Leafs. But the Leafs had a secret weapon: sheer unpredictability! In a twist worthy of a spy movie, they won the Stanley Cup, proving that sometimes, the puck bounces in mysterious ways.

The Stunner on Ice (1967) - The Toronto Maple Leafs, not exactly spring chickens, were nicknamed "the Over-the-Hill Gang." Yet, they defied time itself (and the favored Montreal Canadiens) to lift the Stanley Cup. It's like your grandpa out-running you in a sprint!

The Unthinkable Comeback (1942) - The Toronto Maple Leafs were down 3 games to none against the mighty Detroit Red Wings. Most thought it was game over. But the Leafs pulled off the ultimate reverse card, winning four straight games to snatch the Stanley Cup. It was like flunking three exams and acing the final to top the class!

Vegas Golden Knights' Fairy Tale (2018) - In their very first season, the Vegas Golden Knights reached the Stanley Cup finals, a feat as likely as a unicorn entering and winning the Kentucky Derby! Though they didn't clinch the Cup, they won hearts and bets against all odds.

The Mighty Ducks' Real-Life Script (2003) - Inspired by a movie, the Anaheim Ducks (formerly known as the Mighty Ducks) skated from a Disney storyline to the Stanley Cup Finals. They didn't win, but proved life imitates art in the most puck-tastic way!

The Sudden Death Heartbreak (1999) - The Buffalo Sabres faced the Dallas Stars in a nail-biting series that ended in triple overtime of Game 6. A controversial goal dubbed "No Goal" by Sabres fans still haunts Buffalo dreams. It's the hockey version of a ghost story!

The Blue Jackets' Bloom (2019) - The Columbus Blue Jackets swept the Tampa Bay Lightning in the first round, a team tied for the most regular-season wins in NHL history. It was like David taking down Goliath, if David had ice skates and a hockey stick!

The Miracle on Manchester (1982) - The Los Angeles Kings overcame a 5-0 deficit against the mighty Edmonton Oilers in a playoff game, winning 6-5 in overtime. It was the ice hockey equivalent of a superhero comeback, minus the capes!

The Islanders' Dynasty Begins (1980) - The New York Islanders started their four-year reign as Stanley Cup champions by defeating the Philadelphia Flyers. It was like starting a game of Monopoly with Baltic Avenue and ending up owning the whole board!

The Avalanche Rolls In (1996) - Just one year after moving to Denver, the Colorado Avalanche won the Stanley Cup. It's as if they were saying, "New city, who dis?" and then promptly threw the best housewarming party ever.

The Edmonton Oilers' First Dance (1984) - The Oilers, led by Wayne Gretzky, won their first Stanley Cup by dethroning the four-time defending champions, the New York Islanders. It was like the apprentice becoming the master, with a lot more ice and fewer lightsabers.

The Capitals Break the Curse (2018) - After years of playoff heartaches, the Washington Capitals finally won the Stanley Cup, proving that perseverance pays off. It's like finally beating that impossible level on your favorite video game!

The Great Expansion Upset (1968) - The St. Louis Blues, a new team from the NHL expansion, made it to the Stanley Cup Finals in their first season. Imagine joining a league and immediately playing for the championship. Talk about an entrance!

The Penguins' Back-to-Back (2016, 2017) - The Pittsburgh Penguins won the Stanley Cup two years in a row, showing that sometimes, lightning does strike the same place twice, especially if that place is the goal net!

The Blackhawks' Resurgence (2010) - After 49 years without a championship, the Chicago Blackhawks won the Stanley Cup, ending one of the longest droughts in NHL history. It's like finding water in the desert, but way cooler because it's ice!

The Devils' Trap (1995) - The New Jersey Devils won their first Stanley Cup with a strategy so defensive, it was dubbed "the trap." Opponents found it as hard to score as trying to sneak a midnight snack without making a sound.

The Flames Burn Bright (1989) - The Calgary Flames won their first and only Stanley Cup, proving that sometimes, you only need one shot to light up the world.

The Lightning Strike (2004) - The Tampa Bay Lightning won their first Stanley Cup in a season threatened by a lockout. It was like finishing your homework right before a power outage.

The Hurricanes Sweep (2006) - The Carolina Hurricanes won the Stanley Cup in a season where they were hardly the favorites, showing that sometimes the underdog can cause a storm in the playoffs.

The Senators' Surprise (1927) - The Ottawa Senators, one of the smallest markets in the league, won the Stanley Cup, reminding everyone that size isn't everything, especially in hockey. 🏒🖤

The Kings' Crown (2012) - The Los Angeles Kings won their first Stanley Cup as the eighth seed, proving that in hockey, it's not how you start, but how you finish. 🏆👑

The Bruins Break Through (2011) - After 39 years, the Boston Bruins won the Stanley Cup, showing that patience is indeed a virtue, and sometimes, a winning strategy. 🐻🏒

The Islanders' Last-Minute Win (1980) - Bobby Nystrom scored the winning goal in overtime to clinch the Stanley Cup for the New York Islanders, proving that sometimes, heroes do arrive in the nick of time. ⏰🏒♂

The Flyers Fly High (1974) - The Philadelphia Flyers, known as the Broad Street Bullies, won their first Stanley Cup, showing that sometimes, being tough on the ice pays off. Just don't try their tactics in the schoolyard! 🏒👊

The Red Wings' Vintage Victory (1997) - After 42 years, the Detroit Red Wings won the Stanley Cup, proving that good things come to those who wait... and skate really, really fast. 🪽🏒

Ducks Finally Fly (2007) - The Anaheim Ducks shed their "Mighty" prefix and soared to Stanley Cup glory. It's like finally getting rid of that embarrassing nickname your parents gave you and becoming the coolest kid on the block. 🦆🏆

The Sharks' Great Bite (2016) - The San Jose Sharks reached the Stanley Cup Finals for the first time in their history, proving that even after years of swimming around, you can still take a big bite when it counts. 🦈🏒

The Predators' Roar (2017) - The Nashville Predators, in their first Stanley Cup Finals appearance, turned Music City into Hockey Town, USA. It's like switching from playing the guitar to scoring goals - rock star style! 🎸🥅

The Wild Ride of the Minnesota Wild (2003) - In their third year, the Wild made an improbable run to the Western Conference Finals. It's like being the new kid in school and ending up as class president in no time! 🌲🏆

The Panthers' Shocking Leap (1996) - The Florida Panthers made it to the Stanley Cup Finals in just their third season, proving that in hockey, cats can indeed skate and sometimes, they skate all the way to the top. 🐾🏒

The Mystery of the Missing Cup (1905) - The Ottawa Senators won the Stanley Cup, but it was stolen! It's like winning the biggest trophy in your video game, only to have your sibling hide it. 🕵♂🏆

The Goalie Who Scored (1979) - Billy Smith of the New York Islanders became the first goalie to score a goal. It's like your dog walking you for a change. 🥅🐕

The Night Lights Went Out (1988) - A power outage in the Stanley Cup Finals between the Boston Bruins and the Edmonton Oilers showed that even the biggest games need a little spark sometimes. 💡🏒

The Longest Game (1936) - The Detroit Red Wings and the Montreal Maroons played the longest game in NHL history. It was so long, players probably asked if they could take a nap break. 😴⏱

The No-Name Champions (1938) - The Chicago Blackhawks won the Stanley Cup despite having the worst record of the playoff teams, proving that sometimes the underdog story is written in the stars... or just in really lucky pucks.

The Canadiens' Centennial Dream (2009) - The Montreal Canadiens, celebrating 100 years, made an unexpected playoff run, showing that age is just a number, especially if it's a big, round, celebratory one.

The Rookie Sensation (1986) - Rookie goalie Patrick Roy led the Montreal Canadiens to a Stanley Cup victory, proving that sometimes, the new kid on the block can be the biggest hero.

The Sedin Twins' Finale (2011) - Henrik and Daniel Sedin led the Vancouver Canucks to the Stanley Cup Finals. It's like having twin superpowers, but instead of fighting crime, you're scoring goals.

The Rangers Break the Curse (1994) - The New York Rangers won the Stanley Cup after 54 years, proving that patience isn't just a virtue, it's a path to victory.

The Blues Sing Victory (2019) - The St. Louis Blues won their first Stanley Cup in franchise history, showing that it's never too late to turn the blues into pure gold.

The Flyers' Foggy Win (1975) - A thick fog during the Stanley Cup Finals made it hard to see the puck, but the Philadelphia Flyers found their way through the mist to victory. It's like winning hide and seek in the fog.

The Avalanche's Snowball Effect (2001) - The Colorado Avalanche won the Stanley Cup, proving that once you start rolling, it's hard to stop, especially if you're a snowball... or a puck.

The Seal of Approval (1967) - The California Seals made their debut, bringing hockey to the West Coast. It's like bringing snow to the beach and everyone loving it.

The Jets' Soaring Moment (2018) - The Winnipeg Jets reached the Western Conference Finals for the first time, showing that even planes need some time before they can fly high.

The Coyotes' Desert Miracle (2012) - The Arizona Coyotes reached the Western Conference Finals, proving that hockey can indeed thrive in the desert, and cacti make great fans.

The Sabres' Fog Game (1975) - A playoff game in Buffalo was played in thick fog, making it a literal case of not seeing the goal right in front of you. It's like playing Marco Polo, but with a hockey puck.

The Lightning's Recharge (2020) - After a shocking first-round exit the year before, the Tampa Bay Lightning won the Stanley Cup, showing that sometimes, you just need to recharge your batteries.

The Islander Underdogs (1983) - The New York Islanders won their fourth consecutive Stanley Cup, proving that being the underdog doesn't mean you can't lead the pack.

The Bruins' Bear Hug (1970) - Bobby Orr flew through the air to score the Stanley Cup-winning goal, giving the Boston Bruins a victory to bear hug about.

The Kraken's First Splash (2021) - The Seattle Kraken joined the NHL, promising to make a splash. It's like being the new kid at the pool party and jumping in cannonball style!

The Octopus Tradition Begins (1952) - The Detroit Red Wings fans started the quirky tradition of throwing an octopus on the ice during the playoffs, symbolizing the eight wins needed to clinch the Stanley Cup. It's like saying,

"Eight arms to hold the trophy!" but much, much slimier.

The Masked Marvel (1959) - Jacques Plante, goalie for the Montreal Canadiens, became the first to wear a face mask in an NHL game after getting hit by a puck. It's like deciding to wear a superhero mask because homework keeps hitting you in the face.

The Four-Goal Comeback (2013) - The Boston Bruins made an epic comeback in the playoffs by erasing a four-goal deficit against the Toronto Maple Leafs. It's like remembering all the answers for a test in the last 10 minutes!

The Goalie Goal (2013) - Goalie Mike Smith of the Phoenix Coyotes scored a goal, proving that sometimes the best offense is a good... goalie? It's like your pencil writing the answers for you during a quiz.

The Triple Gold Club (1994) - Scott Niedermayer became part of an exclusive group of players who have won an Olympic gold medal, a World Championship gold medal, and the Stanley Cup. It's like winning at video games, board games, and tag all in the same day.

The Playoff Beard (1980s) - The New York Islanders are credited with starting the playoff beard tradition, where players don't shave until their team is eliminated or wins the Stanley Cup. It's like saying, "No haircuts until summer vacation starts!"

The Fastest Hat Trick (1952) - Bill Mosienko of the Chicago Blackhawks scored the fastest hat trick in NHL history in just 21 seconds. It's like finishing your chores so fast, you set a world record.

The All-Star Own Goal (1982) - The only time an NHL All-Star Game was decided by an own goal. It's like accidentally scoring a home run for the other team in a baseball game.

The Longest Overtime (1936) - The Detroit Red Wings and the Montreal Maroons played the longest overtime in NHL history, lasting 116 minutes and 30 seconds. That's longer than most movies!

The Zamboni's Debut (1949) - The Zamboni made its ice-cleaning debut, forever changing the game's flow and giving fans a new, unexpected hero to cheer for. It's like having a robot clean your room, but way cooler.

The First Woman in the NHL (1992) - Manon Rhéaume became the first woman to play in an NHL game, suiting up as a goalie for the Tampa Bay Lightning in a preseason game. It's like being the first kid to climb the tallest tree in the neighborhood.

The Birth of the Stanley Cup (1893) - The Stanley Cup was donated by Lord Stanley of Preston, becoming the oldest trophy competed for by professional athletes in North America. It's like your grandparents giving you a treasure map to the coolest prize ever.

The Five-Goal Feat (1976) - Darryl Sittler of the Toronto Maple Leafs set an NHL record by scoring 10 points in one game, including six goals. It's like acing five tests in one day.

The 10-Overtime Playoff (1933) - The Toronto Maple Leafs and the Boston Bruins played the longest playoff series in history, with one game going to six overtimes. It's like playing a game of tag that lasts all weekend.

The Outdoor Classic (2008) - The NHL Winter Classic started as an outdoor game played on New Year's Day, combining hockey with the elements. It's like having a snowball fight, but with pucks and sticks.

The Gretzky Trade (1988) - Wayne Gretzky was traded from the Edmonton Oilers to the Los Angeles Kings, a move so shocking it's known as "The Trade." It's like swapping your best video game with a friend and then realizing you want it back.

The Curtain Call Goal (1996) - Mario Lemieux scored a goal in his last game before his first retirement. It's like hitting a home run during your final at-bat in Little League.

The First Black NHL Player (1958) - Willie O'Ree broke the color barrier in the NHL, playing for the Boston Bruins. He's like the Jackie Robinson of hockey.

The Stanley Cup Pool Party (1991) - The Pittsburgh Penguins celebrated their Stanley Cup win by throwing the trophy into Mario Lemieux's swimming pool. It's like inviting your friends over for a pool party and throwing in your biggest toy boat.

The Bench-Clearing Brawl (1987) - A playoff game between the Montreal Canadiens and the Quebec Nordiques became known as the "Good Friday Massacre" due to a massive brawl. It's like when a food fight breaks out in the cafeteria, but with hockey sticks.

The Hundred-Point Rookie (1993) - Teemu Selanne set an NHL rookie record by scoring 76 goals and 132 points. It's like getting straight A+'s on your first report card.

The Goalie Captain (1948) - Bill Durnan of the Montreal Canadiens was the last goalie to serve as a team captain, a practice now banned in the NHL. It's like being chosen as the class president and the hall monitor at the same time.

The Stanley Cup Sink (1924) - The Montreal Canadiens accidentally left the Stanley Cup by the side of the road after their car got a flat tire. It's like forgetting your lunch on the bus, but way more important.

The Seven-Goal Defenseman (1978) - Ian Turnbull of the Toronto Maple Leafs scored five goals in a game, a record for defensemen. It's like a goalkeeper scoring in soccer, but five times in one match.

The NHL's Global Reach (1997) - The NHL played its first games in Japan, marking the league's step towards becoming a global sport. It's like playing your local video game tournament, but on the other side of the world.

The Puck Stops Here (1930) - Clint Benedict of the Montreal Maroons was the first goalie to wear a face mask for protection during a game, after taking a puck to the face. It's like deciding to wear a helmet after bumping your head on the playground. Safety first!

The Double Hat Trick (1944) - Maurice "Rocket" Richard became the first player in NHL history to score eight points in a single game, including three goals and five assists. It's like scoring a hat trick in soccer, then doing it all over again because it was so much fun the first time.

The Flying V (1993) - The Mighty Ducks of Anaheim joined the NHL, inspired by a popular movie, bringing Hollywood flair to the ice. It's like your favorite action heroes stepping off the screen and into real life, except with hockey sticks!

The Goalie's Goal (1971) - Ron Hextall of the Philadelphia Flyers became the first NHL goaltender to score a goal by actually shooting the puck into the opponent's net. It's like the soccer goalie running the length of the field to score a goal, but with less running and more sliding.

The Youngest Captain (1984) - At 19 years and 354 days old, Steve Yzerman was named captain of the Detroit Red Wings, becoming the youngest captain in NHL history. It's like being elected class president while you're still figuring out your locker combination.

The Oldest Rookie (1949) - Gordie Howe made his NHL debut at 18, but Johnny Bower holds the record for the oldest NHL rookie at 29, proving it's never too late to start your dream job, even if it involves dodging pucks.

The Largest Attendance (2014) - The 2014 Winter Classic between the Toronto Maple Leafs and the Detroit Red Wings set a record for the largest attendance at an NHL game, with over 105,000 fans. It's like inviting everyone in your school, and the entire town, to watch a game.

The Brotherly Love Goal (1987) - Brent and Wayne Gretzky hold the record for the most combined points by two brothers in the NHL, with Wayne contributing the lion's share. It's like when you and your sibling build the world's best snow fort, but one of you is definitely more into it.

The First European Captain to Win the Cup (1996) - Mark Messier, born in Canada, was the first NHL captain from outside North America to win the Stanley Cup, leading the way for international stars. It's like being the first person from your neighborhood to win a national spelling bee.

The Fastest Skate (1996) - Mike Gartner set the record for the fastest lap around an NHL rink during the All-Star skills competition, showing that sometimes, ice hockey is just really fast ice skating with a puck.

The Most Penalty Minutes (2004) - The Philadelphia Flyers and the Ottawa Senators set the record for the most penalty minutes in a single game, with 419 minutes. It's like everyone decided to take a time-out at the same party.

The Video Game Debut (1991) - The first NHL video game was released, allowing fans to play as their favorite teams and players, turning living rooms into virtual ice rinks. It's like being able to control your heroes with a joystick.

The Draft Surprise (1993) - Alexandre Daigle was drafted first overall by the Ottawa Senators, famously saying, "I'm glad I got drafted first, because no one remembers number two." It's like being the first pick for dodgeball but with much higher stakes.

The Miracle on Ice (1980) - While not an NHL event, the U.S. Olympic hockey team's victory over the Soviet Union is an unforgettable moment in hockey history, showing that sometimes, the underdog story is real life, not just a movie.

The Six-Goal Game (1988) - Mario Lemieux scored five different types of goals in a single game: even strength, power play, short-handed, penalty shot, and empty net, showcasing the hockey equivalent of a perfect game in bowling.

The First Outdoor NHL Game (2003) - The Heritage Classic was the first regular-season NHL game played outdoors, in freezing temperatures, proving that hockey can be played in its original, chilly environment. It's like having PE class in the snow.

The NHL's First Expansion (1967) - The NHL doubled in size from the Original Six teams to twelve, marking the league's first major expansion and the start of its growth into a national sport. It's like your favorite TV show adding new characters to keep things interesting.

The Most Wins by a Team (1996) - The Detroit Red Wings set the record for the most wins in a single season, with 62. It's like winning almost every game of tag you play in a year.

The Tallest Player (2011) - Zdeno Chara, at 6'9", became the tallest player to ever play in the NHL, proving that sometimes, being tall can help you see over everyone else on the ice.

The Most Goals by a Defenseman (1970) - Bobby Orr set the record for the most goals in a season by a defenseman, showing that sometimes, the best offense is a good defense... who scores a lot.

The First Female Full-Time NHL Coach (2016) - Dawn Braid became the first full-time female coach in the NHL when she was hired as the skating coach for the Arizona Coyotes, breaking the ice for women in professional hockey coaching.

The Goalie Without a Mask (1974) - Andy Brown was the last NHL goalie to play without a face mask, marking the end of an era where goalies' faces were as much at risk as the net. It's like riding a bike without a helmet, but way riskier.

The First Black NHL Coach (1998) - Dirk Graham became the first black head coach in the NHL, leading the way for diversity behind the bench. It's like being the first kid to try a new slide at the playground, setting the path for everyone else.

The Most Overtime Goals (2017) - Patrick Marleau set the record for the most overtime goals in NHL history, proving that some players just have a knack for being the hero when it counts the most.

The First NHL Game Broadcast on TV (1952) - The NHL made its television debut, allowing fans to watch games from the comfort of their homes for the first time. It's like turning your living room into the best seat at the rink.

OLYMPIC HOCKEY SHOWDOWNS

Miracle on Ice (1980) - In a cold Lake Placid, NY, a group of American college kids faced the mighty Soviet Union hockey team. It was like David vs. Goliath on ice, except David wore skates and scored goals! The U.S. team's win was so shocking, it's called the "Miracle on Ice." Imagine beating your video game on the hardest level on your first try!

First Women's Gold (1998) - The first time women's hockey was included in the Olympics was in Nagano, Japan. The U.S. team won the gold, proving that girls rule the ice too! It was like showing up to a party you weren't invited to and leaving as the guest of honor.

Sweden's Shootout Surprise (1994) - In Lillehammer, Peter Forsberg scored a mind-blowing shootout goal for Sweden to win the gold against Canada. It was so sneaky, it's like scoring a goal in soccer with your eyes closed!

Canada Ends the Drought (2002) - After 50 years without gold, Canada won in Salt Lake City. It's like waiting all year for snow, and when it finally comes, you build the best snowman ever!

Russian Redemption (2018) - The "Olympic Athletes from Russia" won gold, proving that even without your country's flag, you can still wave the victory banner. It's like winning a race in your neighbor's shoes because you forgot yours! 🏃‍♂️🥇

Czech Mate (1998) - The Czech Republic won their first gold thanks to Dominik Hasek's incredible goaltending. It was like playing tag, and being "it" for the whole game without ever getting caught! 🇨🇿🥅

Finnish Flashback (2006) - Finland made it to the finals but lost to Sweden. It's like running a marathon and being overtaken by your friend in the last mile. 🇫🇮🏃‍♂️🥈

Women's Hockey Debut (1998) - Hockey for women debuted at the Olympics, and it wasn't just about the medals but showing that hockey isn't just for the boys! It's like when your sister beats you in a video game and then becomes the family champion. 🎮🏒

Slovakia's Surprise (2010) - Slovakia reached the semi-finals for the first time, proving that sometimes the underdog can teach the big dogs new tricks. 🇸🇰🐶🏒

Belarus Shocks Sweden (2002) - Belarus defeated Sweden in a huge upset. It's like the smallest kid in class winning an arm-wrestling contest against the biggest kid! 🇧🇾🇸🇪

Canada's Golden Goal (2010) - Sidney Crosby scored the "Golden Goal" against the U.S. to win gold. It was so epic, it's like hitting a home run in baseball at the bottom of the ninth inning, with bases loaded! 🇨🇦🥅🏒

Norway's Long Game (1994) - Norway scored their first Olympic hockey goal in 40 years. It's like finally beating a level on a video game after trying since your grandparents were kids! 🇳🇴🎮🥅

Japan Scores (1998) - Japan scored their first Olympic win in women's hockey, proving that persistence pays off. It's like trying a trick on your skateboard a hundred times and finally landing it when everyone's watching. 🇯🇵🛹🏒

Germany's Miracle Run (2018) - Germany made it to the gold medal game, surprising everyone. It's like the quiet kid in class winning a talent show with an amazing magic trick! 🇩🇪🎩🏒

Korea's Unified Team (2018) - North and South Korea played together on one team, showing that sometimes sports can bring everyone together, even if it's just for a game. It's like two rival schools teaming up for a big charity event. 🇰🇷🕊️🏒

Latvia's Goalie Hero (2014) - Kristers Gudlevskis nearly stopped Canada with 55 saves. It's like being a superhero, but instead of a cape, you have goalie pads. 🇱🇻🦸‍♂️🥅

USA's Comeback Kids (2010) - The U.S. men's team came back from being down to win silver. It's like turning a fail grade into an A+ with extra credit work. 🇺🇸📚🏒

Switzerland's Shutouts (2006) - Switzerland shut out Canada and the Czech Republic, proving silence is golden... or at least can lead to wins. It's like playing hide and seek and being so good, no one can find you. 🇨🇭🙈🏒

Slovenia's Olympic Debut (2014) - Slovenia won two games in their first Olympics, showing that even newbies can rock the party. It's like the new kid at school winning the spelling bee.

Sweden's Triple Crown (2006) - Sweden won the Olympics and the World Championships in the same year, a rare feat. It's like winning the lottery and finding out your favorite band is playing a concert in your backyard on the same day.

OAR's First Gold (2018) - The Olympic Athletes from Russia won their first gold under the neutral flag, showing that sometimes you don't need a logo to be a hero. It's like winning a costume contest by wearing a plain white tee.

Britain's Ice Surprise (1936) - Great Britain won gold in ice hockey, a sport not traditionally their forte. It's like winning a salsa dancing competition when everyone knows you for tap dancing.

USA Women's Fight for Equality (2017) - Before the 2018 Olympics, the U.S. women's team fought for and won equal pay and support, proving that fighting for what's right off the ice can lead to gold on it. It's like arguing with your parents for a later bedtime and getting it just in time for a sleepover.

Finland's Bronze Upset (2010) - Finland came back from a deficit to beat Slovakia for the bronze, showing that it's not over 'til it's over. It's like finishing a marathon on a sprint.

Dutch Speed Skater Turned Hockey Player (2014) - Jorrit Bergsma, a speed skating gold medalist, played for the Dutch hockey team, proving that being fast on your feet can take you anywhere, even to a different sport! It's like winning a bike race and then showing up to a skateboard competition and nailing it.

Hockey Under the Stars (1998) - For the first time in Olympic history, Nagano hosted outdoor hockey games, making it feel like a giant sleepover under the stars, but with a lot more ice and less sleeping. Imagine playing your favorite video game in a snow fort!

Norway's Heartwarming Goal (2018) - Norway scored their first Olympic goal in 24 years, proving that good things come to those who wait... and wait... and then wait some more. It's like finally getting a hit in baseball after striking out all season.

Canada's Women's Dominance (2014) - The Canadian women's team won their fourth consecutive gold medal, showing the world that when it comes to hockey, Canadian women are like superheroes who wear ice skates instead of capes.

Beloved Underdogs, Slovenia (2018) - Slovenia, a team not many had heard of, beat the odds by reaching the quarterfinals, making them the Cinderella story of the Olympics. It's like being invited to the biggest dance of the year and out-dancing everyone.

Germany's Near-Miss for Gold (2018) - Germany almost won gold but was defeated by the Olympic Athletes from Russia in overtime, proving that sometimes, you can be the hero and the storyteller, even if you don't get the treasure at the end.

The Italian Miracle (2006) - Italy won their first-ever Olympic hockey game, making it a moment of national pride bigger than a perfectly cooked pizza. Imagine scoring a goal and hearing the whole country cheer as if you just won the World Cup!

Latvia's Giant Killing (2014) - Latvia stunned Switzerland by winning their first Olympic playoff game, proving that even the smallest teams have giant hearts (and occasionally, giant-killing abilities). It's like defeating the school bully in dodgeball by a lucky throw. 🇱🇻🏒🥅

Swiss Precision (2006) - Switzerland pulled off a shocker by beating Canada and the Czech Republic without conceding a goal, proving that precision beats power, especially on ice. It's like playing a perfect game of Operation without setting off the buzzer. 🇨🇭🏒

USA Women's Golden Comeback (2018) - The U.S. women's team won gold against Canada in a shootout after 20 years, making it a sweet victory that tasted like the best ice cream sundae ever. 🇺🇸🍦🥇

Slovakia's Historic Win (2010) - Slovakia reached the Olympic hockey semi-finals for the first time, showing that with enough determination, even new kids on the block can dance with the stars. 🇸🇰💃🥅

The Kiwi Dream (2018) - New Zealand qualified for the Olympic hockey qualifiers, showing that even countries without ice can dream of playing in the snow. It's like a fish deciding to take a walk on land and loving it! 🇳🇿🐟

Britain's Ice Shock (1936) - Great Britain won their only gold in ice hockey, reminding everyone that sometimes, the quiet ones have the loudest roars. It's like finding out the quiet kid in class is a karaoke superstar. 🇬🇧🎤🥇

Czech's Golden Era Begins (1998) - The Czech Republic captured gold with a team full of NHL stars, showing the world that when you bring your best to the party, you leave with the biggest slice of cake. 🇨🇿🏒🥇

Sweden's Perfect Run (2006) - Sweden won gold without losing a single game, proving that perfection is attainable, especially when you're on skates. It's like acing every test without even needing to use a pencil eraser. 🇸🇪✏️

Kazakhstan's Olympic Debut (1998) - Kazakhstan made their first appearance in Olympic ice hockey, proving that you can come from a country better known for steppes than slapshots and still make a splash on the ice. It's like showing up to a skateboard park on a horse and nailing the half-pipe. 🇰🇿🏒🐎

The Swiss Miss (2006) - Switzerland's women's team scored their first Olympic goal, showing that even small steps (or shots) can lead to big leaps for a country's hockey history. It's like finally hitting the bullseye after dozens of tries in darts, except with a puck. 🇨🇭🎯🏒

China's Ice Hockey Introduction (2022) - China competed in men's ice hockey at the Olympics for the first time, diving into the deep end of the ice pond. It's like deciding to learn to swim by jumping into the ocean! 🇨🇳🏊‍♂️

Denmark's Historic Qualification (2022) - Denmark qualified for the Olympic ice hockey tournament for the first time, proving that Vikings can be just as fierce on ice as they were on the seas. It's like discovering your rowboat can turn into a speedboat. 🇩🇰🚣‍♂️🚤

Belarus's Memorable Upset (2002) - Belarus knocked Sweden out of the Olympics, a victory so unexpected it was like a mouse scaring away a cat. 🇧🇾🐭🇸🇪🐱

Slovenia's Standout Star (2014) - Anze Kopitar, from tiny Slovenia, shone on the Olympic stage, proving that great talent can come from small places. It's like the smallest pumpkin in the patch winning the prize for best in show. 🇸🇮🎃🏒

Women's Hockey Expansion (2010) - The Olympic women's ice hockey tournament expanded to include 8 teams, showing that the ice is big enough for everyone. It's like realizing your sandbox can fit all your friends, not just a few.

Norwegian Resilience (2018) - Despite a tough tournament, Norway's team played with heart, embodying the spirit of "never giving up." It's like keeping a smile while learning to ride a bike, no matter how many times you fall. N O

South Korea's Olympic Debut (2018) - South Korea's men's team played for the first time, bringing new energy to the ice. It's like the new kid at school jumping into the talent show and bringing down the house. K R

The Unified Korean Team (2018) - North and South Korea competed together, showing the world that sports can build bridges. It's like two rival summer camps teaming up for the ultimate canoe race. K P K R

India's Ice Hockey Challenge (1998) - India, a country known for its heat, debuted in the Winter Olympics for ice hockey, proving that you can do anything, even if it means swapping the cricket bat for a hockey stick. It's like deciding to build a snowman in the desert. I N

Luxembourg's Dream (2014) - Luxembourg, one of the smallest countries, aimed for the Olympics in ice hockey, showing that even the tiniest nations have big Olympic dreams. It's like a mouse dreaming of out-cheesing a cat. L U

Poland's Olympic Return (2022) - After a long hiatus, Poland returned to the Olympic ice hockey stage, proving that it's never too late for a comeback. It's like finding an old video game console and realizing it still works perfectly. P L

Spain's Ice Hockey Quest (2022) - Spain, where ice is more often found in drinks than on rinks, pursued Olympic qualification in ice hockey, showing that passion can come from the most unexpected places. It's like a cactus deciding to grow apples. E S

The Goalie Swap (2018) - In a unique Olympic twist, South Korea's women's team included goalies from both North and South Korea, proving that some barriers can be broken on the ice. It's like two rival superheroes teaming up to save the world. K R ♀ K P

Britain's Last Stand (1948) - Great Britain made its last Olympic ice hockey appearance, marking the end of an era. It's like saying goodbye to your favorite pair of shoes because they've walked too many miles. G B

Hungary's Hungry for Hockey (2018) - Hungary aimed for the Olympics, showing that their hunger for hockey was as big as their famous appetite for goulash. It's like deciding to enter a food contest not just to eat but to win. H U

Bulgaria's Bold Bid (2014) - Bulgaria, a country not known for its ice hockey prowess, threw its hat in the ring for Olympic qualification, proving that boldness knows no bounds. It's like wearing flip-flops in a snowstorm because you're sure summer is just around the corner. B G

Mexico's Ice Ambition (2018) - Mexico, where ice typically means a cool drink, aimed for the ice hockey rinks of the Olympics, blending the heat of competition with the chill of the ice. It's like salsa dancing on skates. M X

Israeli Ice Breakers (2022) - Israel, a country more associated with deserts than ice, pursued its Olympic ice hockey dreams, showing that you can aim for the ice even if you live in the heat. It's like deciding to ski down sand dunes. 🇮🇱⛷️🏜️

Jamaica's Cool Runnings on Ice (2018) - Inspired by their famous bobsled team, Jamaica set its sights on Olympic ice hockey, proving that the spirit of "Cool Runnings" can translate from sleds to skates. It's like swapping a sled for a hockey stick and still aiming for the finish line. 🇯🇲🏒

Australia's Down Under-Up Over (2022) - Australia, a land of surf and sun, chased its icy Olympic dreams, showing that where there's a will, there's a way, even if it means swapping the surfboard for a hockey stick. It's like surfing on ice waves. 🇦🇺🏄‍♂️

The Thai Ice Challenge (2018) - Thailand, known for its tropical climate, embraced the cold challenge of Olympic ice hockey, proving that passion for the game knows no temperature. It's like choosing to have a snowball fight in a tropical paradise. 🇹🇭🌴

Estonia's Ice Odyssey (2022) - Estonia, with a heart as cold as their winters, warmed up to the idea of Olympic glory in ice hockey, showing that small countries have big hearts when it comes to the ice. It's like a small spark turning into a roaring fire. 🇪🇪🔥

The Olympic Debutants (2022) - Several countries aimed to make their Olympic ice hockey debut, reminding us that the Olympic dream is universal, whether you're from a land of snow or sun. It's like everyone from around the world joining hands to play the biggest game of hockey. 🌐🏒

Liechtenstein's Lofty Goals (2022) - Liechtenstein, a tiny country with big ambitions, aimed for the ice hockey rinks of the Olympics, proving that you don't need to be a giant to dream big. It's like a kitten dreaming of roaring like a lion. 🇱🇮🐱🦁

The International Ice Melting Pot (2018) - The Olympics showcased players from all over the world, turning the ice rink into a melting pot of cultures, proving that hockey can bring the world together, one puck at a time. It's like having a potluck dinner where every country brings its best dish. 🍽️🌍

South Africa's Icy Aspirations (2022) - South Africa, more known for its safaris than slapshots, set its sights on Olympic ice hockey, blending the heat of the savannah with the cool of the ice. It's like seeing a lion on skates. 🇿🇦🦁

Greece's Olympic Odyssey (2022) - Greece, the birthplace of the Olympics, pursued its modern-day quest for ice hockey glory, showing that ancient heroes can inspire modern-day warriors. It's like Hercules deciding to play hockey. 🇬🇷🏛️🏒

The Olympic Dreamers (2022) - Every Olympic cycle, new countries join the quest for ice hockey glory, reminding us that the spirit of competition and the love for the game transcends borders. It's like the whole world deciding to play in one giant backyard game. 🌐🏒

Morocco's Ice Milestone (2022) - Morocco, a country where deserts are more common than ice rinks, set its sights on Olympic ice hockey, aiming to slide from sand dunes to icy arenas. It's like trading a camel for a Zamboni and heading straight for the Olympics. 🇲🇦🐪

Portugal's Puck Pursuit (2022) - Portugal, known for its soccer passion, laced up skates to chase Olympic ice hockey dreams, blending the art of the beautiful game with the speed of hockey. It's like swapping a football for a puck and scoring goals on ice. 🇵🇹

The Philippines' Cool Quest (2022) - The Philippines, a tropical paradise, embraced the chill of Olympic hockey, proving that you can dream of winter sports even while living in a summer climate. It's like deciding to build a snowman on the beach. 🇵🇭

Algeria's Ice Ambition (2022) - Algeria aimed to carve its name on Olympic ice, showing that love for hockey can flourish even in the Sahara's shadow. It's like finding an oasis of ice in the desert. 🇩🇿🌵

Iceland's Viking Spirit (2022) - Iceland, land of fire and ice, channeled its Viking spirit into a quest for Olympic hockey glory, proving that warriors of old can inspire athletes of today. It's like Vikings trading their longboats for hockey sticks. 🇮🇸⚔️

Croatia's Icy Challenge (2022) - Croatia, a nation celebrated for its water polo prowess, dived into the challenge of Olympic hockey, showing that skills in the water can translate to magic on ice. It's like swimmers deciding to race on frozen pools. 🇭🇷♂️

Mongolia's Winter Warriors (2022) - Mongolia, known for its horseback archers, aimed to become winter warriors on the ice, proving that the spirit of Genghis Khan lives on in sports. It's like exchanging arrows for hockey pucks. 🇲🇳🏹

Tunisia's Desert on Ice (2022) - Tunisia embarked on a journey from the heat of the Sahara to the cold of Olympic ice hockey arenas, blending the heat of the desert with the cool of the game. It's like making ice sculptures under the scorching sun. 🇹🇳

Serbia's Slapshot Dream (2022) - Serbia, where basketball reigns supreme, showed its passion for puck and ice, aiming for a spot in the Olympic rink. It's like basketball players deciding the court is cool but an ice rink is cooler. 🇷🇸🏀

Vietnam's Vision on Ice (2022) - Vietnam, a country with no winter, envisioned its athletes competing in the chill of the Olympic ice hockey tournament, proving that dreams know no climate. It's like dreaming of snowflakes in a tropical rain. 🇻🇳

Kenya's Cool Run (2022) - Inspired by their long-distance runners, Kenya pursued the dream of long glides on Olympic ice, merging endurance running with ice hockey. It's like marathon runners lacing up skates instead of sneakers. 🇰🇪♂️

Cyprus' Icy Ambitions (2022) - Cyprus, an island bathed in sunshine, embraced the dream of winter Olympic glory, showing that the warmth of their heart matches the coolness they seek on ice. It's like sunbathers deciding to chill in an igloo. 🇨🇾

Guatemala's Glacial Goals (2022) - Guatemala, a land of eternal spring, set its sights on the icy challenge of Olympic hockey, proving that you can reach for the ice stars no matter where you start. It's like planting a pine tree in a rainforest and watching it thrive. 🇬🇹

MIRACULOUS ON-ICE COMEBACKS

The Miracle on Manchester (1982) - The Los Angeles Kings faced the mighty Edmonton Oilers in the playoffs and were down 5-0. But like a superhero team, they rallied to win 6-5 in overtime. It's like flunking five tests and then acing the final to pass the class!

The Easter Epic (1987) - The New York Islanders and the Washington Capitals battled in a playoff game that went to four overtimes, ending after midnight! Pat LaFontaine finally scored, making it a bedtime story with a very late ending. Imagine playing hockey so long you need a midnight snack break!

Toronto's Titanic Comeback (1942) - Down 3 games to none in the Stanley Cup Finals against the Detroit Red Wings, the Toronto Maple Leafs did the unthinkable and won four straight games to take the cup. It's like turning a homework disaster into a report card miracle!

The St. Patrick's Day Massacre (1993) - The Quebec Nordiques were up 2-0 against the Montreal Canadiens with just 8 minutes left in the game. Montreal scored three quick goals to win, proving that hockey miracles can happen faster than finding a four-leaf clover.

The Monday Night Miracle (1986) - The St. Louis Blues were trailing the Calgary Flames in Game 6 of the conference finals. They rallied from a 5-2 deficit in the third period to win in overtime, showing that it's not over until the final buzzer. It's like doing all your weekend homework in one crazy Sunday night!

Penguins' Perfect Comeback (1992) - Down by three goals against the Washington Capitals, the Pittsburgh Penguins stormed back to win in overtime during the playoffs. It's like being down in a video game with one life left and coming back to win the championship.

Flyers Fly High (2010) - The Philadelphia Flyers became the third NHL team to win a series after being down 3-0, beating the Boston Bruins. It's like starting a race three laps behind and zooming past everyone to win the gold.

Capitals' Cool Comeback (2018) - The Washington Capitals were down in the series and in Game 5 against the Columbus Blue Jackets but came back to win the series. It's like being the last one picked for a team, then scoring the winning goal!

Islanders' Impossible Rally (1975) - Down by three goals in Game 3 against the Pittsburgh Penguins, the New York Islanders fought back to win the game and eventually the series. It's like being stuck on a difficult level of a game and then having a moment of brilliance to beat it.

Senators' Stunning Save (2017) - The Ottawa Senators were down to the Montreal Canadiens but managed a comeback to win the game in overtime, showing that every second counts. It's like finishing a huge project five minutes before it's due.

The Flames' Fierce Fight (1989) - Trailing the Vancouver Canucks in the playoffs, the Calgary Flames came back from a 4-1 deficit to win the game in overtime, proving that a little flame can start a big fire.

Ducks' Dramatic Turnaround (2017) - The Anaheim Ducks were down 3 goals in Game 5 against the Edmonton Oilers but rallied to win in double overtime. It's like finding out you aced a test you thought you failed.

Blackhawks' Big Battle (2013) - The Chicago Blackhawks were down 3-1 in the series against the Detroit Red Wings but won three straight games to advance. It's like pulling off a magic trick nobody thought you could do.

Rangers' Remarkable Revival (2015) - The New York Rangers were down by a goal in Game 5 against the Washington Capitals but came back to win the series. It's like being the hero in your own action movie, making the comeback just in the nick of time.

Wild's Wonderful Win (2003) - The Minnesota Wild made NHL history by overcoming three-goal deficits in two playoff games against the Colorado Avalanche, showing that in hockey, it ain't over till it's over. It's like turning a day full of chores into an epic adventure and finishing with a treasure.

Sharks' Shocking Surge (2019) - Down 3-0 against the Vegas Golden Knights in a decisive Game 7, the San Jose Sharks scored four goals on a single power play to eventually win in overtime. It's like hitting a grand slam in the bottom of the ninth to win the game.

Oilers' Overtime Odyssey (1997) - Edmonton Oilers were down 3 goals against the Dallas Stars but rallied back to win in triple overtime, proving that perseverance pays off, even if it means playing hockey till sunrise.

Devils' Daring Comeback (2000) - The New Jersey Devils were down by a goal late in Game 6 against the Philadelphia Flyers but scored twice in the last minutes to win the Eastern Conference Finals. It's like solving a puzzle just when you're about to give up.

Kings' Courtly Comeback (2014) - The Los Angeles Kings were down 3-0 in the first round against the San Jose Sharks but won four straight games to advance, later winning the Stanley Cup. It's like flunking the first quiz but acing the rest to become class valedictorian.

Bruins' Bold Battle (2013) - The Boston Bruins were down by two goals with 90 seconds left in Game 7 against the Toronto Maple Leafs, yet they tied the game and won in overtime. It's like finishing a marathon with a sprint.

Canucks' Victory from the Verge (1994) - The Vancouver Canucks were down 3-1 in the series against the Calgary Flames but clawed back to win in double overtime of Game 7, showing that hope is the best strategy.

Avalanche's Amazing Achievement (2001) - Down 3-2 in the series to the Los Angeles Kings, the Colorado Avalanche won the next two games to advance, eventually winning the Stanley Cup. It's like climbing a mountain, slipping near the top, but reaching the peak anyway.

Predators' Prey Turned Predator (2017) - The Nashville Predators were down in Game 3 against the Anaheim Ducks but fought back to win the game and the series, proving that sometimes, the hunted becomes the hunter.

Maple Leafs' Majestic Moment (1942) - The only team to come back from a 3-0 deficit in the Stanley Cup Finals, the Toronto Maple Leafs made history against the Detroit Red Wings, showing that miracles do happen on ice.

Islanders' Impossible Dream (1980) - Down by a goal in the final minute against the Philadelphia Flyers, the New York Islanders tied Game 6 of the Stanley Cup Finals and won in overtime, proving that sometimes, dreams do come true with just seconds to spare.

Capitals' Capital Comeback (2018) - In the Stanley Cup Finals, the Washington Capitals were down in the series against the Vegas Golden Knights but came roaring back to win their first-ever Stanley Cup. It's like starting a puzzle upside down and realizing it's a map to treasure!

Senators' Sensational Surge (2003) - The Ottawa Senators were on the brink of elimination against the New Jersey

Devils but rallied back to force a Game 7 in the Eastern Conference Finals. It's like being the last one standing in a game of tag and dodging everyone until you're it.

Jets' Jumbo Jet Lift-Off (2018) - The Winnipeg Jets made a stunning comeback in the series against the Nashville Predators, overcoming early losses to advance in the playoffs. It's like building a plane from scratch and then flying it to the moon.

Flames' Fiery Fightback (2004) - Down and almost out against the Vancouver Canucks, the Calgary Flames ignited a comeback flame to win the series and eventually reach the Stanley Cup Finals. It's like a phoenix rising from the ashes, but with hockey sticks.

Blackhawks' Windy City Whirlwind (2015) - Trailing in the series against the Anaheim Ducks, the Chicago Blackhawks orchestrated a comeback that led them to the Stanley Cup Finals and ultimately to victory. It's like turning a whirlwind into a victorious tornado.

Oilers' Oil Change (1997) - Down and seemingly out against the Colorado Avalanche, the Edmonton Oilers engineered a comeback to advance in the playoffs. It's like fixing a broken-down car mid-race and then speeding past everyone to win.

Canadiens' Houdini Act (2010) - The Montreal Canadiens, the eighth seed, stunned the top-seeded Washington Capitals by coming back from a 3-1 series deficit to win in the first round of the playoffs. It's like pulling a rabbit out of a hat, but the rabbit is holding a hockey stick.

Lightning's Shocking Surge (2011) - The Tampa Bay Lightning made a dramatic comeback against the Pittsburgh Penguins in the playoffs, overturning a 3-1 series deficit to advance. It's like turning a game of checkers into a masterful chess move.

Ducks' Dramatic Duckling-to-Swan Transformation (2017) - Down in the series and facing elimination against the Edmonton Oilers, the Anaheim Ducks mounted a historic comeback to win the series. It's like the ugly duckling turning into a swan, but the swan is wearing hockey pads.

Bruins' Beantown Breakthrough (2011) - The Boston Bruins, facing a crucial game against the Vancouver Canucks in the Stanley Cup Finals, flipped the script to come back and win the championship. It's like rewriting the end of a story where the hero triumphs just in the nick of time.

Sharks' Sea Change (2016) - The San Jose Sharks turned a series on its head against the Los Angeles Kings, coming back from a deficit to win in the playoffs. It's like finding a treasure map in a bottle at the beach and following it to find gold.

Golden Knights' Vegas Victory (2018) - In their inaugural season, the Vegas Golden Knights came back multiple times during the playoffs to reach the Stanley Cup Finals, showing that even the new kids on the block can dance with the stars.

Rangers' Broadway Revival (2014) - Down in the series against the Pittsburgh Penguins, the New York Rangers staged a dramatic comeback to advance, proving that the city that never sleeps also never gives up.

Predators' Music City Miracle (2017) - The Nashville Predators, down in the series against the Anaheim Ducks, orchestrated a comeback that led them to their first Stanley Cup Finals appearance. It's like playing a country song backwards and getting your truck, dog, and house back.

Wild's Wilderness Trek (2014) - Minnesota Wild, facing elimination against the Colorado Avalanche, came back to win the series, proving that sometimes the path less traveled leads to victory. It's like finding a secret shortcut in a video game that takes you straight to the boss battle.

Blue Jackets' First Bloom (2019) - The Columbus Blue Jackets, in their first-ever playoff series win, swept the top-seeded Tampa Bay Lightning in a historic upset. It's like the smallest seed in the garden growing into the biggest tree.

Stars' Lone Star Comeback (1999) - The Dallas Stars came back in the Stanley Cup Finals against the Buffalo Sabres to win their first Stanley Cup. It's like a cowboy riding into the sunset, but the cowboy is on skates, and the sunset is a championship.

Panthers' Prowl from Behind (1996) - The Florida Panthers, in their Cinderella run to the Stanley Cup Finals, made several comebacks in the playoffs. It's like a house cat deciding to become a lion and ruling the jungle.

Avalanche's Rocky Mountain Rise (2001) - Down in the playoffs, the Colorado Avalanche climbed back to win the Stanley Cup, proving that the higher the mountain, the sweeter the victory. It's like climbing a giant snow hill and sliding down into a victory parade.

Kings' Regal Return (2012) - The Los Angeles Kings, as the eighth seed, overcame odds and opponents alike to win the Stanley Cup, showing that in hockey, every team has a shot at the throne. It's like the knight in shining armor saving the kingdom against all odds.

Islanders' Long Island Leap (1993) - Coming back from a deficit against the Pittsburgh Penguins, the New York Islanders advanced in a playoff series that no one thought they could win. It's like winning a race on foot against sports cars.

Flyers' Flight to Victory (1987) - The Philadelphia Flyers, facing elimination against the Edmonton Oilers in the Stanley Cup Finals, fought back to force a decisive game, showcasing the heart of a champion. It's like being down in a superhero battle but finding your superpower in the final moment.

Hurricanes' Storm Surge (2006) - The Carolina Hurricanes, trailing in the Stanley Cup Finals against the Edmonton Oilers, rallied to win their first-ever championship. It's like steering a ship through a storm and finding calm waters just as all seems lost.

Maple Leafs' Last Minute Magic (2013) - In a regular-season game against the Boston Bruins, the Toronto Maple Leafs scored two goals in the last minute to tie the game, showcasing that miracles can happen even when the clock is ticking down. It's like finishing an essay in the last minute before it's due and getting an A.

Flames' Comeback Blaze (1989) - In the Stanley Cup Finals, the Calgary Flames fought back against the Montreal Canadiens to win their first and only championship, proving that a single spark can ignite a blaze of glory. It's like lighting a campfire that turns into a bonfire celebration.

CULTURE AND TRADITIONS

HOCKEY SLANG AND EXPRESSIONS

Hat Trick (1940s) - Scoring three goals in one game is called a "hat trick." Originally from cricket, the term migrated to hockey when fans in Toronto threw their hats onto the ice to celebrate a player scoring three goals. It's like hitting the jackpot three times in a row at the arcade! 🎩🏒

Biscuit in the Basket (1950s) - A puck is often called a "biscuit," and scoring a goal is putting that "biscuit in the basket." Imagine playing a giant game of kitchen where scoring means baking the best cookie ever! 🍪🥅

Gordie Howe Hat Trick (1950s) - Named after the legendary Gordie Howe, this is not your usual hat trick. It involves a player scoring a goal, assisting on another, and getting into a fight all in one game. It's like being the star of the show, the best supporting actor, and the stunt double all at once! 🌟🥊

Sin Bin (1950s) - The penalty box is affectionately known as the "sin bin." It's where players go to think about what they've done, kind of like a timeout corner, but with way more spectators. 📦🐷

Top Shelf (1960s) - When a player scores by shooting the puck into the upper part of the net, it's called "top shelf," where grandma hides the cookies. It's the sweet spot every kid (and player) aims for! 🍪🥅

Barnburner (1970s) - A highly exciting game that's back and forth is a "barnburner." It's like a movie that's so good you can't even blink because you might miss something awesome! 🏚️🔥

Chirping (1980s) - Trash talking on the ice is known as "chirping." It's like the birds talking back and forth, but with a lot less tweeting and a lot more sass.

Celly (1990s) - Short for celebration, "celly" is what players do after scoring a goal. It could be anything from a fist pump to a full-on dance routine, like your own victory dance after beating a level in your favorite video game.

Beauty/Beautician (2000s) - A player who is not only good on the ice but also has great character off it is a "beauty." It's like being voted both most valuable player and class president.

Apple (2010s) - An assist is sometimes called an "apple." It's like setting up the perfect play so your teammate can score, similar to giving your friend the perfect setup for a joke.

The Five-Hole (1950s) - The space between the goalie's legs where players love to score is known as the "five-hole." It's like the secret passage in a video game that leads directly to the treasure.

Goon (1970s) - A player known more for their fighting and physical play than scoring is a "goon." Think of them as the bodyguards of the ice, making sure everyone plays nice... or else.

Twig (1960s) - A player's hockey stick is often called a "twig." Back when sticks were actually made of wood, this term really stuck. It's like calling your trusty pen your "magic wand" during a test.

Pylon (1980s) - A player who is slow or not very good at defense might be called a "pylon," as in, they're as easy to skate around as those orange cones on the road. It's the hockey version of being the last one picked in dodgeball.

Sieve (1990s) - A goalie that lets a lot of goals through is sometimes jokingly called a "sieve," like a kitchen strainer that can't seem to keep anything out. It's like when your backpack has a hole, and all your pencils fall out.

Zamboni (1940s) - The machine that cleans and smooths the ice is named after its inventor, Frank Zamboni. It's like the magic carpet of the ice world, making everything nice and shiny for the players.

Bucket (1970s) - A player's helmet is often referred to as a "bucket." It's like your battle armor when going into the epic world of ice hockey.

Bender (2000s) - A player with skates that bend at the ankle due to poor skating form is called a "bender." It's like when your shoes are too big, and you end up walking like a clown at a circus.

Gino (1990s) - A goal scored in a game is sometimes called a "gino." It's like hitting a home run in baseball, but for hockey.

The Blue Line (1940s) - Not slang, but essential hockey lingo. The blue lines divide the ice into zones. It's like the boundaries in a game of tag that you dare not cross unless you're ready for action.

The Enforcer (1970s) - Similar to a goon, but with a noble twist. This player protects teammates and keeps the peace, like a knight in shining armor... if the knight carried a hockey stick.

Grinder (1980s) - A player known for hard work and perseverance rather than flashy play is a "grinder." It's like being the person who studies hard and aces the test through sheer determination.

The Point (1960s) - The area just inside the opponent's blue line. Players here are poised to score or pass, like a quarterback ready to make the winning throw.

Wraparound (1990s) - A move where a player takes the puck around the back of the net and tries to score. It's like sneaking around the back of the playground to surprise your friends.

The Healthy Scratch (2000s) - When a player is left out of the lineup for a game, they're a "healthy scratch." It's like being all dressed up with nowhere to go, except you have to watch your friends go to the party.

The Office (2010s) - Behind the opponent's net, where playmakers like to set up shop and plan their next scoring move. It's like the secret clubhouse where all the best plans are hatched.

Duster (1980s) - A player who spends most of the game on the bench, collecting "dust." It's like being the class pet; you're part of the team but don't get out much.

Garbage Goal (1990s) - A goal that's not pretty but counts just the same, usually scored by scrambling in front of the net. It's like turning a messy room into a masterpiece by finding a lost treasure under a pile of clothes.

Grocery Stick (2000s) - The player who sits on the bench between the forwards and defensemen, separating them like a grocery stick separates groceries on the conveyor belt. It's like being the referee of rock, paper, scissors.

Howitzer (1970s) - A powerful, fast shot. It's like launching a rocket from your hockey stick, aiming straight for the stars... or, in this case, the back of the net.

Lettuce (2010s) - Referring to a player's hair, especially when it flows out from under their helmet. It's like having a personal salad bowl, but cooler and much more stylish.

Mitts (1980s) - A player's hands, especially when they're good at handling the puck. It's like having magic gloves that make the impossible, possible.

Muzzy (1990s) - A mustache, often grown by players, especially during the playoffs for good luck. It's like a facial fur trophy that shows you're in it to win it.

Pigeon (2000s) - A player who picks up easy goals or feeds off the hard work of others. It's like being the one who waits for the pizza to arrive and then swoops in for the first slice.

Plumber (1990s) - A hardworking player who isn't afraid to do the gritty, dirty work, much like a real plumber. It's like being the hero who unclogs the sink of the game.

Saucer Pass (1960s) - A pass that floats off the ice like a flying saucer, making it harder for opponents to intercept. It's like sending a secret message through the air that only your friend can catch.

Silky (2000s) - Used to describe smooth, skilled play. It's like gliding on ice as if you're dancing on clouds.

Snipe (2010s) - A precise, accurate shot that results in a goal, often from a distance. It's like hitting the bullseye from the other side of the carnival.

Tape-to-Tape (1980s) - A pass that goes directly from one player's stick tape to another's without interruption. It's like sending a text message that gets an instant reply.

Tilt (1970s) - A fight during a hockey game. It's like arguing over the last slice of pizza, but with more rules and referees.

Twig (1960s) - Another term for a hockey stick, especially when they were made of wood. It's like calling your best pencil your "magic wand" during a test.

Wheel (1990s) - To skate fast or to have great speed. It's like having rocket-powered rollerblades in a race against bikes.

Yard Sale (2000s) - When a player gets hit hard and their equipment scatters across the ice like items at a yard sale. It's like tripping with a backpack full of toys and watching everything spill out.

Zebra (1980s) - A referee, named for the black and white stripes of their uniform. It's like having a jungle guide to navigate the wild game of hockey.

Ghosting (2010s) - When a player is so fast or skilled, they seem to disappear from opponents. It's like playing hide and seek, but you're invisible.

The Kitchen (2000s) - The area directly in front of the net, where a lot of action and "cooking" up plays happen. It's like being the chef in a fast-paced restaurant during dinner rush.

Lumber (1970s) - Another term for a hockey stick, referring to its wooden origins. It's like calling a sword your "battle stick" in a knight's tale.

Pylon (1980s) - Used to describe a slow or ineffective player, as easy to move around as a traffic cone. It's like being the statue in a game of tag.

Rocket (1960s) - A fast skater or a powerful shot. It's like having jet engines on your skates.

Sweater (1920s) - The term for a hockey jersey, dating back to when they were actually made of sweater material. It's like wearing your coziest winter gear, but for going into battle.

CLASSIC HOCKEY FOODS

Poutine Power Play (1950s, Quebec, Canada) - In the heart of hockey country, poutine became the ultimate comfort food for fans. Imagine gooey cheese curds and gravy on fries, like a warm hug in a bowl during those cold hockey nights. It's like the edible version of a hat trick—cheese, gravy, and fries scoring all at once!

Stanley Cup of Chowder (Boston, USA) - In Boston, fans celebrate with a hearty bowl of clam chowder. It's like the soup version of a body check: it hits you with flavor and warms you up for the game. Imagine eating a cloud made of clams and cream, floating towards a goal of deliciousness.

Hockey Sushi Roll (Early 2000s, Vancouver, Canada) - In Vancouver, sushi rolls became an unexpected hockey favorite. Picture seaweed and rice rolling around the ice, with salmon playing forward and avocado on defense. It's a culinary power play that brings the ocean to the rink.

The Penalty Box Pretzel (Germany, 1970s) - Big, soft pretzels found their way from German Christmas markets to hockey arenas worldwide. Eating one is like getting a warm, salty hug from your favorite player—minus the sweaty jersey. Imagine a doughy defenseman that fights hunger instead of opponents.

Zamboni Pizza Slice (North America, 1950s) - Named after the iconic ice-resurfacing machine, this pizza slice is a fan favorite for its quick, easy, and satisfying nature. It's like having your own Zamboni, but instead of smoothing ice, it satisfies your hunger, one cheesy slice at a time.

The Hat Trick Hot Dog (USA, 1920s) - A staple at hockey games, the hot dog became synonymous with quick, delicious game-day food. Imagine a hot dog that scores three times: once with the bun, once with the sausage, and a final time with all the toppings. It's the MVP of arena snacks.

The Slapshot Soda (Canada, 1960s) - A fizzy drink to wash down all the snacks, soda became the go-to beverage for fans shouting and cheering. It's like a carbonated pep talk for your taste buds, getting them ready for the next big play.

Breakaway Bagel (Canada, 1990s) - In the colder regions, the bagel became a warm, comforting snack for early morning games. Imagine a bagel breaking away from the pack, dodging cream cheese and lox, to score the perfect breakfast goal.

Overtime Onion Rings (USA, 1980s) - For those tense moments that stretch into overtime, onion rings offered a crispy, satisfying way to deal with the nerves. They're like edible stress balls, but much tastier and less squishy.

The Goalie's Garlic Fries (California, USA, 2000s) - Garlic fries burst onto the hockey scene, offering a pungent, savory snack option. Eating them is like blocking a slapshot with flavor—bold and unforgettable. Just remember, they might repel more than just vampires in the stands.

Faceoff Fish Tacos (California, USA, 2010s) - As hockey's popularity surged in warmer climates, fish tacos became a go-to game snack. Imagine a taco so fresh and full of zest, it feels like a beach day during a power play.

The Defenseman's Donut (Canada, 1950s) - Sweet, circular, and perfect for those early morning games or late-night munchies. It's like having a sugary shield against hunger, with sprinkles for extra protection.

Power Play Popcorn (North America, 1940s) - Easy to eat and share, popcorn became the unofficial snack of suspenseful moments. Each kernel is like a tiny puck, ready to pop into action at the drop of a hat.

The Checker Chili (Canada, 1990s) - A hearty bowl of chili became the ideal warm-up for fans braving the cold. It's like a body check for your taste buds, cozy and bold with every spoonful.

Blue Line Burrito (Southwestern USA, 2000s) - A hefty, all-inclusive meal for the hungriest of fans, offering a full game's worth of energy in every bite. It's like a defenseman you can eat, blocking hunger all game long.

Hat Trick Hummus (International, 2010s) - A newer addition to the hockey food lineup, offering a healthier option for fans. Each scoop is a goal: one for taste, one for health, and one for innovation.

Slapshot Smoothie (North America, 2010s) - For those looking for a quick, nutritious boost, the smoothie offers fruits, veggies, and a blast of energy. It's like getting a pep talk from your favorite player in liquid form.

Penalty Shot Peanuts (USA, 1930s) - A classic snack that's easy to share and even easier to spill in excitement. Each peanut is like a mini penalty shot, offering a crunchy chance to fuel up before the next faceoff.

The Enforcer's Energy Bar (International, 2000s) - For fans and players needing a quick boost, the energy bar offers sustenance without missing a play. It's like having your own personal trainer in your pocket, ready to pep you up.

Breakaway Bratwurst (Germany, 1970s) - Introduced to North American hockey by German fans, the bratwurst became a savory sensation. It's like a sausage on skates, speeding towards the goal of your appetite.

Icing Ice Cream (North America, 1950s) - For those sweet victories or to soothe the sting of defeat, ice cream serves as the perfect treat. It's like celebrating a win or nursing a loss with a cold, creamy friend.

Sudden Death Sundaes (USA, 1980s) - A dessert reserved for the most nail-biting overtime games, where every bite is as suspenseful as the game's final moments. It's like a shootout, but with spoons.

The Grinder's Grilled Cheese (Canada, 2000s) - Simple, reliable, and comforting, much like the player who gives it their all. It's like getting a warm, cheesy hug every time your team hits the ice.

Hat Trick Hot Chocolate (Canada, 1960s) - For those chilly rinkside games, hot chocolate offers warmth and sweetness, like scoring three cozy goals against winter.

The Netminder's Nachos (USA, 1990s) - A shareable snack that's as chaotic and messy as a scramble in front of the net. It's like a team effort in a tray, where every chip supports the others with cheesy, jalapeño-laden goodness.

Face-Off Fondue (Switzerland, 1960s) - In the heart of hockey-loving Switzerland, fondue became a game-day tradition. Imagine dipping bread like you're scoring goals, with each dip a pass through the defense of melted cheese. It's the communal pot where strategy meets snack time.

The Checkerboard Cake (Sweden, 1970s) - Celebrating hockey victories in Sweden often includes a checkerboard cake, symbolizing the ice rink. Each square is like a section of the ice, sweet victory in every bite. It's like planning your game strategy with dessert.

Power Play Pierogies (Eastern Europe, 1980s) - In regions where hockey and hearty meals go hand-in-hand, pierogies became the ultimate power play snack. Stuffed with potato, cheese, or meat, they fuel fans like a well-executed play fuels a team. Imagine each pierogi as a mini puck, ready to slide into the net of your appetite.

Slapshot Smoked Meat (Canada, 1950s) - Montreal's love for hockey is matched by its love for smoked meat. Piling high on rye bread, it's a sandwich that tackles hunger as fiercely as a defenseman checks an opponent. It's like a culinary body check that leaves you satisfied.

The Goalie's Goulash (Hungary, 1960s) - A hearty, warming bowl of goulash became synonymous with watching hockey in Hungary. It's like having a goalie in your stomach, making sure hunger doesn't score. Every spoonful is a save against the chill of the ice.

Breakaway Borscht (Russia, 1950s) - In Russia, the vibrant beet soup known as borscht is a staple for hockey fans. Its bright red color and hearty warmth are like a breakaway on the ice, rushing to comfort your taste buds.

Hat Trick Haggis (Scotland, 1990s) - Though not traditionally associated with hockey, haggis found its way into the hearts of Scottish hockey fans as a celebratory meal. It's like scoring three times with flavor, texture, and tradition, all in one dish.

Puck Drop Pancakes (Canada, 2000s) - For early morning games, pancakes became a way to kick off the day. Each pancake is like a puck ready for the drop, with syrup as the sweet victory to follow. It's breakfast with a side of anticipation.

Overtime Oysters (Eastern Canada, 2010s) - In maritime regions, oysters became a sophisticated snack for watching the game. Each one is like a mini adventure, diving into the ocean's flavor as you wait for the game's next twist.

Penalty Box Popovers (USA, 1970s) - Light, airy, and a bit unpredictable, popovers are like the penalty box moments of hockey—tense, exciting, and filled with potential. They're a delightful surprise, much like a short-handed goal.

Zamboni Ziti (Italy, 1980s) - In Italian hockey-loving households, ziti pasta, baked with layers of cheese and sauce, fuels fans. It's like a Zamboni for your stomach, smoothing over hunger with every cheesy layer.

The Grinder's Gravy Train (USA, 1990s) - In the spirit of hardworking "grinders" on the ice, gravy-smothered dishes represent the culinary equivalent of grit and determination. It's like a delicious reward for all the tough battles won in the corners of the rink.

Hat Trick Hummus Wrap (Middle East, 2000s) - A healthier option for fans, the hummus wrap became a game-day favorite, offering a trifecta of flavor, nutrition, and convenience. It's like a well-rounded player that excels in all aspects of the game.

Blue Line Blinis (Russia, 2000s) - Mini pancakes topped with caviar or smoked salmon, blinis are a luxurious way to enjoy hockey. Each one is like a slapshot of flavor, aiming straight for the culinary goal.

The Enforcer's Elk Stew (Sweden, 1970s) - In colder climates, a robust elk stew provides the warmth and energy needed to cheer through overtime. It's like having your own enforcer to fend off the cold.

Sudden Death Sushi (Japan, 1990s) - In Japan, sushi represents the precision and skill of hockey's most tense moments. Each piece is a calculated play, a blend of timing and artistry, much like scoring the winning goal in sudden death overtime.

Power Play Poutine Pizza (Canada, 2010s) - Combining two beloved foods, this dish is for fans who refuse to choose. It's like having the best of both worlds on your plate, ready to tackle hunger with a one-two punch of fries and pizza.

Slapshot Schnitzel (Germany, 1980s) - A crispy, breaded piece of meat that's as satisfying as a clean slapshot goal. It's like the culinary equivalent of a perfect shot from the point—crisp, golden, and hitting the spot every time.

Breakaway Bruschetta (Italy, 1990s) - Fresh, vibrant, and quick to disappear, bruschetta represents the simple yet thrilling aspects of hockey. It's like a breakaway goal—quick, fresh, and immensely satisfying.

The Checker Chili Dog (USA, 2000s) - Combining spicy chili with the classic hot dog, this snack is a game-day essential for those who like a bit of heat with their hockey. It's like adding a fiery forward to your culinary lineup.

Penalty Box Pierogi (Poland, 1980s) - In Eastern Europe, pierogi are a comfort food staple, perfect for those penalty box moments when you need a comforting bite. It's like a warm hug in dumpling form, offering solace during the game's tense moments.

Hat Trick Hamburger (North America, 1950s) - The hamburger, a classic at hockey games, offering three layers of perfection: bun, patty, and toppings. It's like scoring three times with taste, satisfaction, and tradition.

Overtime Olives (Mediterranean, 2000s) - A simple yet sophisticated snack, olives are the perfect bite for those nail-biting overtime moments. They're like the veterans of the snack world—reliable, seasoned, and full of character.

The Grinder's Gyro (Greece, 1990s) - Packed with flavor and ready to tackle hunger, the gyro is like the hardworking grinder of hockey foods. It delivers a solid performance of taste in every bite, much like a player who gives their all on the ice.

Breakaway Breakfast Burrito (Southwestern USA, 2000s) - For early morning games, the breakfast burrito scores with fans, offering a portable feast to start the day. It's like executing a perfect breakaway play, but instead of a puck, you're navigating a delicious, egg-filled wrap to victory.

FAN CHANTS AND RITUALS

The Octopus Toss (Detroit Red Wings, 1952) - The tradition began when two brothers hurled an octopus onto the ice during the playoffs, its eight tentacles symbolizing the eight wins needed to clinch the Stanley Cup at the time. It's like throwing your hat for a hat trick, but way more slippery and eight times as lucky!

The Hat Trick Hats (General Tradition, 1940s) - When a player scores three goals in a game, fans show appreciation by tossing their hats onto the ice. It's like giving a standing ovation, but with headgear, turning the rink into a milliner's dream.

The Montreal Canadiens' "Ole" Song (2000s) - Adapted from soccer, Canadiens fans sing "Ole, Ole, Ole" to cheer on their team, blending the worlds of hockey and football with each chant. It's like bringing a bit of the World Cup to the ice.

The Nashville Predators' Fang Fingers (1998) - Fans imitate a chomping motion with their hands during power plays, a ritual that's both intimidating and a bit like trying to scare someone with shadow puppets.

The Winnipeg Jets' Whiteout (1987) - Fans dress in all white during playoff games, creating a blizzard-like effect in the stands. It's like attending a giant hockey-themed toga party, but cooler and with more goals.

The New York Islanders' Yes! Yes! Yes! Chant (2010s) - Borrowed from wrestling, fans extend their arms and chant in unison after each goal, turning the arena into a giant pep rally. It's like agreeing with everyone about how awesome your team is, but louder and with more high-fives.

The "Potvin Sucks!" Chant (New York Rangers, 1979) - Rangers fans have been chanting this for decades whenever they play against the Islanders, a long-standing tradition of rivalry and ribbing that's like telling your sibling they're bad at video games, but in front of thousands of friends.

The Toronto Maple Leafs' "Go Leafs Go!" (General) - A simple but powerful chant that fills the arena, uniting fans in a chorus of support that's as straightforward as asking for extra ketchup for your fries, but way more passionate.

The Chicago Blackhawks' National Anthem Cheering (1985) - Fans cheer loudly throughout the singing of the national anthem, a unique tradition that turns patriotism into a participatory sport. It's like singing in the shower, but with thousands of friends and way more flags.

The "Knighting" Ceremony (Vegas Golden Knights, 2017) - Before home games, a knight on the ice "defeats" an enemy representing the visiting team, blending medieval fantasy with hockey in a spectacle that's part Renaissance fair, part pre-game hype.

The "Woo!" (Carolina Hurricanes, 2010s) - After each home win, fans and players alike let out a loud "Woo!" echoing wrestling legend Ric Flair, making it feel like a victory party where everyone's invited to the conga line.

The "Towel Power" Wave (Vancouver Canucks, 1982) - Inspired by a coach's penalty box protest, fans wave white towels during playoff games, a sign of solidarity that's like giving the team a giant, cozy, visual hug.

The "Thunderstick" Bang (Anaheim Ducks, 2000s) - Fans bang together inflatable sticks to create thunderous noise, turning the arena into a storm of support. It's like giving applause with giant balloons, but with more boom.

The "Puck Off" Chant (Philadelphia Flyers, 1960s) - A cheeky play on words, fans chant this at the start of games, blending humor with the intensity of the moment. It's like telling the other team it's time to leave, but in the politest hockey way possible.

The "Sea of Red" (Calgary Flames, 1980s) - Fans wear red to home games, creating a visual show of support that's like being part of a living, breathing team jersey. It's like going to a giant costume party where everyone decided to come as their favorite hero.

The "Beard-a-thon" (Playoff Beards, General) - Fans and players grow beards during the playoffs, a symbol of unity and superstition that's like not washing your lucky socks during a winning streak, but for your face.

The Goal Song Sing-Along (General, 1990s) - After a home team goal, fans sing along to a specific song, turning each goal into a mini concert. It's like karaoke night, but with better music and more high-fives.

The "Sieve" Taunt (General, 1970s) - Fans chant "sieve" at opposing goalies after a goal, a playful jab that's like telling someone they have a hole in their pocket after they drop their change.

The "Hats Off" Salute (General, 2000s) - When a player scores a hat trick, fans throw hats onto the ice, a tradition that's like giving a standing ovation, but with headwear. It's like saying "I tip my hat to you," but literally.

The "Air Horn" Blast (General, 1980s) - Fans use air horns to celebrate goals and big plays, a tradition that's like announcing dinner's ready, but for excitement and in a language only hockey fans understand.

The "Kiss Cam" Love (General, 2000s) - During game breaks, the "kiss cam" encourages fans to smooch, blending romance with hockey in a way that's like mixing Valentine's Day with game day.

The "Dance Cam" Break (General, 2010s) - Fans show off their dance moves on the jumbotron during breaks, turning the arena into a giant dance floor. It's like being in a flash mob, but with more hockey jerseys and less rehearsal.

The "Boo the Ref" Chorus (General, 1960s) - Disagreeing with a call, fans collectively boo the referees, a shared expression of disapproval that's like telling your video game it cheated, but with thousands of voices.

The "Seventh Player Award" (Boston Bruins, 1960s) - Fans vote for the player who goes beyond expectations, embodying the spirit of the team. It's like electing the class president, but for hockey heroics.

The "Home of the Brave" Line Roar (Chicago Blackhawks, Present) - Fans cheer loudly at the line "home of the brave" during the national anthem, a tradition that's like hitting the high note in your favorite song, but with national pride.

"Green Men" Antics (Vancouver Canucks, 2000s) - Two fans dressed in full-body green spandex suits became famous for their hilarious antics beside the penalty box, distracting opposing players and entertaining everyone else. It's like having your own personal comedians at the game, except they're dressed as green beans.

The Teddy Bear Toss (Minor Leagues, 1993) - Originating with the Kamloops Blazers, fans throw teddy bears onto the ice after the home team scores their first goal. The toys are then donated to children's charities, turning a moment of celebration into a wave of kindness. It's like scoring a goal in hockey and in hearts.

"You Suck" Chant (New Jersey Devils, 2000s) - To the tune of "Rock and Roll Part 2," Devils fans add their own flavor by chanting "you suck" at the opposition, combining music with mischief in a way only New Jersey can. It's like joining a choir, but the lyrics would make your grandma blush.

The Rally Towel Wave (General, 1980s) - Popularized by the Pittsburgh Penguins, fans wave towels during crucial moments for a visual show of unity and support. It's like signaling for a superhero, but instead of a bat signal, it's a sea of towels.

"Jump Around" Tradition (Wisconsin Badgers, Before Hockey Games) - While not exclusive to hockey, fans jumping to the song "Jump Around" before the third period has become a staple in some arenas, energizing the crowd and team alike. It's like turning the stadium into the world's largest bounce house.

The Horn Blast (Montreal Canadiens, 1950s) - A tradition where a train horn blasts after every Canadiens goal, echoing Montreal's history and adding an auditory punch to each score. It's like having your own victory trumpet, but much, much louder.

"The Good Old Hockey Game" Sing-Along (Canada, 1970s) - Fans across Canada often break into Stompin' Tom Connors' "The Hockey Song" during games, a musical tribute to the sport they love. It's like your favorite campfire song, but with thousands of backup singers.

The Siren Sound (Washington Capitals, 2000s) - A tradition where a celebrity or notable figure cranks a siren before the game and during key moments, like summoning warriors to battle but with less sword fighting and more slap shots.

"The Wave" (General, 1980s) - While not exclusive to hockey, the wave has become a fan-favorite way to boost energy in the arena, making a human rollercoaster of excitement that ripples around the stands. It's like doing the hokey pokey, but you're the rollercoaster.

Hat Collection Display (Detroit Red Wings, After Hat Tricks) - The Red Wings collect and display hats thrown onto the ice for hat tricks, creating a museum of fan enthusiasm and memorable moments. It's like keeping a scrapbook, but with way more hats and hockey history.

"The Oil Drum" Cheer (Edmonton Oilers, 2000s) - Oilers fans bang on oil drums outside and inside the arena, a nod to the city's industry and a unique way to drum up support. It's like calling the troops to dinner, but the meal is hockey and the bell is a drum.

"Sweet Caroline" Sing-Along (Boston Bruins, 2000s) - Adopting Neil Diamond's hit, Bruins fans belt out "Sweet Caroline" during the third period, making a communal moment of joy, regardless of the score. It's like karaoke night where the whole bar is your backup band.

The Goal Light Ritual (General, 1990s) - Fans replicate the flashing of the arena's goal light at home whenever their team scores, creating a synchronized celebration that lights up neighborhoods. It's like having a party signal, but for goals and glory.

The Viking Clap (Multiple Teams, 2010s) - Inspired by Icelandic soccer fans, some hockey crowds have adopted the slow, thunderous clap and chant to intimidate opponents and rally their team. It's like summoning thunder, but with hands and team spirit.

Lucky Seat Upgrade (General, 2000s) - Some teams randomly upgrade fans' seats as a surprise, turning regular tickets into VIP experiences. It's like buying a lottery ticket and finding out you've won a golden ticket to the chocolate factory, but for hockey.

"Who Are Ya?" Chant (General, 2000s) - Fans question the identity of the opposing team with a chant, poking fun and asserting dominance in a playful manner. It's like asking someone for their ID, but in a massive, echoing voice.

The Kiss Cam (General, 1990s) - A tradition where couples are encouraged to kiss when featured on the arena's big screen, adding a dash of romance to the rink. It's like Valentine's Day meets game day, with the entire crowd playing Cupid.

Intermission Races (General, 2000s) - Young fans often participate in races or mini-games on the ice during intermissions, a tradition that's like halftime entertainment, but slipperier and with more pint-sized athletes.

The Playoff Beard (General, 1980s) - Players and fans grow beards during the playoffs as a sign of solidarity and superstition. It's like not shaving until your homework is done, but the homework is winning the Stanley Cup.

The "Celery" Chant (Buffalo Sabres, 2010s) - Unique to Sabres fans, this chant celebrates a peculiar local tradition involving celery as a good luck charm. It's like having a rabbit's foot, but crunchier and part of your veggie platter.

The "We Want Tacos" Chant (Los Angeles Kings, 2010s) - If the Kings score a certain number of goals, fans are rewarded with taco coupons, turning goal-scoring into a deliciously incentivized activity. It's like hitting a piñata, but instead of candy, out come tacos.

"Thank You, Fans!" Salute (General, Post-Game) - Teams often raise their sticks to the crowd in a post-game salute, a thank-you for the support. It's like taking a bow at the end of a play, but with more helmets and less stage fright.

The "Loser Lap" (General, Youth Leagues) - In some youth leagues, the losing team takes a lap around the rink, acknowledging the fans and learning sportsmanship. It's like saying, "We'll get 'em next time," but with more skating and team spirit.

The "Gordie Howe Hat Trick" Chant (General, Honoring Players) - When a player achieves a goal, an assist, and a fight in one game, fans and teammates honor the achievement with cheers, celebrating the rare feat named after the legendary Gordie Howe. It's like completing a triathlon, but for hockey tough guys.

The "Hockey Hug" (General, After Goals) - Players embracing in a group hug after a goal captures the camaraderie and joy of the sport, a tradition that's like group hugging at a family reunion, but with more pads and less awkward questions.

GREAT NHL MOMENTS

INCREDIBLE GOALIE SAVES

The Dominik Hasek Flip Save (1994) - Imagine doing a cartwheel while catching a fly – that's what Dominik Hasek did against the New Jersey Devils, except the fly was a speeding puck. This save not only showcased his flexibility but also his nickname, "The Dominator," proving he could stop goals in his sleep, probably while dreaming about flying. 🤸🚫

The Ron Hextall Score (1987) - Goalies are known for stopping goals, but Ron Hextall broke the mold by scoring one himself! He shot the puck across the ice into an empty net, making history as the first NHL goalie to score by actually shooting the puck. It's like if the school's safety patrol officer suddenly decided to run for class president – and won! 🥅🏒

The Martin Brodeur Scorpion Save (2012) - Like a scorpion flicking its tail, Martin Brodeur kicked his leg up behind him to stop the puck against the New York Rangers. This save wasn't just impressive; it was like watching a ninja in goalie pads, proving that age is just a number when you're as flexible as gum. 🦂🥅

The Jonathan Quick Behind-the-Back Glove Save (2014) - Jonathan Quick performed a magic trick against the New York Islanders by snagging the puck from behind his own back. It's like he had eyes on the back of his head, or maybe he's just part owl. 🦉🎩

The Marc-Andre Fleury "The Save" (2009 Stanley Cup Finals) - With seconds left, Fleury dove across the goal to stop a shot from Nicklas Lidstrom, clinching the Stanley Cup for the Pittsburgh Penguins. This wasn't just a save; it was like slamming the door on a monster trying to sneak into your room, heroically preserving bedtime peace.

The Carey Price Superman Save (2017) - Price flew across the crease like Superman to deny Tampa Bay Lightning's Nikita Kucherov, proving that you don't need a cape to fly or to have superhero reflexes. Just a goalie stick and a sense of dramatic timing.

The Braden Holtby "The Save" (2018 Stanley Cup Finals) - In Game 2, Holtby stretched out his stick in a last-ditch effort to block a sure goal, a move that preserved the Washington Capitals' lead and ultimately helped them secure their first Stanley Cup. It's like catching a falling glass with a spoon - improbable, impressive, and immensely satisfying.

The Curtis Joseph Double Save (1998 Playoffs) - Against the Dallas Stars, Joseph made not one, but two jaw-dropping saves in quick succession. It's like playing a video game on hard mode and beating the boss with one life point left - twice.

The Mike Smith Butt Save (2017) - Yes, you read that right. Mike Smith stopped the puck with his backside, proving that in hockey, it's not just hands and feet that matter, but sometimes your bottom gets to be the hero too. It's like winning a dance battle with a move you didn't know you had.

The Henrik Lundqvist Windmill Save (2013) - Lundqvist flashed his glove with a windmill-like motion to snatch a goal-bound puck out of the air, turning what looked like a certain goal into just another save. It's like snatching a hat off a friend's head just as they're about to leave - smoothly executed and slightly show-offy.

The Jean-Sebastien Giguere Leg Pad Stack (2003 Playoffs) - Giguere stacked his pads in a classic yet dramatic style to make a series of saves that helped the Mighty Ducks of Anaheim reach the Stanley Cup Finals. It's like building a fort out of pillows to stop a sibling invasion - effective and surprisingly solid.

The Tim Thomas Stick Save (2011 Stanley Cup Finals) - Thomas deflected a sure goal with the narrow part of his stick, a move that required timing, luck, and a bit of wizardry. It's like catching a fly with chopsticks - everyone's shocked when you actually pull it off.

The Pekka Rinne Behind-the-Back Save (2017) - Rinne somehow stopped the puck with a blind, behind-the-back grab against the Chicago Blackhawks, showcasing reflexes and a bit of showmanship. It's like reaching behind the couch without looking and finding the remote on the first try.

The Roberto Luongo Glove Save (2007) - Luongo leaped and stretched his glove to make a save that defied gravity and expectations, turning the air above the crease into his personal stage. It's like doing a high jump, but instead of a bar, you're catching a speeding puck.

The Antti Niemi Flexible Save (2013) - Niemi twisted and contorted his body in ways that seemed to defy human anatomy to stop the puck, proving that sometimes, being a goalie means being part acrobat, part rubber band.

The Sergei Bobrovsky Full Split Save (2019) - Bobrovsky executed a full split to deny a goal, showcasing flexibility that would make gymnasts envious. It's like doing the splits to pick up a dropped pencil in class – showy, unnecessary, but undeniably cool.

The Tuukka Rask Top Corner Denial (2020) - Rask flashed his glove to snatch a puck headed for the top corner, a save that combined anticipation with a flair for the dramatic. It's like catching a popcorn thrown at your mouth from across the room – unexpected, but a crowd-pleaser.

The Cam Ward Scorpion Tail Save (2011) - Ward mimicked a scorpion's tail with his leg to stop the puck, a move that looked more like a yoga pose than a traditional hockey save. It's like inventing a new dance move in the middle of a game, and it just so happens to work.

The Jimmy Howard Glove Snatch (2016) - Howard reached out with his glove to catch a puck that seemed destined for the net, a save that was part intuition, part reflex, and all heart. It's like snatching a hat out of the air on a windy day – satisfying and a little bit heroic.

The Semyon Varlamov Desperation Dive (2014) - Varlamov threw himself across the goal to make a save, a moment of desperation that turned into triumph. It's like diving to catch a bus as the doors are closing – desperate, but when it works, you feel like you've won the lottery.

The Andrei Vasilevskiy Behind-the-Back Save (2018) - Vasilevskiy blindly stopped a puck with his glove behind his back, a save that seemed to defy logic and physics. It's like guessing the right answer on a test without studying – lucky, impressive, and a relief.

The Carey Price Paddle Save (2015) - Price used the paddle of his stick to stop a puck, a reminder that sometimes, the best saves come from the most unexpected moves. It's like using a broom to catch a falling vase – unconventional, but effective.

The Marc-Andre Fleury Diving Stop (2008) - Fleury dove across the crease to make a save in the Stanley Cup Finals, a moment that combined athleticism with sheer willpower. It's like leaping to save a plate of cookies from falling to the floor – heroic and deliciously rewarding.

The Ben Bishop Stick Save (2015) - Bishop used just his stick to deflect a puck away, proving that sometimes all you need is a good stick and a prayer. It's like using a magic wand to turn a frog back into a prince, but with more ice and less fairy tale.

The Connor Hellebuyck Windmill Save (2020) - Hellebuyck channeled old-school goalies with a windmill glove save, a blend of classic style and modern skill. It's like reviving disco in the middle of a modern dance party – retro, flashy, and totally cool.

J.S. Giguere's 2003 Playoff Marathon - In the 2003 playoffs, Jean-Sebastien Giguere of the Mighty Ducks of Anaheim faced a staggering 63 shots in a single game against the Dallas Stars and stopped 60 of them in a triple-overtime win. It's like being the last kid standing in a dodgeball game that lasts all recess, except with more pads and a puck.

Henrik Lundqvist's Winter Classic Magic (2012) - In the final moments of the 2012 Winter Classic, Lundqvist stopped a penalty shot by Danny Briere of the Philadelphia Flyers, preserving the New York Rangers' 3-2 victory. It was like stopping time itself, or at least stopping a puck that felt as heavy as a snowball aimed at clinching the game.

Jordan Binnington's Rookie Record (2019 Playoffs) - Binnington, a rookie for the St. Louis Blues, stepped into the net and rewrote history by leading his team to their first Stanley Cup, showcasing saves with the calm of a librarian in a room full of silent bookworms, but with much more at stake.

Patrick Roy's Statue of Liberty Save (2002 Playoffs) - Roy made a dramatic glove save and held his pose, reminiscent of the Statue of Liberty, against the Detroit Red Wings. It was a moment of pure showmanship, like pulling a rabbit out of a hat in the middle of a magic trick that the whole world was watching.

Roberto Luongo's Game 5 Performance (2007 Playoffs) - Facing elimination, Luongo made 72 saves for the Vancouver Canucks in a quadruple-overtime game against the Dallas Stars. It was like being the last one standing in a marathon dance competition, except on ice and with more dramatic falls.

Mike Richter's Penalty Shot Stop (1994 Stanley Cup Finals) - Richter denied Pavel Bure of the Vancouver Canucks on a penalty shot, a pivotal moment that helped the New York Rangers end their 54-year Stanley Cup drought. It was like stopping a meteor from hitting the Earth, if the meteor was a hockey puck and the Earth was the net.

Dominik Hasek's Top of the Crease Tumble (2002 Playoffs) - Known for his unconventional style, Hasek made a series of acrobatic saves for the Detroit Red Wings, often leaving the crease and diving headfirst into plays. It was like watching a gymnast perform a routine, but with more ice and high stakes.

Marty Turco's Behind-the-Back Save (2007) - Turco, in a game for the Dallas Stars, reached behind his back to catch the puck, denying a sure goal. It was like catching a fly with chopsticks blindfolded, showing off skills that seem to defy physics and expectation.

Curtis Joseph's Diving Save Against Avalanche (1996 Playoffs) - "Cujo" lunged across the crease to rob Claude Lemieux of the Colorado Avalanche, a save that epitomized his nickname's ferocity. It's like a superhero dive to save the world, only the world is a hockey net.

Ron Hextall's Paddle Save (1987 Stanley Cup Finals) - Hextall, known more for his scoring ability as a goalie, made a remarkable paddle save in the finals, showcasing that sometimes, the best defense is a good... stick. It's like using a broom to fend off a swarm of bees – unconventional, but effective.

Marc-Andre Fleury's "The Flower Blooms" Save (2018 Playoffs) - Fleury made a jaw-dropping save against the Winnipeg Jets, fully extending his body across the goal line. It was like watching a flower bloom in fast-forward, if the flower was a goalie glove stopping a puck.

Carey Price's "Blind" Save (2015) - Price, without seeing the puck, instinctively lifted his leg to stop it, a move that combined luck, skill, and perhaps a bit of goaltender's sixth sense. It's like guessing the right answer on a test about a book you didn't read – lucky, but genius.

Tim Thomas' "Flying Squirrel" Save (2011 Stanley Cup Finals) - Thomas leaped and contorted his body in mid-air to make a save, earning the nickname "flying squirrel" for the play. It's like if a superhero decided that flying wasn't just for getting around, but for stopping goals too.

Steve Mason's Stick Save (2014) - Mason, in an almost horizontal leap, used his stick to deny a goal, proving that sometimes, all you need is a good piece of wood and some air time to make hockey history. It's like being a drummer who decides to catch the stick mid-solo for the finale. 🥁🥢

Andrei Vasilevskiy's "Behind-the-Back" Glove Save (2018) - With his back to the shooter, Vasilevskiy blindly snagged the puck with his glove, a save that seemed more like a magic trick than a sports play. It's like pulling a coin from behind someone's ear, but with more cheering and less "how did you do that?" 🎩🧤

Ed Belfour's "Eagle Eye" Save (1999 Stanley Cup Finals) - Belfour, nicknamed "Eagle," showcased his sharp vision and reflexes by making critical saves that helped lead the Dallas Stars to victory. It's like having the eyesight of a hawk, but for stopping rubber discs instead of spotting mice. 🦅🚫

Henrik Lundqvist's "King's Court" Save (2014 Playoffs) - Lundqvist made a series of saves in a game against the Montreal Canadiens that were so regal, they could only befit a king. It's like ruling a kingdom where the subjects are pucks, and the castle is a net. 👑🥅

Cam Talbot's "Ghostbuster" Save (2017) - Talbot, for the Edmonton Oilers, made a save that was so improbable it looked as if he had caught a ghost, solidifying his nickname "Ghostbuster" among fans. It's like wearing a proton pack on the ice, but instead of ghosts, you're catching pucks. 👻🚫

Jake Allen's "Blind Luck" Save (2019) - Allen, not seeing the puck, instinctively made a save that left both teams in disbelief. It's like guessing where the ball will land in a game of pinball and getting it right, without ever seeing the ball. 🎮·

Jonathan Quick's "Split Second" Save (2012 Stanley Cup Finals) - Quick performed an unbelievable split to stop a goal, a move that showcased not just his skill but his name's literal accuracy. It's like being named "Fast" and winning a race before it even starts. 🏁🏆

Ilya Bryzgalov's "Humongous Big" Save (2010 Playoffs) - Bryzgalov, known for his quirky interviews, made a save so significant against the Detroit Red Wings, it could only be described in his own words as "humongous big." It's like catching a beach ball, but if the beach ball was fired out of a cannon. 🏖️🎯

Pekka Rinne's "No-Look" Block (2017 Stanley Cup Finals) - Rinne, facing away from the shooter, blocked a shot with a no-look save, relying purely on instinct and perhaps a bit of goaltender telepathy. It's like texting without looking at your phone, but with much higher stakes and more protective gear. 📱🥅

Connor Hellebuyck's "Game Changer" Save (2020 Playoffs) - Hellebuyck made a save that turned the tide of a game, proving that sometimes, a single moment of brilliance can shift the momentum. It's like being the quiet kid in class who answers the question that stumps everyone else. 🧐🏆

Sergei Bobrovsky's "Bobrovsky on the Case" Save (2017) - Bobrovsky, inspired by a commentator's catchphrase, made a detective-worthy save, solving the mystery of how to keep the puck out of the net. It's like cracking a code, but the code is a 100 mph slap shot. 🕵️‍♂️🔒

Kirk McLean's "The Save" (1994 Stanley Cup Playoffs) - In a critical moment against the Calgary Flames, McLean stretched out for a double overtime pad save that kept the Vancouver Canucks' playoff hopes alive. It's like catching a frisbee just before it hits the ground during the most intense game of ultimate frisbee ever played. 🥏🥏

Bill Ranford's Acrobatic Diving Save (1990 Stanley Cup Finals) - Ranford, of the Edmonton Oilers, made a diving, acrobatic save that not only denied a goal but also clinched the Finals MVP title for him. It was as if he was part goalkeeper, part circus performer, and all hero.

Grant Fuhr's "The Impossible Stop" (1987 Canada Cup) - Playing for Team Canada, Fuhr made an unbelievable save that seemed to defy physics, keeping the puck out of the net with a last-second glove grab against the USSR. It's like pulling a rabbit out of a hat, but the rabbit is a puck, and the hat is a hockey net.

Mikka Kiprusoff's "The Scorpion Kick" (2004 Playoffs) - Kiprusoff executed a save so unique and flexible that it looked more like a martial arts move than a hockey play, kicking his heels up behind him to stop the puck. It's as if he momentarily transformed into a scorpion, tail sting and all, but on ice.

Henrik Lundqvist's "The King's Denial" (2013 Eastern Conference Semifinals) - Lundqvist made a series of critical saves in a do-or-die game against the Washington Capitals, including a point-blank stop that preserved the New York Rangers' lead. It was like he had a force field around the net, only penetrable by his royal decree.

Gerry Cheevers' "Stitch Save" (1970s Regular Season) - Notable more for the aftermath, Cheevers had stitches painted on his mask for every shot that would have injured him had he not been wearing it, turning his mask into a badge of honor and bravery. It's like collecting scars, but without the actual pain and with way cooler stories.

Jonathan Quick's "Goal Line Stand" (2014 Stanley Cup Playoffs) - Quick made a save so close to the goal line that it required a video review to confirm it hadn't crossed. It was like guarding the last piece of pizza with your life at a party; no one was getting past him, not even the puck.

Roberto Luongo's "Desperation Save" (2011 Stanley Cup Finals) - In a pivotal game against the Boston Bruins, Luongo stretched every fiber of his being to make a toe save, keeping the Vancouver Canucks in contention. It was like stopping a door from closing with just a pinky toe, except with millions watching.

Patrick Roy's "Statue of Liberty Save" Redux (2001 Playoffs) - Roy, known for his dramatic flair, made a series of iconic glove saves throughout his career, but one against the Los Angeles Kings where he confidently hoisted the puck in the air post-save was pure theatrics. It was as if he was saying, "Look what I found!" with the swagger of a magician.

Matt Murray's "Rookie Wonder" Save (2016 Stanley Cup Finals) - Murray, then a rookie for the Pittsburgh Penguins, showcased maturity and skill beyond his years with a critical save that helped secure the Stanley Cup. It's like acing an exam in a class you skipped all semester; no one expected it, but he delivered.

Braden Holtby's "Holtbeast Mode" (2018 Playoffs) - Holtby earned his nickname with a series of monstrous saves, including a pivotal stick save that helped the Washington Capitals capture their first Stanley Cup. It was as if he turned into a superhero, complete with cape and theme music, at the most crucial moment.

Terry Sawchuk's "The Save" (1950s Regular Season) - A pioneer of modern goaltending, Sawchuk made countless remarkable saves, but one iconic photo capturing him mid-save, eyes focused, body contorted, encapsulates his legendary career. It's like the hockey version of a Renaissance painting, only much cooler because it's in ice.

Marc-Andre Fleury's "Diving Save" (2009 Stanley Cup Playoffs) - Fleury's athleticism was on full display when he made a diving save against the Detroit Red Wings, helping to clinch the Stanley Cup for the Pittsburgh Penguins. It was like diving into a pool, but instead of water, it was glory he plunged into.

Ken Dryden's "The Stand" (1970s Playoffs) - Known for his calm demeanor, Dryden made a stand against the Boston Bruins, literally leaning on his stick while making pivotal saves. It was as if he was waiting for a bus, but instead, he was stopping some of the most powerful shots in hockey.

Tom Barrasso's "Against All Odds" Save (1992 Stanley Cup Finals) - Barrasso, facing a barrage of shots from the Chicago Blackhawks, made a save that seemed to defy logic, keeping the puck out against all odds. It was like solving a Rubik's Cube while riding a roller coaster; complicated, but he made it look easy.

Glenn Hall's "Mr. Goalie" Save (1960s Regular Season) - Hall, nicknamed "Mr. Goalie," made a save that was so emblematic of his career: reliable, unflappable, and always spectacular. It's like being the dependable friend who always catches the popcorn in their mouth, no matter how far it's thrown.

Mike Vernon's "Clutch Save" (1997 Stanley Cup Finals) - In a high-pressure situation against the Philadelphia Flyers, Vernon made a save that not only showcased his skill but also his ability to perform under pressure. It was like defusing a bomb with seconds to spare, except the bomb was a hockey puck.

Evgeni Nabokov's "The Glove" (2008 Regular Season) - Nabokov, with a lightning-fast glove save, robbed the opposing team of what seemed like a guaranteed goal. It was as if he had a magnet in his glove, attracting the puck with supernatural force.

Jacques Plante's "Masked Marvel" Save (1959) - After returning to the ice with a mask following an injury, Plante made a save that not only marked the acceptance of masks in hockey but also showcased his resilience. It's like turning up to a duel with a shield; unconventional at the time, but undeniably effective.

Felix Potvin's "The Cat" Reflexes (1990s Playoffs) - Potvin, known as "The Cat" for his quick reflexes, made a save that epitomized his nickname, springing into action with feline agility. It was as if he had whiskers sensing the puck's movement, pouncing at just the right moment.

Curtis Joseph's "Cujo's Leap" (2002 Playoffs) - Facing a determined opponent, Joseph leaped across the crease, making a save that seemed to bend the laws of physics. It was like watching a superhero fly, but instead of saving the world, he saved the game.

Antti Niemi's "Finnish Fortress" (2010 Stanley Cup Playoffs) - Niemi, standing tall for the Chicago Blackhawks, made a series of saves that fortified his net like a fortress, denying entry with the determination of a medieval gatekeeper.

Ilya Bryzgalov's "Humongous Big Universe" Save (2012 Playoffs) - Bryzgalov, known for his philosophical musings, made a save that was as vast and impressive as the universe he often pondered. It was like catching a star; improbable, dazzling, and a bit humongous big.

Ryan Miller's "Millertime Miracle" (2010 Olympics) - Representing Team USA, Miller made a save against Canada that kept American hopes alive, turning "Millertime" into a moment of patriotic pride. It was like catching an eagle in flight, symbolizing freedom and the American dream, but with a hockey stick.

DRAMATIC OVERTIME GOALS

Bobby Orr's Flying Goal (1970 Stanley Cup Finals) - Bobby Orr scored "The Goal" to win the Stanley Cup for the Boston Bruins, launching into the air in celebration. It was like Superman taking flight, except instead of a cape, Orr had a hockey stick and skates. This iconic moment is immortalized in a statue outside TD Garden, proving heroes don't always wear capes; sometimes, they wear hockey jerseys.

Patrick Kane's Stealthy Clincher (2010 Stanley Cup Finals) - Kane scored a sneaky goal nobody saw enter the net except him, clinching the Chicago Blackhawks' first Stanley Cup in 49 years. It was like performing a magic trick that fooled everyone, including the goalie, the fans, and even the cameras, but ultimately won the ultimate prize.

Brett Hull's Controversial Toe in the Crease (1999 Stanley Cup Finals) - Hull scored the triple-overtime winner with his skate in the crease, a goal that remains one of the most debated in NHL history. It's like sneaking into a secret club through the back door and then finding out you're the guest of honor.

Alec Martinez's Double OT Glory (2014 Stanley Cup Finals) - Martinez scored to win the Stanley Cup for the Los Angeles Kings in double overtime, a moment that turned him into an instant legend. It was like hitting the winning home run in the bottom of the ninth at the World Series, except on ice and with a puck.

Henrique's Rookie Dream (2012 Eastern Conference Finals) - Adam Henrique, a rookie, scored in overtime to send the New Jersey Devils to the Stanley Cup Finals, proving that sometimes, fairytales do come true, and yes, rookies can be heroes too. It was like the new kid at school leading the team to victory at the big game.

Stephane Matteau's "Matteau! Matteau!" (1994 Eastern Conference Finals) - Matteau scored a wraparound goal in double overtime for the New York Rangers, a goal so famous it's simply known by his last name, chanted twice. It's like scoring the winning goal in a schoolyard pick-up game, and everyone chants your name as if you've just saved the world.

Max Talbot's Shhh (2009 Stanley Cup Playoffs) - Not an overtime goal but a moment of brilliance: Talbot scored two goals to silence the Philadelphia crowd, embodying the "silencing the critics" mantra. It's like telling a ghost story so spooky, even the skeptics start to shiver.

Chris Drury's Late Heroics (2007 Eastern Conference Semifinals) - Drury scored with 7.7 seconds left in regulation to send the game into overtime, where the Buffalo Sabres would win. It's like turning in a test with seconds to spare and finding out you scored the highest in the class.

Eberle's NHL Debut Dream (2010 Regular Season) - Jordan Eberle scored an unforgettable goal in his NHL debut, a moment that promised the start of an exciting career. It's like nailing a solo at your first school concert; the crowd goes wild, and you know you've just begun a thrilling journey. 🎵🚀

David Volek's Underdog Surprise (1993 Patrick Division Finals) - Volek, an unlikely hero, scored in overtime to eliminate the Pittsburgh Penguins, proving that sometimes, the underdog gets their day. It's like the quiet kid in class answering the question that stumps everyone else. 🐶🏆

Gretzky's High Stick (1993 Western Conference Finals) - While not a goal, Gretzky's high stick on Doug Gilmour that went uncalled, leading to a game-winning goal later, remains one of the most controversial moments. It's like sneaking a cookie from the jar and not getting caught; thrilling, but oh so naughty. 🍪😼

Ray Bourque's Cup Lift (2001 Stanley Cup Finals) - After winning his first Stanley Cup, Bourque lifting the trophy is an enduring image of fulfillment and joy, a reminder that perseverance pays off. It's like working all summer on a lemonade stand and finally buying the bike you've been dreaming of. 🍋🚲

Sidney Crosby's Golden Goal (2010 Olympics) - Not NHL, but Crosby's overtime goal for Canada in the Olympics against the USA is a moment of national pride and a highlight of his career. It's like hitting the game-winning shot in backyard basketball, but your whole country is cheering you on. 🇨🇦🏀

Joe Sakic Passing the Cup to Bourque (2001 Stanley Cup Finals) - Sakic immediately handing the Stanley Cup to Bourque, foregoing the tradition of the captain taking the first skate, is a moment of ultimate respect and teamwork. It's like winning the spelling bee and giving the trophy to your study buddy because you couldn't have done it without them. 🐀🏆

Mike Bossy's 50 in 50 (1981 Regular Season) - Bossy achieving the feat of 50 goals in 50 games solidified his place as one of the greatest scorers in history. It's like finishing a marathon, then running another because you just love running. 🏃‍♂️💨

Mario Lemieux's Comeback Goal (2000) - Lemieux scoring on his first game back from retirement showed that legends never really leave; they just take breaks. It's like your favorite superhero coming out of retirement to save the day once more. 🦸‍♂️🏒

Martin St. Louis' Mother's Day Goal (2014 Playoffs) - Scoring in overtime shortly after the passing of his mother, St. Louis' goal was a poignant reminder of the human element in sports. It's like hitting the winning home run the day you forgot your lunch, and finding out your mom packed your favorite sandwich anyway. 🥪🖤

Jaromir Jagr's Ageless Wonder (2013 Regular Season) - Jagr becoming the oldest player to score a hat trick showed that age is just a number, especially if you're a hockey legend. It's like your grandpa out-dancing you at a family wedding; surprising, impressive, and a bit humbling. 🕺👴

Darryl Sittler's 10 Point Game (1976 Regular Season) - Sittler's record-setting game for the Toronto Maple Leafs remains one of the most impressive individual performances in NHL history. It's like acing every test in a single day; unheard of, unlikely, but totally awesome. 📚🚀

Paul Henderson's Summit Series Winner (1972) - Again, not NHL, but Henderson's goal for Canada against the USSR is a defining moment in hockey history, a goal that transcended the sport. It's like scoring the winning point in an epic game of capture the flag that spans your entire neighborhood. 🏁

Henrik Zetterberg's 2008 Conn Smythe Performance - Zetterberg's entire playoff run, capped with a Stanley Cup and the Conn Smythe Trophy, was a masterclass in leadership and skill. It's like leading the school project team to an A+, but the project was building a rocket ship. 🚀

Wayne Gretzky's 802nd Goal (1994 Regular Season) - Breaking Gordie Howe's record, Gretzky became the NHL's all-time leading scorer, a monumental moment in sports history. It's like beating the high score on the arcade game at the pizza place, except the previous high score was held by a legend. 🕹️🏆

Bryan Bickell's Final Shootout Goal (2017 Regular Season) - Bickell, diagnosed with MS, scored in his final NHL game, a bittersweet moment of triumph over adversity. It's like hitting the game-winning shot in your final game of backyard basketball, knowing it's your last game before moving away. 🏀💚

Ovechkin's 700th Goal (2020 Regular Season) - Ovechkin joining the exclusive 700-goal club cemented his status as one of the greatest goal scorers in history. It's like joining a secret society, but instead of secret handshakes, there are slap shots and celebrations. 🎉

Teemu Selanne's Farewell Lap (2014 Regular Season) - Selanne's final lap around the rink, greeted by teammates and opponents alike, was a tearful goodbye to a beloved player. It's like the last day of summer camp, where even the friends you made yesterday feel like family. 👋

The Miracle on Manchester (1982 Stanley Cup Playoffs) - The Los Angeles Kings completed the largest comeback in NHL playoff history against the Edmonton Oilers. Down 5-0 entering the third period, the Kings rallied to win 6-5 in overtime. It was like turning a disaster movie into a feel-good comeback story, where the underdog saves the day against all odds. 🎬

Peter Forsberg's Stamp Goal (1994 Olympics) - Although not in the NHL, Forsberg's one-handed shootout goal for Sweden in the Olympic gold medal game was so iconic, it was immortalized on a stamp. It's as if his move was so smooth, even the post office wanted to deliver his finesse to every household. 🇸🇪

Auston Matthews' Four-Goal Debut (2016 Regular Season) - Matthews made history by scoring four goals in his first NHL game, setting the stage for a career under the brightest of spotlights. It's like showing up to your first day at school and solving a math problem even the teacher couldn't crack. 🍁🎩

Gordie Howe's Final Shift (1980 Regular Season) - Howe took to the ice for one last shift at the age of 52, an unmatched testament to longevity in professional sports. It's like your grandpa entering a marathon and not just finishing it but sprinting the last mile. 👴

Mario Lemieux's Return from Retirement (2000 Regular Season) - Lemieux returned to the NHL after three and a half years and immediately proved he still belonged among the elite, scoring a goal and two assists in his first game back. It's like riding a bike after years away, except the bike is in a professional race, and you still finish first. 🚴‍♂️

Wayne Gretzky's 50 Goals in 39 Games (1981-82 Regular Season) - Gretzky shattered the record for the fastest 50 goals scored in a season, a feat that seemed as unimaginable as finding a unicorn in your backyard.

The Five Overtime Marathon (2000 Eastern Conference Semifinals) - The Philadelphia Flyers and the Pittsburgh Penguins battled through five overtimes, the longest game in modern NHL history, a testament to endurance, will, and the love of the game. It was like running a marathon, then deciding to run another because you're having so much fun.

The Easter Epic (1987 Patrick Division Semifinals) - The New York Islanders defeated the Washington Capitals in the fourth overtime, a game that ended on Easter Sunday. It was as if the game was so good, not even the Easter Bunny wanted to interrupt.

Ray Bourque's Boston Farewell (2001 Regular Season) - Bourque, a long-time Boston Bruin, received a standing ovation from Boston fans in his return as a Colorado Avalanche, a moment of pure respect and admiration that transcends team loyalty. It's like coming home for Thanksgiving and getting the biggest piece of pie, even though you've been away.

John Scott's All-Star MVP (2016 All-Star Game) - Enforcer John Scott, voted into the All-Star Game as a fan vote campaign, scored two goals and earned MVP honors, a Cinderella story on ice. It was like the class clown winning prom king, then dancing like Fred Astaire.

Saku Koivu's Return from Cancer (2002 Regular Season) - Koivu returned to the ice after battling cancer, receiving an emotional standing ovation from the Montreal crowd. It was like watching a superhero return from a battle with the greatest villain and winning.

The Double Hat Trick Game (2011 Regular Season) - Sam Gagner of the Edmonton Oilers scored four goals and four assists in one game, a rare "double hat trick" that made it seem as if he was playing a video game on rookie mode.

Alex Ovechkin's 500th Goal (2016 Regular Season) - Ovechkin became the fifth-fastest player to reach 500 NHL goals, a milestone that cemented his place among the greats. It was like hitting a home run in every game of the season; you're not just playing, you're making history.

The St. Louis Blues' First Stanley Cup (2019) - After 52 years, the Blues won their first Stanley Cup, proving that patience isn't just a virtue, it's a pathway to victory. It's like waiting all year for Christmas, and when it finally comes, Santa brings you a real, live unicorn.

Patrick Roy's Wink (1993 Stanley Cup Finals) - Roy winked at Tomas Sandstrom of the Los Angeles Kings after making a save, a moment of confidence and swagger that defined Roy's career. It's like answering the final question on a test with a smiley face, knowing you've aced it.

Sidney Crosby's Outdoor Game Winner (2008 NHL Winter Classic) - Crosby scored the shootout winner in the first-ever Winter Classic, an iconic moment in snowy conditions that was like winning a snowball fight with a perfectly crafted ice sculpture.

Bobby Nystrom's Cup-Winning Goal (1980 Stanley Cup Finals) - Nystrom scored in overtime to win the New York Islanders their first Stanley Cup, starting a dynasty. It was like the first domino falling in a line of dominoes that spelled out "champions."

The Lightning's Cup in the Bubble (2020 Stanley Cup Finals) - The Tampa Bay Lightning won the Stanley Cup in a pandemic "bubble," a unique achievement in sports history. It was like playing the biggest game of your life in your backyard, but the whole world was watching through the fence.

Teemu Selanne Breaks Rookie Goal Record (1993 Regular Season) - Selanne's 76 goals in his rookie season shattered the previous record, a feat so impressive it was like rewriting the rulebook on what rookies could achieve.

Jean Beliveau's 10th Stanley Cup (1971) - Beliveau retired after winning his 10th Stanley Cup as a player, a record that's as towering as the man himself. It's like finishing a decade-long game of Monopoly as the undisputed champion, owning everything on the board.

The Blackhawks' 17 Seconds (2013 Stanley Cup Finals) - Chicago scored twice in 17 seconds to clinch the Cup, a whirlwind finale that was like watching a magician pull off the ultimate trick with the world as his audience.

Zdeno Chara's Fastest Shot (2012 All-Star Game) - Chara set the record for the hardest shot, unleashing a blistering 108.8 mph slapshot. It was like throwing a fastball so fast, it could turn back time.

Doug Gilmour's Double-Overtime Goal (1993 Playoffs) - Gilmour's wraparound goal in double overtime for the Toronto Maple Leafs was a masterpiece of endurance and skill, like running a two-marathon and finishing with a sprint.

The Red Wings' 25-Year Playoff Streak (2016) - Detroit's quarter-century of consecutive playoff appearances is a testament to consistency and excellence, like getting straight A's every year from kindergarten through graduate school.

Jagr Moves to Second in Points (2017 Regular Season) - Jaromir Jagr passed Mark Messier to become second on the all-time NHL points list, a feat that's like climbing Mount Everest and then deciding to go just a little bit higher to see if there's a better view.

David Ayres' Emergency Goalie Win (2020) - When both of the Carolina Hurricanes' goalies were injured during a game, 42-year-old Zamboni driver David Ayres stepped in as an emergency goalie and helped secure a win against the Toronto Maple Leafs. It was like the guy who mows the lawn at a soccer stadium getting called in to take a penalty kick – and scoring.

Alex Ovechkin's "The Goal" (2006) - Ovechkin scored one of the most remarkable goals in NHL history against the Phoenix Coyotes, while sliding on his back and facing away from the net. It was like pulling off a magic trick while blindfolded, on ice.

The Miracle at Molson (1993 Playoffs) - The Montreal Canadiens rallied from a 2-0 deficit in the final minutes of Game 3 in the Adams Division Semifinal against the Quebec Nordiques, winning in overtime. This comeback was like finishing a marathon after losing a shoe at mile 20.

Joe Sakic's Handoff to Ray Bourque (2001 Stanley Cup Finals) - After winning the Stanley Cup, instead of hoisting it first, Joe Sakic immediately handed it to Ray Bourque, allowing him to lift it for the first time in his 22-year career. It was like giving the last piece of cake to your friend who's had a really bad day.

Darryl Sutter's Coaching Record (2012-2014) - Sutter led the Los Angeles Kings to two Stanley Cup victories in three years, emphasizing a defense-first approach. It was as if he turned a group of chess pieces into a fortress that could move and attack.

The First Winter Classic (2008) - The Pittsburgh Penguins and Buffalo Sabres faced off in the first-ever Winter Classic, an outdoor game played in a snowstorm. It was like holding a ballet on a frozen pond, where the dancers are wearing skates and pads.

Wayne Gretzky's Final Game (1999) - The Great One's last NHL game was met with tributes from teams, fans, and even non-hockey followers, marking the end of an era. It was like watching the final episode of your favorite show, knowing there will never be anything quite like it again.

Mario Lemieux's Five Goals, Five Ways (1988) - Lemieux scored five goals in a single game, each in a different manner: even strength, power play, short-handed, penalty shot, and empty net. It was like hitting a home run, scoring a touchdown, making a basket, scoring a soccer goal, and winning a race all in one day.

The Triple Gold Club - Only a select few players have won the Stanley Cup, an Olympic gold medal, and a World Championship. Joining this club is like getting into the most exclusive club in town, where the membership fee is sweat, tears, and unparalleled skill.

Bryan Trottier's Six-Point Period (1978) - Trottier set a record for most points in one period with four goals and two assists. It's like solving six Rubik's cubes in under five minutes – a burst of brilliance that leaves everyone else marveling.

The Sedin Twins' Retirement (2018) - Henrik and Daniel Sedin, who played their entire careers with the Vancouver Canucks, retired together, ending a remarkable era of sibling success in the NHL. It was like watching your favorite dynamic duo ride off into the sunset, except they're on ice skates instead of horses.

Steve Yzerman's Double Overtime Goal (1996 Playoffs) - Yzerman's laser of a shot in double OT against the St. Louis Blues is one of the most replayed goals in NHL history, a moment of individual brilliance that lifted an entire city. It was like hitting the bullseye in darts, but the dartboard is moving, and the dart is a puck.

The Battle of Alberta (1980s) - The fierce rivalry between the Calgary Flames and Edmonton Oilers defined a decade of hockey, with both teams frequently clashing in high-stakes games. It was like having two superhero teams in the same city, battling not just for victory but for the heart of Alberta.

Pat LaFontaine's Easter Epic Goal (1987 Playoffs) - Scoring in the fourth overtime against the Washington Capitals, LaFontaine ended one of the longest games in NHL history. It was like finishing an epic novel in one sitting, with the final twist happening as the sun rises.

The Montreal Canadiens' 24th Cup (1993) - The Canadiens won their 24th Stanley Cup, the most by any team, solidifying their status as the most successful franchise in NHL history. It's like winning the school science fair so many times they retire the trophy and just give it to you.

Gordie Howe's Six-Decade Career (1980) - Howe retired after playing professional hockey in six different decades, a feat unmatched in sports. It's like being part of a band that tops the charts in every era from the Beatles to Billie Eilish. 🎵

The 2010 Golden Goal (Olympics) - Sidney Crosby's overtime goal for Canada against the USA in the Vancouver Olympics, while not an NHL moment, captured the hearts of a nation. It was like hitting a walk-off homerun in the bottom of the ninth at the Olympics, if baseball were played on ice.

The NHL's 100th Anniversary (2017) - The league celebrated a century of hockey with ceremonies, documentaries, and special events. It was like throwing a birthday party where every guest has brought a story more incredible than the last.

Jarome Iginla's 600th Goal (2016) - Iginla became the 19th NHL player to score 600 goals, joining an elite group of hockey legends. It's like joining a club where the only other members have discovered new planets.

The Return of the Winnipeg Jets (2011) - The NHL returned to Winnipeg after a 15-year absence, reigniting the passion of a city for its beloved team. It was like getting back together with your first love, but this time, it's forever. 🤍

Henrik Lundqvist's 400th Win (2017) - Lundqvist became the 12th goalie in NHL history to reach 400 wins, all with the New York Rangers, blending consistency with excellence. It's like being voted class president every year from kindergarten through high school.

The Vegas Golden Knights' Inaugural Season Run (2018) - The expansion team made it to the Stanley Cup Finals in their first season, a fairy tale start for the new franchise. It was like the new kid at school leading the team to a championship in their first year.

Ovechkin and Crosby's Rookie Duel (2006) - The rookie seasons of Alex Ovechkin and Sidney Crosby reignited the excitement for the future of the NHL, a rivalry and showcase of talent that promised great things for hockey. It was like watching two chess grandmasters, both prodigies, facing off for the first time.

The 2004-05 Season Lockout - The entire NHL season was canceled due to a lockout, a sobering moment that ultimately led to significant changes in the league. It was like pressing pause on your favorite TV show, only to have the next season come back with a plot twist you never saw coming.

Maurice Richard's 50 in 50 (1944-45 Season) - Richard was the first player to score 50 goals in 50 games, setting a standard for scoring excellence. It was like being the first person to run a four-minute mile, except on skates and with a puck.

FIERCE RIVALRIES

The Battle of Alberta: Edmonton Oilers vs. Calgary Flames - This rivalry is as heated as a pot of chili left on the stove all day. When these two teams meet, it's not just a game; it's a battle for bragging rights in Alberta. The rivalry peaked in the 1980s when both teams were vying for Stanley Cups, creating a series of unforgettable playoff clashes. It's like having two siblings fighting over the last cookie, but the cookie is a giant, shiny, silver cup. 🏆

Montreal Canadiens vs. Boston Bruins - This rivalry is older than your grandpa's favorite chair and twice as intense. With over 34 playoff meetings, these teams have a history of epic battles that have left fans on the edge of their seats. It's like a never-ending chess match where each move is more cunning and bold than the last, except the chess pieces are hockey players, and the board is ice.

Toronto Maple Leafs vs. Montreal Canadiens - As two of the Original Six NHL teams, this rivalry is like the classic tale of two knights jousting for the kingdom's honor. Their confrontations are legendary, showcasing the rich history of hockey in Canada. Imagine a superhero versus villain showdown, but every year, and sometimes the heroes wear blue and white.

Pittsburgh Penguins vs. Washington Capitals - This modern rivalry has been defined by the battle between two of hockey's greatest stars: Sidney Crosby and Alex Ovechkin. Every game feels like a blockbuster movie where the lead actors refuse to let the other steal the scene. It's like watching two chefs trying to out-cook each other on a cooking show, except the kitchen is an ice rink.

Chicago Blackhawks vs. Detroit Red Wings - With over 800 regular-season and playoff games between them, this rivalry is as iconic as pizza in Chicago or cars in Detroit. It's like two old friends who can't decide whether to hug or wrestle, so they do a bit of both.

New York Rangers vs. New York Islanders - The battle for New York is as fierce as a Broadway diva-off. When these teams clash, it divides families, friends, and even neighborhoods, all vying for the title of New York's top team. It's like deciding whether pizza or bagels are the ultimate New York food – impossible.

Philadelphia Flyers vs. Pittsburgh Penguins - Known as the Battle of Pennsylvania, this rivalry splits the state in two. The intensity of their matchups is akin to a superhero showdown, with each team fighting to prove they're the true protectors of Pennsylvania. It's like having a snowball fight where every snowball is made of hard, unyielding ice.

Los Angeles Kings vs. San Jose Sharks - This California rivalry is hotter than a sunny day at the beach. With both teams often competing for dominance in the Pacific Division, their contests are as unpredictable as LA traffic. Imagine surfing where the waves fight back, and you've got the idea.

Ottawa Senators vs. Toronto Maple Leafs - The Battle of Ontario is like a polite argument over who makes the best maple syrup, but with more body checks and less maple trees. These matchups are always marked by high stakes and higher emotions, proving that even Canadians can turn up the heat when hockey's on the line.

Detroit Red Wings vs. Colorado Avalanche (1990s) - This rivalry was born out of playoff intensity and grew into one of the most heated feuds in NHL history. With brawls, high-stakes matchups, and unforgettable playoff series, it was like a drama series where every episode ended with a cliffhanger. It's like if two magicians were rivals, each trying to outdo the other with a more spectacular trick.

Vancouver Canucks vs. Chicago Blackhawks (Late 2000s/Early 2010s) - This rivalry was defined by several intense playoff series that left fans breathless. It's like watching a series of epic movies, where each sequel is more thrilling than the last, and you can never guess the ending.

Buffalo Sabres vs. Ottawa Senators (Mid-2000s) - Sparked by playoff battles and on-ice incidents, this rivalry had all the makings of a classic feud: intensity, passion, and unforgettable moments. It's like a food fight that started over something small but escalated into an epic showdown with mashed potatoes and pie flying everywhere.

Edmonton Oilers vs. Los Angeles Kings (Late 1980s) - Fueled by high-scoring playoff confrontations, including the famous "Miracle on Manchester," this rivalry is a testament to the unpredictability and excitement of hockey. It's like a rollercoaster that only goes up, with twists and turns that leave you screaming for more.

Calgary Flames vs. Vancouver Canucks - The intensity of this Western Canadian rivalry burns as fiercely as a forest fire, with both teams often leaving everything on the ice in their quest for supremacy. It's like a dance-off where the floor is lava, and the only way to win is to keep moving.

Tampa Bay Lightning vs. Florida Panthers - The Battle of Florida might be a newer rivalry, but it's as intense as the summer heat in the Sunshine State. When these teams meet, it's like watching two alligators wrestle; it's fierce, unpredictable, and you can't look away.

Minnesota Wild vs. Colorado Avalanche - Born out of playoff clashes, this rivalry has all the elements of a classic showdown: close games, overtime thrillers, and a mutual respect born from hard-fought battles. It's like a long hike where every turn brings a new, breathtaking view, and sometimes, a bear.

San Jose Sharks vs. Vegas Golden Knights - Though the Golden Knights are the new kids on the block, their matchups with the Sharks have quickly become must-see TV, full of drama, comebacks, and intense playoff series. It's like the new student at school who ends up being the lead in the school play – a star is born.

Montreal Canadiens vs. Quebec Nordiques - Before the Nordiques moved to Colorado, the Battle of Quebec was one of the most passionate rivalries in hockey, rooted in provincial pride and cultural identity. It was like having two chefs from the same town, each claiming to make the best poutine, and every meal is a culinary showdown.

St. Louis Blues vs. Chicago Blackhawks - This rivalry is as intense as a game of musical chairs where the music never stops. With both teams part of the Original Six expansion teams, their long history is filled with memorable playoff matchups. It's like a never-ending dance-off between two tap-dancing pros, each step more intricate than the last.

Winnipeg Jets vs. Nashville Predators - A newer rivalry that quickly gained steam with a high-octane playoff series in 2018. It's like the new action movie that outdoes all previous blockbusters with its heart-stopping chases and dramatic showdowns.

Boston Bruins vs. Philadelphia Flyers - Known for their physical play, the matchups between these teams often feel like watching a superhero movie where every character is The Hulk. It's a battle of strength, grit, and determination, where the ice might just crack from the intensity.

Detroit Red Wings vs. Toronto Maple Leafs - An Original Six rivalry that has cooled and heated over the decades, it's like a friendship that endures through thick and thin, with occasional arguments over who ate the last slice of pizza.

New York Rangers vs. Philadelphia Flyers - The Broadway Blueshirts and the Broad Street Bullies have a rivalry that's as classic as Rocky vs. Apollo. Each game is a bout that could fill the seats of any arena or movie theater.

Colorado Avalanche vs. Detroit Red Wings (Late 1990s and early 2000s) - This rivalry was the stuff of legends, featuring brawls, blood, and Stanley Cups. It was like watching two chess grandmasters play with pieces that could actually fight back.

Pittsburgh Penguins vs. Philadelphia Flyers - Another Battle of Pennsylvania entry, but with all the plot twists of a soap opera. It's a tale of two cities where every game is a chapter adding to an epic saga.

Edmonton Oilers vs. Winnipeg Jets (1980s) - Before the Jets' relocation and eventual return, this rivalry was defined by high-flying offenses and playoff showdowns. It was like a racecar event on ice, with both teams pushing the speedometer to its limits.

Montreal Canadiens vs. Ottawa Senators - A rivalry that has grown with each playoff meeting, it's like a story of an underdog constantly trying to outsmart the established champion, with every encounter adding a new twist.

Vancouver Canucks vs. Chicago Blackhawks (Late 2000s/Early 2010s) - This rivalry was marked by intense playoff series that often ended in heartbreak for one team. It's like a trilogy where each sequel raises the stakes, and you're never sure who will come out on top until the very end.

Buffalo Sabres vs. Toronto Maple Leafs - Proximity breeds rivalry, and the battle for the QEW is as fierce as a snowball fight that spans two cities. When these teams meet, it's like a friendly neighborhood rivalry that everyone talks about but secretly takes very seriously.

San Jose Sharks vs. Anaheim Ducks - The Battle of California part two, where the ice is just as hot as the sand on a California beach. Each game is like a surfing contest where every wave could be the one that makes or breaks your ride.

Los Angeles Kings vs. Anaheim Ducks - And completing the California trifecta, this rivalry is as glamorous and intense as a Hollywood premiere. Every matchup is a blockbuster, with the drama to match any Oscar-winning movie.

Minnesota Wild vs. Dallas Stars - A rivalry with roots in relocation, the Wild and Stars face off with the history of Minnesota's original NHL team moving to Dallas. It's like watching a drama where the protagonist moves away and returns, only to find a new hero has taken their place.

Tampa Bay Lightning vs. Columbus Blue Jackets (2019 First Round Playoffs) - In a stunning turn of events, the Columbus Blue Jackets swept the record-setting Tampa Bay Lightning in the first round of the 2019 playoffs. It was like the school chess champion losing to a newcomer who just learned the game. The Lightning had tied the record for the most wins in a regular season, making this upset one for the history books.

Boston Bruins vs. Vancouver Canucks (2011 Stanley Cup Finals) - This intense seven-game series was filled with dramatic turns, from biting incidents to pivotal game-changing hits. It was like watching a marathon where runners had to dodge unexpected obstacles, like flying pies and rolling barrels. The Bruins ultimately triumphed, capturing their first Cup in 39 years, in a series that had fans on the edge of their seats from start to finish.

Montreal Canadiens vs. Toronto Maple Leafs (2021 First Round Playoffs) - After years without a playoff meeting, these two Original Six teams reignited their historic rivalry in a first-round matchup. The Canadiens, coming back from a 3-1 series deficit, won in Game 7, reminding everyone of their storied past. It was like watching a classic rock band come back for a reunion tour and play their greatest hits better than ever.

Calgary Flames vs. Tampa Bay Lightning (2004 Stanley Cup Finals) - This hard-fought series went to seven games, with Tampa Bay capturing their first-ever Stanley Cup. It was a battle as heated as a summer day in Florida, with both teams leaving it all on the ice. Imagine a cook-off where every dish is spicier than the last, and the final decision comes down to the last bite.

Pittsburgh Penguins vs. Detroit Red Wings (2008 & 2009 Stanley Cup Finals) - These back-to-back finals showcased the height of 2000s hockey, with each team taking home the Cup once. It was like watching two master magicians trying to outdo each other with increasingly spectacular tricks, each finale more breathtaking than the last.

New York Islanders vs. New York Rangers (1970s-80s) - The "Battle of New York" reached peak intensity in the late '70s and early '80s, with the Islanders' dynasty years overlapping with the Rangers' quest for glory. It was like a Broadway showdown, where every performance could be a star-making turn or a dramatic exit stage left.

Edmonton Oilers vs. Dallas Stars (Late 1990s Playoffs) - This series of playoff battles defined late '90s Western Conference hockey, with each team frequently standing in the other's way. It was like a high-stakes game of rock-paper-scissors, where every round was unpredictable and nail-biting.

San Jose Sharks vs. Los Angeles Kings (2010s Playoffs) - Their 2014 first-round series, where the Kings came back from a 3-0 deficit to win in seven games, added a fiery chapter to this California rivalry. It's like watching a movie where the hero is down and out, only to make a miraculous comeback just when all seems lost.

Washington Capitals vs. New York Rangers (2010s Playoffs) - This rivalry has featured numerous memorable playoff series, marked by clutch performances and game 7 dramas. It's like a series of intense arm wrestling matches, where each contestant has one last move that could clinch victory.

Ottawa Senators vs. Buffalo Sabres (Mid-2000s) - The "Battle of the 417" featured several tense playoff matchups, including a brawl-filled game in 2007. This rivalry was as unpredictable as a weather forecast, with every game bringing a new storm.

Chicago Blackhawks vs. St. Louis Blues (2010s Playoffs) - Their 2016 first-round series went to seven games, embodying the historic rivalry's intensity. It was like a tug-of-war where both sides are evenly matched, and the rope is made of pure determination.

Minnesota Wild vs. Chicago Blackhawks (2010s Playoffs) - A newer rivalry that quickly developed a competitive edge with several playoff meetings in the early 2010s. It's like starting a new book series and getting hooked from the first chapter, with each game adding depth to the story.

Vegas Golden Knights vs. San Jose Sharks (2019 First Round Playoffs) - In their second year, the Golden Knights faced the Sharks in a dramatic series that featured a controversial penalty and a comeback for the ages in Game 7. It was like watching a magician pull off an escape act that leaves the audience gasping.

Colorado Avalanche vs. St. Louis Blues (2020s) - With both teams emerging as powerhouses in the West, their matchups have become must-see events, filled with skill, speed, and the promise of a new rivalry for the ages. It's like watching two sprinters who are equally fast, making each race a photo finish.

Toronto Maple Leafs vs. Boston Bruins (2010s Playoffs) - This rivalry was rekindled with several playoff series, including heartbreaking losses for Toronto that added new chapters to their storied history. It's like watching a drama where the same character faces a different challenge every season, with the audience rooting for a happy ending.

Calgary Flames vs. Edmonton Oilers (2020s) - The Battle of Alberta has been reignited with new stars and intense games, proving that some rivalries never lose their fire. It's like a classic rock band going on tour with new hits; the songs might change, but the energy remains.

Montreal Canadiens vs. Boston Bruins (2010s) - Their 2014 second-round playoff series, where Montreal triumphed in seven games, underscored this timeless rivalry's enduring intensity. It's like a saga where each installment is more epic than the last, with heroes and villains who never fail to captivate.

Made in United States
North Haven, CT
28 June 2024